THE ART OF
RADIO TIMES

THE ART OF
RADIO TIMES
The first sixty years

Compiled by David Driver
Introduction by Asa Briggs

BBC

Designer DAVID DRIVER
Interviews PETER HARLE
Decade introductions BRIAN GEARING
Editorial assistant MARTIN JAMES
Researcher AMANDA GLASS
Assistant designer ASHTED DASTOR
Cover illustration PETER BROOKES

We would like to thank the following people
for their contributions:
Wallace Grevatt
for decade introduction research,
Geoffrey Cannon
for the introduction to the 1920s
and The BBC Written Archives Centre,
Caversham

An exhibition of original artwork,
selected by Edward Booth-Clibborn,
opened at the Victoria & Albert Museum, London,
on 21 October 1981
and ran until 10 January 1982.
The exhibition was sponsored by
Designers and Art Directors Association
and European Illustration.

Printed in Japan by Dai Nippon
Filmset by Filmcomposition, London
Paper 128gsm matt coated
Typeface Cheltenham Book

Published jointly by
BBC Publications,
35 Marylebone High Street,
London W1M 4AA.
Distribution:
UK, Commonwealth,
144/152 Bermondsey Street,
London SE1 3TH.

European Illustration,
12 Carlton House Terrace,
London SW1Y 5AH.
Distribution:
USA, Europe and the rest of the world.
No part of this book
may be reproduced in any manner
without written permission.
First published 1981
Copyright © 1981 European Illustration, London
and British Broadcasting Corporation

BBC PUBLICATIONS ISBN 0 563 17906 6
EUROPEAN ILLUSTRATION ISBN 0 904866 19 X

Contents

6
Introduction by Asa Briggs

10
The **1920s**

20
Interview with Eric Fraser

22
The **1930s**

28
Interview with Jack Dunkley

38
Interview with Victor Reinganum

60
Interview with Edward Ardizzone

82
The **1940s**

102
The **1950s**

106
Interview with Leonard Rosoman

110
Interview with Anthony Gross

112
Interview with Robin Jacques

122
Interview with Robert Micklewright

126
Interview with Edward Gage

132
Interview with Susan Einzig

136
The **1960s**

156
Interview with Laurence Scarfe

170
Interview with Val Biro

180
Interview with Terence Greer

184
The **1970s**

186
Interview with Peter Brookes

210
Interview with Nigel Holmes

225
Interview with Ralph Steadman

244
Interview with Bill Tidy

249
Biographies and Index

Introduction

BY ASA BRIGGS

THE RADIO TIMES, ILLUSTRATED FROM
THE START, WAS INTENDED NOT ONLY TO
SET OUT DETAILS OF SPECIFIC PROGRAMMES
BUT TO INTRODUCE AND COMMENT ON THEM

Organised broadcasting is less than a century old. The BBC, indeed, has not yet celebrated its 60th anniversary. In 1947 it was still possible to describe it as 25-years-young.

There are many different sources for the study of broadcasting history – programmes, though many of these in sound or vision have vanished into thin air even since the development of recording; reports, for broadcasting has generated more words than any other medium, including film; individual documents, though documents relating to broadcasting are patchy, often misleading and almost always difficult to interpret; and, not least, pictures, whether they be sketches, cartoons or photographs, for these can often reveal more of mood as well as of style than the most carefully constructed paragraphs. Historians – or at least modern historians – have notoriously been more willing to use documents than pictures, but they are learning fast. They have become far more interested in so-called 'ephemera' too – and in archives. For all these reasons, therefore, if they are interested in contemporary society and culture, they cannot afford to neglect the RADIO TIMES, in which the pictures are as informative and interesting as the words.

Just as there are different sources, there are also different ways of dividing the short history of broadcasting into periods and of relating those periods to the huge changes in politics, society and culture which have taken place since the birth of RADIO TIMES in September 1923.

The biggest break, the Second World War, marked the climax of sound broadcasting in this country and the peak influence of the BBC in other countries. The biggest change in broadcasting itself, the advent of television, was heralded as early as 1936 with the beginning of the BBC's first regular television programmes, yet it was not until 1958 – after a long wartime break – that the total number of combined sound and television licences (over eight million) exceeded the total number of sound licences only (nearly six-and-a-half-million) for the first time. The RADIO TIMES, which was designed to appeal to viewers as well as to listeners after television was introduced, had already reached its all-time highest weekly average of more than eight million copies three years earlier in 1955.

Such statistics are themselves part of the evidence, reflecting as they did the appeal of different media of communication. Yet, even though the growth of huge 20th-century audiences or readerships has been charted and analysed, searching and controversial questions remain. The influence of sound broadcasting on ways of life was often discussed between 1923 and 1939, not least in the pages of the RADIO TIMES, but there was no agreement about it, not least because of the difficulty of isolating the effects of broadcasting from changes due to other 'causes'. Likewise, after the return of television in 1946 there was never any general agreement about its influence on society or, for that matter, about the influence of society on it.

It was only from the early 1950s that much careful attention was being devoted to the relative influence of words and of pictures or the relative impact of different media of communication, a term not used when regular BBC broadcasting began in 1922. It was not until the late 1950s and early 1960s that sound broadcasting and television – with different but related pedigrees – were beginning to be thought of as two elements only in a cluster of media influences.

The RADIO TIMES (like *The Listener*, which was launched six years later) was part of this cluster. In face of opposition in both cases the BBC had weekly magazines at its disposal of very different kinds. The RADIO TIMES, illustrated from the start, was intended not only to set out details of specific programmes (to serve as 'a Bradshaw of Broadcasting') but to introduce and to comment on them and on the framework of programme policy within which they were devised and presented.

To browse through the RADIO TIMES, therefore, is at least as entertaining as browsing through the old numbers of *Punch*, about which so much has been written, and to study it carefully is to learn more of the folklore of broadcasting and the rhythms of the broadcasting week and year than it is possible to learn from any other single source. It was not only that there was no organised listener research until 1936; there was virtually no sociology of broadcasting either. Even after listener research began, one cultivated and experienced BBC official, Lionel Fielden, called 'Listener Research' a 'hellish department', dating the 'real degradation of the BBC' from its introduction: the RADIO TIMES and *The Listener* were good enough for him. As for the sociological lacuna, a social psychologist of the period who was genuinely interested in broadcasting, T. H. Pears, wrote to me in 1961 that it took academic thinkers an inordinate amount of time 'to realise that the machine in the servants' kitchen would soon have such vast social repercussions'. Broadcasting was left to the broadcasters, listeners, a few armchair critics, some of them more noisy than distinguished, and *The Listener* (after 1929). The RADIO TIMES, therefore, is indispensable.

The viewers commanded more attention than the listeners, particularly after the return of television in 1946, and it was shown that out of the first audience research sample of 900 as many as 91 per cent said that they watched the whole night's programmes from 8.30 pm to close-down at 10.30 pm 'Every time the milky light spins across the screen', a BBC official wrote around that time, 'there is a sense of eager anticipation which even the most mediocre programme does not wholly dispel'.

It was in the television age – after the hallowed monopoly went in 1955 (in television not in sound) – that ratings really began to count. The *TV Times* was launched in 1955, and thereafter RADIO TIMES faced competition.

Whatever the structure or the date, however, before or after 1955 the illustrations in the RADIO TIMES are as revealing to the historian of society and culture as are the programme announcements and the articles about them. Indeed, it is remarkable that such a pictureless medium as sound broadcasting could inspire such a wealth of illustrated material outside as well as inside the pages of the RADIO TIMES before the age of television. Moreover, just because the RADIO TIMES penetrated so many homes – well over a million copies a week were being sold by 1929 and over two-and-a-quarter million ten years later when war broke out – it usually throws more light on general attitudes to broadcasting among all sections of society than a study of the attitudes of the broadcasters themselves as expressed in the programmes or in the pages of *The Listener*. They at best – for long, at least – were an élite. The main change in this respect came after 1955, when the language of sound broadcasting began to change – the growth of recording was a condition, not a cause – and television, invaded as it was by a large number of journalists, speeded up the tempo of the day as well as of the week.

One of the most convenient methods of dividing the subsequent history both of broadcasting and of society and culture as a whole is the simplest – and it is the method followed in this book. Different decades are endowed with an identity – increasingly while they are still current. Thus, we talk of the 'warring forties' or the 'swinging sixties'. The seventies are awkward to name, yet at least one writer, Christopher Booker, has called them the 'most significant' decade of the century: 'not a decade however you looked at it, to solace the moralists', wrote another writer, Norman Shrapnel, on the same period, 'it seemed to be coming up with all the wrong answers'.

As this book shows, different decades are sufficiently different to invite controversial historical explanation or interpretation, and the controversy is heightened when one decade is compared with, or preferred to, another. Some fascinating accounts have been given of the changing moods of decades both by professional historians and by other writers, beginning – at least as far as the period since 1922 is concerned – with Malcolm Muggeridge's 'The Thirties' (1940). There is still no one single study, unfortunately, on the twenties, although there have been 'personal accounts', like that of Douglas Goldring. Goldring saw the twenties (choosing to compare them with the 1890s) as 'a beginning' …'Bliss was it in that dawn to be alive'.

WE CAN RELATE THE EVENTS OF A DECADE
TO DEVELOPMENTS WHICH TOOK PLACE
LONG BEFORE…BROADCASTING TO
PUBLISHING AND ELECTRONICS TO PRINT

There are three difficulties in a simple methodology of dividing history into decades which need to be identified. First, the decade is an artifical construct: most decades include phoney years, like the year of the phoney war which began in a September and ended dramatically in the May of the following year. There are other dates, too, which stand out in the middle of decades – like 1945, the year of victory; 1956, the year of Suez, Hungary, 'Look Back in Anger' and Bill Haley and his Comets; or 1973 and 1974, years of war in the Middle East, threats to oil and to security and of political and economic crisis when Britain and the world seemed to be in the course of being turned upside down. Such years often dominate memory, yet they cannot be related simply to the context of one decade.

The second difficulty is that no two people look at the same decade in quite the same way. For Irving Kristol the 1960s, 'one of the more bizarre decades of our history', was also a decade of 'chills and fevers' casting their shadows for years to come. For other writers, however, it was an exciting decade of 'ferment' and 'dynamic vitality', though it had its own shifts of pace and expectation which led a third group of critics to write of 'the crazy sixties' or of 'the over-heated decade'. It was a decade which looked

different, too, in the light of the contrasting experience of the 1970s.

The third difficulty in the methodology is that a decade is too short a unit to be sufficiently 'comprehensive'. For that reason, therefore, the older notion of a 'generation' (30 years or so) has advantages: it was a notion which was strong in the 1920s when there was talk of a missing generation lost during the war, and which came back in the 1960s, when there was endless talk of the 'generation gap'. Other familiar notions are 'century' or 'jubilee'; while Raymond Williams, spanning more than a century, has shown what we can do with the notion of a 'long revolution', particularly when we consider the media. We can relate the events of a decade to developments which took place long before…broadcasting to publishing and electronics to print.

IN GENERAL THE RADIO TIMES UNDER
SUCCESSIVE EDITORS NEVER FORGOT THAT IT
WAS A 'MAJORITY' PAPER. THE FIRST NUMBER
SOLD OVER A QUARTER-OF-A-MILLION

Broadcasting, which will celebrate its diamond jubilee in 1982, took shape in the aftermath of technical and social developments during the 1890s, with a year in the middle of that decade – 1896 – standing out as sharply as 1956 did sixty years (or two generations) later. It was in 1896 that Northcliffe founded the *Daily Mail*, the first regular cinema show was opened in London's West End, the first motor race from London to Brighton was held, and Marconi arrived in London with his wireless patents. A generation later, the 1920s saw the realisation of new social and cultural achievements which had been long in the making, though few people knew it and few people were ready to interpret it.

Leonard Crocombe, the first Editor of the RADIO TIMES, edited *Titbits* from 1918 to 1945. Since *Titbits* was one of Northcliffe's first publishing ventures, there was a direct link here between two phases in the long communications revolution. It was within a few months of the British Broadcasting Company being founded that its Board of Directors resolved, in May 1923, that 'the General Manager make the appointment of an individual to deal with propaganda, publicity and the production of a magazine'. Thereafter Reith handled the complicated arrangements, soon making a business agreement with George Newnes Ltd, which placed editorial control not in the hands of the BBC but of the publishers. The only function of the BBC at first was to supply details of programmes to Crocombe. It was he who asked Sir Ernest Rutherford to write in the first number on 'The Miracle of Broadcasting' and Rex Palmer ('Uncle Rex') to produce a 'Children's Corner'; he invited Reith, too, to write 'What's in the Air?' for the second number. 'Journalism is not my long suit', Reith admitted, but he and Crocombe always got on well.

Crocombe found space, too, in the very first number for an article from a listener somewhat different from the ideal listener envisaged by Reith. 'Frankly', this critical listener, P. J., wrote, 'it seems to me that the BBC are mainly catering for "listeners" who own expensive sets and pretend to appreciate and understand only highbrow music and educational "snob stuff." Surely, like a theatre manager, they must put up programmes which will appeal to the majority, and we must remember that it is the latter who provide the main bulk of their income'.

There is something refreshing in the finding of space at the very beginning for this firm declaration of separate (majority) interest…if there is also something archaic in the column 'Samuel Pepys, Listener'. In general the RADIO TIMES under successive editors never forgot that it was a 'majority' paper. The very first number sold over a quarter-of-a-million copies, and a million copies of the Christmas number were sold in 1927: they carried with them Reith's own Christmas message, 'Wise listening also implies an intelligent use of RADIO TIMES'. Christmas numbers, strikingly illustrated, were to figure prominently in the future. By 1929, when there were 2,717,367 licences, average weekly sales were 1,147,571 (*The Listener* figure was then 27,773). Ten years later, on the outbreak of the Second World War, the comparable figures were 8,968,338; 2,588,433; and 49,692. On one occasion, at least, sales promotion was too vigorous. Henry Hall's song 'Radio Times', composed to boost circulation in 1934, was such a big success that the Newspaper Proprietors' Association complained that it was direct advertising and pressured Hall to stop playing it.

This was not the only occasion when the issue of advertising arose in the history of the pre-1939 RADIO TIMES. As early as 1924 the Newspaper Proprietors' Association had expressed alarm that RADIO TIMES advertising was merely the prelude 'to larger spheres of advertising, perhaps subtle but nevertheless effective and competitive', and although eight years later *The Era* described the RADIO TIMES simply as 'the dry-goods-catalogue of the BBC', less than a quarter of the advertisements in it were concerned directly with 'wireless'. Business enterprise was an essential ingredient in the success of the magazine.

So, too, of course was editorial skill. Crocombe was forthright as well as experienced. When his critics inside the BBC suggested from time to time that he should 'puff' programmes more, he rightly insisted to Gladstone Murray, the BBC's first Director of Publicity (a Canadian 'radioman' who took over in December 1924), that 'the RADIO TIMES would fail as a popular journal and as your official organ if it were edited, as the Programme Department seems to think is possible, by a very scattered committee representing various interests'. Crocombe's successor, Walter Fuller, who became Editor in 1926 under a new arrangement which transferred editorial control from the publishers to the BBC, was more rather than less vulnerable to such pressures, for Gladstone Murray made it clear that he wished the RADIO TIMES to be 'a conscious auxiliary to the programme service'. Nonetheless, Fuller reorganised the editorial structure of the RADIO TIMES as energetically as Gladstone Murray reorganised the information services of the new Corporation, and the signs of his efforts were apparent both in the lay-out and contents of the magazine. There was only one page of pictures in 1926, but soon there were pictures throughout the paper.

MANY OF THE ARTISTS WERE GIVEN
THE FEELING, IN THE WORDS OF ONE
OF THEM, THAT THEY WERE JOINING
'A VERY EXCLUSIVE CLUB'

During the editorship of Eric Maschwitz (1927-1933) and Maurice Gorham (1933-1941) RADIO TIMES blossomed– with the pictures (and not just the pictures in the advertisements) being dealt with as thoughtfully and imaginatively as the words. Maschwitz and Gorham were lively men who were to play an even more important part in broadcasting than in journalism, but their great strength lay in the fact that they were just as interested in the world outside broadcasting as in what was going on first in Savoy Hill and (after 1932) in the less informal and more hierarchical world of Broadcasting House. Their liveliness guaranteed that the RADIO TIMES should always be more than a programme summary. So, too, indeed, did the philosophy they urged (backed by Reith) on listeners–'Plan your Listening in Advance'. Whereas American listeners were content with 'radio on tap', Maschwitz and Gorham were as determined as Reith that they should discriminate.

Gorham had started as Art Editor, and it was under his inspiration that artists with quite different styles were invited to contribute to the magazine. Sometimes they approached him: just as often he approached them (never by telephone). The same tradition of informal approach was maintained under succeeding Art Editors, although the habit of artists submitting non-commissioned drawings, as some of them did in the early years, was dropped. Many of the artists were given the feeling, in the words of one of them, that they were joining 'a very exclusive club'. Certainly, the RADIO TIMES regularly employed more artists, many of them working, of course, for other newspapers or periodicals as well, than any

other magazine of the inter-war years. They all had to work under pressure at weekends–some found this exhilarating, others 'scary', all relentless–and they were artists of very different kinds. At a time when Reith was involved in fascinating exchanges with the Editor of *The Listener* about the merits of Henri Rousseau and Paul Klee–and about 'modern art' in general–RADIO TIMES was prepared to be 'avant-garde'. Eric Fraser was often described in this way, and as Victor Reinganum states, 'The RADIO TIMES was the only magazine before 1939 prepared to take risks with the new'. London Transport and Shell were also prepared to do so, but not 'the run of the mill advertisers or magazines'.

Apart from the regular weekly editions of the RADIO TIMES great attention was paid to special numbers–a superb 'Fireside number', for example, used as the dust cover of a recent book on early broadcasting; 'Women's numbers'; 'Humour numbers' (one of 1936, introduced by Gilroy's famous laughing cat); 'Holiday numbers'; even a 'Memories number'. Above all, there were the Christmas numbers, testimony to the fact that the BBC more than any other institution contributed to a new 20th-century conception of Christmas.

THE INTRODUCTION OF COLOUR INTO THE
PAGES OF THE RADIO TIMES WAS AS
MUCH OF A TECHNICAL – AND CULTURAL –
LANDMARK AS COLOUR TELEVISION

The Christmas numbers reflect the eclecticism of approach by successive Editors and Art Editors–with Douglas Graeme Williams, who started work on the RADIO TIMES as Gorham's office boy, going on to succeed him as Art Editor in 1933 and eventually becoming Editor in 1954. The Christmas covers for 1926 and 1927 were produced by E. McKnight Kauffer, and the French poster artist A. M. Cassandre prepared the 1928 cover. Paul Nash chose wireless hardware and Edward Ardizzone Christmas decorations as the inspiration for their covers in 1930 and 1932. Althea Willoughby made use of toys in the cover for the 1936 number, which included an article by the BBC's Chairman on the tenth anniversary of the Corporation reaffirming the BBC's desire 'to broadcast Wisdom, Beauty and Contentment'.

Avant-garde or traditional, there was never any sign in the pre-1939 Christmas covers of discontent–or of the darkening international scene. Thus, Walter Hodges's 1938 cover recalls Christmases of yesteryear, and even the cover by James Hart for the first Christmas of war, 1939, displayed holly leaves. Although Guinness poster artist John Gilroy showed Santa in a tin hat on the cover of the 1940 number, his Santa was unabashedly traditional. The only difference brought about by war in the cover of the last Christmas number to be published under Gorham's Editorship, was the insertion (because of print rationing) of more verbal material on the cover page.

Artists found it interesting (though sometimes difficult) to integrate design and words on the pages of the magazine; and when these were reduced drastically during the war, one jaded listener/reader pleaded for more 'decoration and embellishment' of the pre-war kind. By then many of the artists were serving in the forces, of course, with some compensation for those remaining to be found both in new programme themes ('community whistling', for example) and in morale-boosting advertisements (like 'up housewives and at 'em'). In general, while the war provided broadcasting with the greatest challenge in its history and (after a difficult start) it responded magnificently, the RADIO TIMES suffered from the fact that its Editors were expected 'to give an example of economy to other publishers'.

The wartime Editors Gordon Stowell (1941-1944) and Tom Henn (1944-1954) faced problems unknown to their predecessors. So, too, did D. G. Williams and Leslie Barringer, who was in charge of art for part of the war. There was still a mood of austerity, indeed, when Ralph Usherwood began his ten-year spell as Art Editor in 1950 and the RADIO TIMES returned to 35 Marylebone High Street, Clothes rationing had ended only the year before, and in the year afterwards, bacon, butter, cheese, meat, eggs (one per person per week), sugar and sweets were still rationed. It was in 1951, too, that the price of the RADIO TIMES was raised to three pence, the first rise since 1923, when it was first published.

The 1950s was one of the decades of this century to which no adjective has yet been tagged, partly, of course, because it was divided down the middle. If austerity was still a key word in 1950, affluence was certainly a key word by 1960. (J. K. Galbraith's 'The Affluent Society' had appeared on the other side of the Atlantic in 1958 and, on this side, the first clothes shop for teenagers had opened in Carnaby Street two years earlier in 1956.) The biggest change inside the BBC – and the RADIO TIMES – was the emergence of television (now competitive) as the major medium; and from 1957 onwards the emphasis in RADIO TIMES covers was on vision, not sound. In the same year there was an argument behind the scenes about the separation of sound and vision in the programme pages, and in December 1957 an unusual plebiscite showed a majority of readers in favour of a return to integration. Advertisers felt the same way and reintegrated pages were eventually restored in a new lay-out of 1960, designed by Abram Games. At the same time the weekly format was changed from Sunday-Saturday to Saturday-Friday.

It is easier to record the chronology of events since 1960 than it is to interpret anything that happened in the broadcasting world or in the greater world which, according to opinion, it registered or helped to transform. (The word 'image' was a key word of this period when, during the hectic moments of the present, the whole long history of communications suddenly began to fall into place.) Williams remained as Editor of the RADIO TIMES until 1968 to be succeeded by C. J. Campbell Nairne (1968-1969), Geoffrey Cannon (1969-1979) and Brian Gearing (1980-the present); while among the Art Editors Peter Harle (1960-1969) almost saw the 'swinging sixties' through, David Driver was in the post for eight years from 1969 to 1977, and Brian Thomas, appointed in 1978, is still there. If the shift from sound to vision (and the subsequent transformation of sound including segmented radio networks and local broadcasting) are major broadcasting themes, each with a complex history, the introduction of colour into the pages of the RADIO TIMES was as much of a technical – and cultural – landmark as the development of colour television. There was full colour on the cover and some of the inside pages of the lavish 'Radio Times Annuals' of the mid-1950s – 1954, 1955 and 1956 – but it was not until 1962, the year when *The Sunday Times* produced its first colour supplement (with a Mary Quant-Jean Shrimpton cover, a James Bond short story and a 'Sharp Look at the Mood of Britain') that the RADIO TIMES carried out a trial run with colour. By 1964 it contained five pages with full colour.

YET SUCCESSIVE EDITORS AND ART-
EDITORS, WHILE RECOGNISING THE NEED
FOR CHANGE AND INITIATING IT, NEVER
BROKE WITH THE CONTINUITIES …

The difference between hue and colour, interesting though it is to students of art and graphics, is less interesting to historians than some of the other social and cultural changes of this period which were reflected in the pictures as much as in the words – the speeding up of the news and the way in which it was presented; educational change, including the growth of comprehensive schools, the enormous expansion of higher education, and new forms of art education and arguments about them; the undercurrent of satire which took some, though not all, of the complacency out of the age of affluence, and which was a feature of Hugh Greene's BBC; the appeal of 'permissiveness' – and the resistance to it – which destroyed the consensus on which the BBC had relied as an institution when its monopoly power was unbroken. In the Report of the Annan Committee on the Future of Broadcasting, the last of a series of

enquiries reaching back to 1923, we read how while 'for years British broadcasting had been able successfully to create, without alienating Government or the public, interesting and exciting popular network programmes from the world of reality as well as the world of fantasy', now 'these began to stir up resentment and hostility, and protests against their political and social overtones'.

Changes in the art of the RADIO TIMES are worth studying in order to approach these issues. Indeed, they often reveal more than a cleverly assembled television programme or even a well-ordered academic argument. Yet successive Editors and Art Editors, while recognising the need for change and initiating it, never broke with the continuities of the magazine: they continued to employ artists who had been working for the paper during the 1930s. They were also in no doubt about the magazine's distinct identity. The Annan Committee wisely refused to accept the suggestion of a 1968/9 House of Commons Estimates Committee that the RADIO TIMES and the *TV Times* should amalgamate in the dubious interest of 'economy'. Each broadcasting organisation, its report stated, 'should be allowed to publish material about their programmes in the manner and style which they think will be the most attractive and helpful to their audiences'.

The Annan Report showed no interest, however, in the story which is unfolded in this book. 'We incline to the view', they stated, 'that the RADIO TIMES, should have fewer articles by prominent writers and better programme notes'. Yet by making no reference at all to the pictures they limited the range of evidence at their own disposal.

'THE RADIO AGE WAS A GOLDEN
PERIOD FOR THE ILLUSTRATOR IN THAT
YOU WERE CREATING VISUAL IMAGES OF
THE SOUNDS PEOPLE WERE HEARING…'

In this book every picture tells a story, and all the pictures put together provide a kind of cavalcade, a word which (like the word panorama) broadcasting made once more fashionable. 'The radio age', Laurence Scarfe told an interviewer in 1979, 'was a golden period for the illustrator in that you were creating visual images of the sounds people were hearing from their radios'. Yet fortunately, as this book shows, gripping illustrations did not come to an end with the advent of television; we can do far more technically in the 1980s with the lay-out of the published text – article, newspaper, magazine or book – than would have been thought conceivable during the 1920s. But the techniques by themselves are never enough – just as they are never enough in broadcasting. The imagination of the artist is essential to get the best of them, and he can reveal the quality of that imagination not only when he is thinking of posterity, but when he is under orders to produce his work between Friday and Monday morning.

As long ago as 1932, the RADIO TIMES was boasting that several of its artists had just held one-man exhibitions, that a Kent art school had organised an exhibition of drawings from the magazine, and that Roland Pym, who had drawn the first page inside the Christmas number – 'all robins and fairy queens' – had just designed a bathroom for a bishop ('newspapers gloating over the fact that bishops bathe').

Broadcasting has changed our conceptions of time in this century – of the minute, hour, the day and tomorrow – and viewed in historical terms, this may stand out (along with its appeal to huge audiences) as a major influence. It has also given us access to generals and prime ministers as well as to bishops. The word 'TIMES' in the title of the RADIO TIMES is not just a reference to the times of particular broadcasts, but a pointer (like the title of *The Times* newspaper) to the changing shapes of a whole society and culture. The pictures make many of the shapes real: they will also help to restore the sense of immediacy when we move out of the age of broadcasting altogether. And some will attract new generations in the future as much as they attracted people in the past.

RADIO TIMES OWES ITS STATURE AS A MAJOR PATRON OF
EDITIORIAL DESIGN IN BRITAIN ORIGINALLY TO A GROUP OF
REMARKABLE MEN WHO EDITED AND ART-EDITED RADIO TIMES
IN THE 1920's

Like other British institutions that work best by goodwill and common understanding–cricket, the Law, Parliament, the BBC itself–RADIO TIMES defies logic.

Founded in September 1923 by John Reith in response to a hostile British press which wanted to charge advertising rates for publishing BBC programmes, RADIO TIMES has always been a commercial enterprise. In 1934 it had achieved a circulation of two million, and its net profit in that year was over one quarter of the total BBC licence income. Immediately before ITV broke the BBC monopoly of British broadcasting in 1955, its circulation was over eight million; and it has remained the weekly periodical with the highest circulation in Britain.

RADIO TIMES owes its well-being, and in particular its stature as a, and sometimes the, major patron of editorial illustration in Britain, originally to a group of remarkable men who edited and art-edited RADIO TIMES in the 1920s. It was founded, as its original masthead proclaimed, as 'the official organ of the BBC'; and has always been seen, in and out of the BBC, if not exactly as BBC publicity, certainly as promotion for the BBC and its programmes. The BBC, after all, is its publisher.

How could–how can–RADIO TIMES have real editorial quality or (not at all the same thing) gain a large and wide circulation, and be profitable, if it is BBC publicity? Or, indeed, if it is bound to reflect the full range of BBC programme activity, including educational and other programmes never designed for a general audience? It was probably a good thing for the BBC that the first Editor of RADIO TIMES, Leonard Crocombe, was never a BBC man, but was seconded from *Titbits*, which he edited from 1918 to 1945, by George Newnes who, for the first few years of the life of RADIO TIMES, were its co-publishers with the then British Broadcasting Company, whose initial role was to supply the programme details and let him get on and edit the journal. In a trenchant memorandum dated 31 August 1925 (which was hung on the wall of the Editor's office during the 1970s), addressed to Gladstone Murray, the BBC's Director of Publicity, and himself a champion of RADIO TIMES, Crocombe wrote, in answer to a protest from the BBC programme staff, as follows: 'The RADIO TIMES would fail as a popular journal and as your official organ if it were edited, as the Programme Department seems to think is possible, by a very scattered committee representing various interests'. Exactly so. Editors should edit.

In 1926 Walter Fuller followed Crocombe as Editor, then came Eric Maschwitz, who was succeeded by Maurice Gorham who, previously, had invented the post of Art Editor for himself. During Maschwitz's time, in the late 1920s and early 1930s, RADIO TIMES also employed Val Gielgud and Laurence Gilliam. These were four of the BBC's great men: Maschwitz went on to be head of radio Variety; Gielgud of radio Drama, Gilliam of radio Features and Gorham, who stayed longest at RADIO TIMES, went on to be head of the radio Light Programme and later, briefly, head of BBC Television. Both Maschwitz and Gorham wrote memoirs of their RADIO TIMES days which show them both as visionaries, buccaneers and indomitable champions of their cause, who earned themselves a good time by hard work. And they made the magazine work by making it lively; enjoyed both by its publishers and its readers.

The 1920s were uniquely exciting years to work for BBC radio and to listen to its programmes. Everything was new. There was a widely shared consciousness that radio was changing British, and world, society. By September 1925, 40 million people were in range of BBC broadcasts. And many of the RADIO TIMES illustrations in the 1920s reflect a sense of changing space and shifting social and family relationships.

It takes certainly several years for any periodical to achieve its own editorial style, and many of the illustrators who worked for RADIO TIMES in the 1920s had earned reputations elsewhere. Even so, the particular requirements of RADIO TIMES, from its beginnings, were reflected in characteristic illustrative treatments. These types of illustration, done as always under excruciating pressure of time, all had a definite editorial purpose: to be, in Gladstone Murray's characteristically somewhat-shaded phrase, 'a conscious auxiliary to the programme service'. Maschwitz put it squarely, in a 1928 memorandum: 'The present policy is based on the belief that what readers of the RADIO TIMES want is every kind of information that can help them to appreciate broadcast programmes'.

During the 1926 General Strike, RADIO TIMES, in common with almost all other journals in the country, was unable to appear. For the BBC, the strike presented a great challenge and a great opportunity–to keep the country cool and informed. Reith kept in constant touch with announcers and made important broadcasts himself–and with the strike over Radio was established as a front-rank communications medium. As RADIO TIMES commented on its return: 'It is not easy to estimate what would have been the effect of the strike if there had been no such thing as wireless communication'.

For RADIO TIMES the best was yet to come. Maschwitz and Gorham saw to it that RADIO TIMES should fully explore its privileged position by attempting, at least on occasion, to publish the very best illustration, which would sometimes contradict received notions of what a popular periodical could or should do. Covers are inevitably the clearest signal of a magazine's vivacity. And in 1926 McKnight Kauffer's spectacular and brilliant Christmas cover design *(right)* of the radio lightning-flash linking London with the Holy Star was published despite doom-laden protests from Newnes, still then co-publishers. It was the most daring and memorable work of illustration published by RADIO TIMES in the 1920s. And it outsold the previous Christmas issues.

By the end of the 1920s the circulation of RADIO TIMES was well over a million copies a week, and rising. There seemed to be no limit to growth.

RADIO TIMES, DECEMBER 17TH, 1926.]

Southern Edition.

CHRISTMAS NUMBER

BBC

6d.

THE

RADIO TIMES

E. McKnight K.

Vol. XIII. No. 168. December 17th, 1926.

Registered at the G.P.O. as a Newspaper. S.

The Philistine (switching off): "Wicked the way this classical stuff is supplanting jazz—what?"

"Does your wife like the wireless?"
"Not a bit.   She can't talk over it."

Voice of Uncle: "Hullo, Chicks!"
Irritated Listener: "Confound it!   Another talk on poultry!"

WIRELESS EDUCATION.
"'Ow did yer like Beethoven's 9th Symphony last night on the old crystal?"
"Bit too 'ackneyed, old boy!   'Ad it three times in the last six months."

RADIO TIMES. Vol. IX. No. 117. December 18th, 1925.
Registered at the G.P.O. as a Newspaper.
THE CHRISTMAS NUMBER
RADIO TIMES
6D.
Abbey

B.B.C. OFFICIALS AS OUR ARTIST SEES THEM
'The Chief Engineer'

Engineer 1929: 'I think it's just about time we faded him out !'

THE BIG NOISE.

Teddy Brown, the master of the xylophone, the man who can play every instrument in his own band, the one London character whom the most unobservant know by sight, is ' on tour ' this week. Make a note of the date when he comes your way : Monday, Cardiff ; Tuesday, Belfast ; Wednesday, Newcastle ; Thursday, Aberdeen ; Friday, Manchester ; Saturday, Glasgow

TOMMY HANDLEY

KEEPING AN EYE ON THE FILMS
Mr. Anthony Asquith

THE MAN WITH THE SCALPEL
Mr. A. G. Gardiner

Here are the Musical Avolos (as Sherriffs sees them). The Avolos have brought xylophone playing to a tremendous art. They make all their own instruments, one of which weighs nearly three hundred pounds. If you have never heard them, you should watch for them this week—the combination of three great xylophones playing at the same time is something quite new in music. The Avolos are broadcasting this week as follows :—

Monday, Newcastle ;   Tuesday, Aberdeen ; Wednesday, Manchester ; Thursday, Belfast ; Saturday, Cardiff.

A VISION OF THE NEAR FUTURE.
Listening and seeing at the same time.

ERIC FRASER WAS BORN IN 1902 AND HAD BEEN DRAWING FOR RADIO TIMES SINCE 1926, SURELY SOMETHING OF A RECORD. HE WAS EDUCATED AT WESTMINSTER CITY SCHOOL UNTIL THE AGE OF 17

Where did you receive your art training?
'I went to Goldsmiths' College at New Cross between 1919 and 1924. To begin with, the college was still full of ex-servicemen and 'women on government grants. They were an exceedingly enthusiastic bunch of students. Until a younger master came, Clive Gardner, we were all drawing hard from The Antique – that kind of work. He introduced a new aspect entirely of more simplified basic design in figure-work. Another member of staff was Edmund J. Sullivan, who was an expert in line work. He probably had the greater influence on me because he showed me how it was possible to draw in straightforward line in a very vigorous manner.

'When I left Goldsmiths' I had heard, through the principal of the college, of R. P. Gossop who had just started an agency for artists. I applied to him and he said he would take me on–which he did in 1925–and I immediately got married on the strength of it. From then to this day they have handled all my work. In 1926, I received my first commission through him for a drawing for RADIO TIMES, which, as far as I can remember, was a humorous drawing of a family listening to a radio with the old horn loudspeaker. In those days we did drawings and submitted them, they were not necessarily commissioned'.

Today you are best known as the 'tragedian' of RADIO TIMES illustrators, the man who does the really heavy stuff: the Greek dramas, the Shakespearian plays, that sort of thing. I believe that in your younger days that was not the way it was.
'Nearly all my drawings in the 20s and early 30s were humorous. I don't remember doing any serious illustrations until RADIO TIMES commissioned me to illustrate a Pirandello play'.

Today and for many years past you have had a very distinctive, strong, almost stark technique. Presumably you had to develop that technique from the style of your humorous illustrations.
'Yes, it has always been my belief that the technique used in a drawing should suit the subject matter. When you come to Greek drama, it's necessary to draw in such a manner that it gives a true impression of Greek design and methods of patterning; the same applies to Shakespeare–all plays which require a more elaborate, crosshatch technique. As to Restoration plays, they definitely require a complicated flowing line and very decorative formal masses'.

Eric, you've mentioned the ways in which you have fitted your technique to the content of the commissions you've been given for RADIO TIMES. Perhaps, by doing so, you have influenced the sort of commisson that RADIO TIMES gave to you. You've mentioned your treatment of Shakespearian plays, and I'm looking as I speak at your drawing for 'The Merchant of Venice,' a good example of what you have been saying. I personally commissioned from you a drawing for 'Arsenic and Old Lace,' for which you used a different technique for what was, of course, a very different kind of play... Perhaps you'd like to say something about that...
'I consider that the artist is similar to an actor, in that he has a part to play and should make up and act that part. The artist receiving a script should adapt himself to interpreting that script. In the case of "Arsenic and Old Lace," which was set in late Victorian or Edwardian America, it seemed to me that the technique I needed to use should be rather more light-hearted. Although the play had a basically serious plot, it was treated in a light-hearted way, and I found I could enjoy myself, almost relaxing, by using a fine pen to produce squiggly lines, gradually building up the masses so that the drawing was rather wiry and much more fun'.

Now we come to a problem in drawing for RADIO TIMES, which has been for some a thorn in the side and to others a challenge, and that is the headings and borders with which the magazine has always decorated its programme pages to mark the great national festivals of the year. The Art Editor would give a layout to the illustrator containing a series of very
awkward shapes within which the artist would decorate in a way which would be true to the feel of whichever festival was in question. How did you feel about this type of commission, of which you did more than any artist I can think of?
'Those commissions were always a considerable problem. It was very necessary to accommodate the lettering, which was probably the most important part of the design–after all it states what the design is all about. I always considered it a challenge when asked to design one of these, and I always enjoyed it. Sometimes they come off and sometimes they didn't but, in the main, I enjoyed the effort of overcoming the difficulties of making designs fit into your odd shapes'.

Obviously there must have been times when you produced a drawing for RADIO TIMES and the Art Editor, for whatever reason, suggested an alteration to you–or even perhaps rejected it out of hand. It is common to any Art Editor/illustrator relationship that it produces the occasional friction of that kind. Can you think of any such?
'Definitely. For example, the illustration I did for a play called "Aaron's Field," by D. G. Bridson. I drew a number of people standing around, and from the centre of them arose the figure of Christ, to illustrate an actual incident in the play. The drawing was sent straight back to me with a request to remove the figure of Christ and insert that of a human figure, albeit a figure with small wings, because on the opposite page to this drawing was a photograph of a comedian and they didn't think the two would mix. So Christ came out and the comedian stayed. I wondered why it

Aaron's Field – 1939
'The drawing was sent straight back to me'.

couldn't have been done the other way round.

'Another case I can think of was one of a series I did to illustrate articles by Maurice Lane Norcott. In one of these I showed the side of a building with pieces of nude statuary set in niches. Back came the drawing with a request that I dress them in robes. I think of this whenever I see the Eric Gill sculptures on Broadcasting House'.

Since 1923, RADIO TIMES has been perhaps one of the major sources of patronage of the graphic arts in this country, and many distinguished artists have drawn for it. Many, many illustrators began their careers by drawing for RADIO TIMES, and are household names today in the graphics world: Eric, were you pleased to be of this number, and did you admire any of them particularly?
'Of course, I was very pleased indeed, because at that time I was still quite young, and to be given the opportunity of joining the band of capable illustrators in such a well-known publication was a great compliment'.

You were commissioned to do a drawing on a Thursday if you were lucky, Friday if the Art Editor was over-worked. This left you the weekend to do your drawing and get it to us by Monday midday. Now, this is very little time to give an illustrator, certainly an illustrator of your technique and character. How did you feel about that?
'I didn't feel at all happy at times. In my case, I got the script on the Friday evening and then had to read it, assemble whatever reference was necessary, which happened very often because the sort of drawings I was asked to do were mainly historical, then I would do a quick rough to get the general feeling of the subject, and then the finished drawing. As it had to be delivered to my agent by Monday morning, or at the very latest Tuesday morning, it certainly left very little time to sit back and make alterations or have second thoughts'.

Yet in spite of these drawbacks, Eric, you maintained a very high standard over a very long time. Perhaps it could be argued that RADIO TIMES was doing you a favour. You produced, strong, original thoughts.
'I think the challenge of having to produce a drawing in such a short time, worrying as it was, did produce an ability to draw upon hidden reserves of energy which are not normally used. When you have a week or more in which to produce a drawing, the mind tends to relax, and those reserves are not called upon at all. I suppose we all have these hidden reserves which are there to call upon in an emergency and, as far as I was concerned, every commission I received from RADIO TIMES was an emergency.

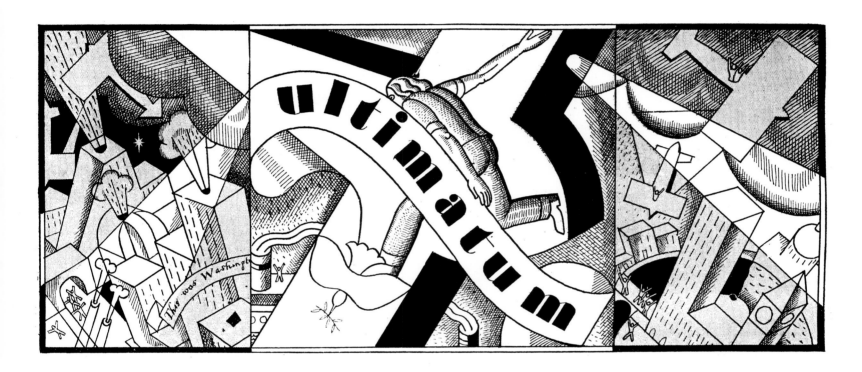

THE RADIO TIMES

THE JOURNAL OF THE BRITISH BROADCASTING CORPORATION

NATION SHALL SPEAK PEACE UNTO NATION

THEIR COVERS GAVE OPPORTUNITIES TO BOTH ESTABLISHED ARTISTS AND NEWCOMERS TO DEVELOP WORK SUITABLE FOR RADIO TIMES AND WILL FOREVER REMAIN SYMBOLIC OF THE GRAPHIC ARTWORK OF THE ERA

The 1930s was a decade of great events and changes culminating in the most dramatic of all–the outbreak of the Second World War. But one feature was a model of stability–the price, at 2d, of RADIO TIMES. As the hungry unemployed marched, as Britain's Monarchy itself trembled under the impact of the Abdication crisis, as the war-clouds gathered, the two-penny price of RADIO TIMES was so secure that they even printed it on rubber door-mats and enamelled advertisements. Indeed, incredible as it may seem today to a world grown accustomed to rampaging inflation, the cover price of RADIO TIMES was unchanged from its birth right through to 1951.

Maurice Gorham (Art Editor from 1926 until 1933 and then Editor until 1941) was the magazine's compelling influence during the 30s. It was he who established the most distinctive feature of the decade–the Special Numbers. Six to eight of these were produced each year. Their covers gave opportunities to both established artists and newcomers to develop work suitable for RADIO TIMES and will forever remain symbolic of the graphic artwork of the era. Probably the most famous of all was John Gilroy's laughing cat on the Humour Number in October 1936. A reader hailed it as '... the jolliest face I ever saw in print'. But there are many others: Edward Ardizzone's Children's Hour Number (1937) and two Women's Numbers are especially memorable, those by Ralph and Mott (1934) and Clixby Watson (1939).

At the appropriate season readers were encouraged out of doors, while the Fireside Numbers (notably Philip Zec's 1935 cover) suggested cosy nights by the fire with the wireless as an ever-present companion. Stanley Herbert's 1937 Outside Broadcasts cover (*right*) was acclaimed.

Eric Maschwitz, who preceded Gorham as Editor, established the fine maxim of 'planning your listening in advance'. This theme led to RADIO TIMES becoming a vehicle for ideas and articles of genuine critical appreciation, rather than merely an agency for noting programmes which were to be broadcast. It also set a pattern which no Editor has ever completely lost sight of to this day.

In 1932, Broadcasting House, that great, gleaming, white liner of a building, dropped anchor in Portland Place and the BBC said farewell to Savoy Hill, where it had lived out its first ten years. A copy of the first issue of RADIO TIMES was deposited beneath the foundation stone of the im-pressive new building.

There were important developments, too, in the printing arrangements for RADIO TIMES. The BBC, as the magazine's publishers, commissioned Waterlow & Sons Limited to construct a custom-built factory at Park Royal in North London. The Duke of Gloucester opened the new premises, and, with their seven huge rotary letterpress machines, they were as modern and well-equipped a print factory as you could find anywhere in the world. The first issue from Park Royal, 8 January 1937, stated that the magazine would be printed there for the next ten years. Forty years later the same plant was still going strong!

The Abdication apart, the 30s saw Royal events which were a rich cause for national celebration–the first Royal wedding to be broadcast (1934), the Silver Jubilee of George V and the Coronation of George VI. The 110-page Coronation issue had a sale of 3,540,547 copies, which was under-stood to be the largest ever recorded by a weekly magazine in any country.

The yearly *pièce-de-résistance* was the Christmas number which until the war had a cover designed by leading artists, including McKnight Kauffer, Paul Nash, C. Walter Hodges and Rex Whistler. On these occasions RADIO TIMES had a special price–6d–but offered a much-enlarged service, including Christmas stories, supplements and items by performers.

Television arrived in the London area in November 1936, and RADIO TIMES marked this with a special supplement for distribution throughout the capital. Later, details of the television programmes, which were still available only in a limited area, were carried on one page in all copies.

Sunday programme pages throughout the 30s reflected faithfully the Reithian influence. Until the war only serious music, religious programmes and news bulletins were permitted. Gorham did his best to keep Reith at bay. But Reith was a frequent visitor to the RADIO TIMES offices and once demonstrated his authority by insisting that a Harpic advertisement was removed from the Sunday page.

During the rest of the week broadcasting on Radio's seven channels–one national and six regional–was dominated by the full range of music. Talks, stories, drama, news, religion, outside broadcasts and, of course, *Children's Hour* were also there but, for hour after hour, the airwaves of Britain were filled by music.

Gorham had clearly stated his aims in 1934–to produce a journal 'with the largest possible circulation and to give the most helpful kind of service ancillary to broadcasting'. He aimed to aid the 'average listener' to 'understand and appreciate the programme' and maintained that the journal must not be too highbrow but not go down-market.

When war came in September 1939 dramatic changes occurred in RADIO TIMES. Immediately, the size of the journal was drastically reduced. And, at this strenuous period of adjustment, RADIO TIMES actually went to press three times in five days, surely a unique achievement for a weekly journal. Its normal Friday issue containing the next week's programmes (never broadcast) was already on sale. The previous day it had gone to press with the issue for the week after (this number, of course, never saw the light of day). The first war-time issue, already in part prepared against such a need, was at once put under way and within three days, on Monday, 4 September 1939, was on sale with details for the rest of that week.

The world was at war–but RADIO TIMES, to John Reith 'the connecting link of the service', was firmly establshed as part of the British way of life.

Radio Times, June 4, 1937 Vol. 55 No. 714   Registered at the G.P.O. as a Newspaper   Price Twopence

RADIO TIMES

OUTSIDE BROADCASTS NUMBER

2d

We want Robespierre —

the Horse Show —

the Eclipse of the Moon —

Sand-blasting in a bell foundry —

— and Winston Churchill

Now go away

We go away

We ponder

We consult

We confer, and—

on Monday we submit

ROBESPIERRE—

('Very good of Nelson Keys'
says the Art Editor)

— THE HORSE SHOW —
('Enlarged cross-section of some
rare microbe, I take it' says the
Intelligence Department)

— THE ECLIPSE —
('Besides' says the Engineer 'you
don't get headphones that size')

— SAND-BLASTING —
('A.R.P., what?'
says Puzzle Corner)

AND WINSTON CHURCHILL—

('Postponed', says the Editor, 'take it
away and make it into the Forth Bridge')

We are removed — and on Friday the Editor
says to us 'We want—'

The Radio Times, May 18, 1934

JACK DUNKLEY

JACK DUNKLEY WAS BORN IN 1906 IN HOLLOWAY AND WAS EDUCATED AT THE SIR HUGH MIDDLETON CENTRAL SCHOOL, WHICH HE LEFT AT THE AGE OF 16 AND GOT A JOB IN WARDOUR STREET DOING SUBTITLES FOR ADVERTISING FILMS, WHITE LETTERING ON BLACK CARD. HE STAYED WITH THEM DOING FREELANCE WORK IN HIS SPARE TIME FOR ABOUT EIGHT YEARS

'During that time I was earning about 17-and-six a week, working Saturday mornings and running all the way to play football on Hackney Marshes in the afternoon. However, while I was there I won an evening scholarship which entitled me to go to the Central School of Arts and Crafts in Southampton Row for three evenings a week. I also got £3 a year for travelling expenses. The scholarship was for three years but, if I kept up a minimum of 80 per cent attendances, I could get another free year – which I did. By keeping up that level of attendance I managed to get eight years of free attendances working at general drawing, doing a bit of everything. I had no aspirations to becoming a "fine" artist, I was commercial minded right from the start, had to be. Anyway, I left the film studio in about 1930. I'd developed a few freelance connections with newspapers, so I started sending cartoons around. I got my first real commission from *The Daily Mirror* in 1932, which was about the same time as I got my first drawing in RADIO TIMES, so they're my oldest customers.

'I read a letter in RADIO TIMES which I illustrated and then took it around to Savoy Hill and showed it to a fellow who became a great friend of mine, Maurice Gorham, and a young office boy called Douglas Graeme Williams. The Editor then was Eric Maschwitz. I got on very well with Maurice: he was a likeable, jovial fellow, a man after my own heart. He was an Irishman and had a slight stammer when he got excited and talked too fast.

'When my first, tiny drawing was published in RADIO TIMES I was awfully proud of it. In those early days I remember Maurice asking me to illustrate a series called something like "Radio Through the Ages," a sort of comic-historical series; things like *The Mayflower* sailing from Plymouth with a loudspeaker blaring away and somebody on the quay shouting, "Clear out, we've had enough of that noisy rubbish".

Incidentally, I do remember that I drew them all on scraperboard. RADIO TIMES definitely saw me as a humorous artist in those days. In fact, I always have specialised in humour and sport'.

You were in good company – Eric Fraser was regarded by RADIO TIMES *as a comic artist at that time. When did you start covering sport for us?*
'I have difficulty remembering dates, but it was about the time you moved from Savoy Hill to Broadcasting House. I remember meeting Clixby Watson then. I thought he was a brilliant artist and very jovial. He was a tall fellow, carried quite a bit of weight and had a weak leg which had to be supported by a leg-iron. Most of us, when we had delivered our drawings to RADIO TIMES in the afternoon, used to go on to the pub in the evening, playing darts and table-tennis. Clixby was the champion at both in spite of his handicap; how he got around so fast as he did I just don't know, he was a very agile hopper.

'As Douglas Williams progressed in his career he took us all along with him, all pals together. Douglas became a very fine Art Editor and I have very pleasant memories of him. He could always suggest ideas to his illustrators in a way that eliminated a lot of hard work. I can't remember him ever turning one of my drawings down, which is rather remarkable. Right at the beginning of the war, before I went overseas, I used to phone up on a Monday from wherever I was stationed to see if there was anything he wanted drawing. Usually there would be an order for a couple of drawings and they would be finished and in the post that night'.

I remember asking you over the phone, at 3.30 in the afternoon, to do a football drawing. I described it to you and gave you the size and said that I needed it the following day. I shall always remember you saying, 'Well, I've nearly got it finished, I'll drop it off on the way home'. I ask every illustrator that I've interviewed a stock question: what did they feel about the pressures of working to the short deadlines of RADIO TIMES? *Quite obviously the question is pointless in your case.*
'Well, yes, I've always worked very quickly – it's one of my few assets. Working as I have all my life for daily papers made it a necessity, it was a problem that was never a bother to me'.

Tell me something about the way you draw, how you set about it, what tools you use and so on.
'Pen and brush were my main tools. For RADIO TIMES nearly all my drawings were done with a fine brush. With a soccer match I always had to check on the strip the teams would be wearing. I was well placed at the *Mirror* to get quick reference from their library or check it out with the sports-desk. Although I worked there as a freelance I had my own studio, I still have it to this day – 40 years later, even though I only go in once a week. As far as I know this is a unique privilege. I'd start scribbling, trying to get some feel of action into the drawing – in pencil on paper, then transfer it on to a piece of drawing board and then ink it in. Usually by that time a messenger from the BBC would be downstairs waiting for it.

'This had the advantage for me that, being "pinch-hitter" for RADIO TIMES, I got a wide variety of subjects to draw over the years: illustrating play scripts, variety programmes and even drawing caricature portraits. Always my first need was to know the shape and size and then I would think my drawing into it. I found this very useful when you asked me to draw headings for Christmas or Easter on the programme pages. I didn't mind at all that the shapes were difficult, I could always fill them, even if it was a case of RADIO TIMES ringing and saying, "One-and-three-quarter-inches wide, half-an-inch deep, subject: Wembley Stadium on an international football match day." '

At the beginning of the war, Jack, when you were about 33, I believe you and Douglas Williams went to Bristol where the BBC Variety and Light Music departments had found refuge.
'We had a cousin of Basil Rathbone with us to write the copy and I had to draw the life and times of all the broadcasting artists. I remember Sir Frank Dobson the sculptor was there, too, and did some portraits for you. The actors were rehearsing all over the shop – in church halls and all sorts of curious places. "Garrison Theatre" with Jack Warner and his "lil gel" – Joan Winters, who was the daughter of the conductor of the Variety Orchestra Charles Shadwell. I drew them all: Dorothy Carless, Vera Lynn, Anne Shelton, Max Kester, Kenaway and Young, I drew them while Rathbone interviewed them.

'I went overseas in 1942 so that finished my contact with RADIO TIMES for a while. We landed in Algeria in November 1942 and stayed there for two years. I was a radar specialist and I went to two officer-selection boards – I'm still waiting to hear from them'.

When the war eventually ended what happened to you?
'My demob number came up in early 1946 and, the day after I got out, I went round to the *Express* and sold them a strip I'd been working on while waiting for demob. I started straight away again with the *Mirror* but I was also working for the *News Chronicle*, the *Express* and the *Daily Sketch*. As I'd started up again immediately with RADIO TIMES as well I was pretty busy'.

Douglas Williams came back from the War Office and was succeeded in 1950 by Ralph Usherwood with whom you also got on very well, I remember; I became his deputy at the same time. At that time you were drawing practically every week; sometimes, indeed, three or four times a week. You must have done more drawings for RADIO TIMES *than any other illustrator in its history.*
'Yes, I think that's probably true over the long time which I worked for you. I think I did all your sporting drawings for over 30 years. I even did a couple of covers for you – one for the Grand National and one for the Olympic Games, in which I used chalk to do a figure of the athlete carrying the torch to light the Olympic flame, as I remember. They were certainly the biggest jobs I ever did for RADIO TIMES, I remember being very impressed at getting them'.

Another stock question, Jack. Of all the other illustrators who drew for RADIO TIMES, *for which of them did you have a particular respect or liking?*
'Oh, most of them, but perhaps particularly Clixby Watson, Eric Fraser, Bob Sherriffs, Arthur Watts – they all drew better than I did. I suppose Eric was the most brilliant draughtsman.

'Incidentally, going back a bit to the beginning of the war, RADIO TIMES was evacuated to the Park Royal printing works in Wembley and I remember going down there with my pen and little bottle of ink every Wednesday asking if there were any drawings needed. I did them on the spot, so I can claim to have had a desk in RADIO TIMES as well'.

Hanging a bat out to dry; Bumper and Duck – 1938: 'I always have specialised in humour and sport'.

'A Mr. Funf would like to speak to you, sir'

MOTORING
versus
WALKING
As a means of seeing the countryside
A discussion between
L. DU GARDE PEACH
and
P. M. OLIVER, M.P.
To be broadcast tonight at 9.15

'...and now, if you will just tune down your sets a little...'

GENTLEMEN
v. PLAYERS

THE RADIO TIMES

SUMMER NUMBER

They say a Garden is a Lovesome Thing
By BEVERLEY NICHOLS

The World we Listen in
By FILSON YOUNG

A Masque of Neptune
By HERBERT FARJEON

The Voice that Cured a King
By ROBIN HEY

Treasure Upon Earth: A Radio Play
By L. DU GARDE PEACH

A Chinaman Visits the Proms
By W. R. ANDERSON

'I have Fallen in Love with a Lady-oh!
By E. V. KNOX

The D.O.I. : An Interview of the Future
By WINIFRED HOLTBY

BATT

THE
RADIO TIMES

THE JOURNAL OF THE BRITISH-BROADCASTING CORPORATION

NATION SHALL SPEAK PEACE UNTO NATION

Vol. 38. No. 493. [Registered at the G.P.O. as a Newspaper.] MARCH 10, 1933. Every Friday. TWO PENCE.

'MACBETH'

A broadcast version of Shakespeare's tragedy will be given on Sunday afternoon

SCHUBERT . . . . . A LITTLE MAN BUT A GIANT

BEETHOVEN: THE MAN

THE PROMS : ONE OF THE MOST REMARKABLE SIGHTS IN BRITAIN

reinganum.

VICTOR REINGANUM WAS BORN IN LONDON IN 1907 AND EDUCATED AT HABERDASHERS SCHOOL IN HAMPSTEAD, AND BEGAN HIS ART EDUCATION FIRST AT HEATHERLEY AND THEN AT THE ACADEMIE JULIAN IN THE QUARTIER LATIN, PARIS. DURING HIS YEAR IN PARIS HE WAS ONE OF ONLY SIX STUDENTS ACCEPTED BY THE DISTINGUISHED PAINTER LEGER AND, ONCE A WEEK, ATTENDED HIS TEACHING STUDIO IN MONTMARTRE

'In 1926 I tramped round London with a folio of rather poor drawings, and I went to RADIO TIMES at Savoy Hill and saw Maurice Gorham, who was the Art Editor, and much to my surprise and delight he actually bought one of the drawings I had in my folio. It was a drawing in airbrush of a rather dashing dancing girl, slightly sexy, and he used it in RADIO TIMES for one of the many cabaret-type programmes which were all the rage at the time.

'I was rather typecast to begin with as "a bright young thing", and I was asked to draw subjects like cocktail bars, dancing girls, the sort of swinging-20s kind of thing. Eventually I graduated to the sort of drawing I preferred to do. Gorham would try you out, when he got to know you, by giving you very different types of things.

'In those days you were called to Savoy Hill. Gorham never commissioned by telephone, you would just get a message to come down and see him. But time was very tight then, as I believe it is now, for an illustrator. One had to work over the weekend and deliver the drawing on Monday morning, but I'm very glad that I had that sort of training because it was an extremely good discipline. This sort of short-order working didn't happen only with RADIO TIMES, the advertising agencies always needed their work in a frantic hurry too.

'Three guineas was the going rate and, in real money terms, I think I was rather better paid then than your illustrators are now. I lived fairly comfortably on about six guineas a week while supporting a wife and two children.

'I was always very happy to work for RADIO TIMES because I had a very good chance that anything I did was going to be used; in consequence I felt free to let myself go, far more so than with any other job. Occasionally Maurice Gorham would turn a drawing down flat, and then I would have to re-do it by working right through the night, and bring back a new drawing the next morning.'

On a Friday morning you were asked to do a drawing needed by Monday midday, how did you go about it?
'The size and shape of the drawing came first. What I always did was to draw a series of small rectangles to the proportion given, quite small, postage-stamp size, and fiddle around with them and pick the one I thought to be the best composition. I'm a good visualiser and I usually started with a pretty clear picture in my head of what I wanted the drawing to end up looking like – there are very few "accidents" in my work.

'I was mainly a pen man. For a short time I used scraperboard, but I gave it up because I found I could do more with a pen to create black and white shapes. I always found my drawings getting too "tight" on scraperboard. I did buy an airbrush when they became fashionable in the 20s, but I used it very rarely in my work for RADIO TIMES because I never thought it a suitable method for a magazine printed by letterpress on newsprint.'

On the great national festivals of the year it was always our policy to ask illustrators to decorate the top and sides of a double-spread of pages. The shapes given to you by the Art Editor were precise and very awkward ones – a very difficult job for an illustrator. How did you feel about it?
'I didn't find it difficult at all, in fact quite the reverse. I have always found it easy to decorate, in some ways too easy for my own good. They were nothing like as much of a challenge as a straight illustration of, say, Ibsen or Shaw. Mind you. I enjoyed the lettering, which I think I was always rather good at.'

In 1941 you took over from Bob Sherriffs the job of illustrating the diary pages of RADIO TIMES which, in those days were called 'Both Sides of the Microphone.' How did you find that as a job, and did you enjoy it?
'It was enormous fun to do because there was so much variety. It also gave me an opportunity to introduce a bit of humour into my drawing. They were very small drawings, but this wasn't a problem as I was always apt to put in too much detail in my larger drawings and these small ones proved to be a very good discipline.'

You must have been very aware of the other illustrators: in a way your competitors. What did you feel?
'In my early days there was considerable prestige attached to drawing for RADIO TIMES, and there were some very considerable artists who contributed quite regularly. There were several I admired enormously: Eric Fraser, of course, Pearl Falconer, Len Rosoman later, and John Minton.'

When you started, Victor, I'm sure most of the readers would have regarded you and, shall we say, Eric Fraser, as very much avant-garde. *Was it not adventurous of RADIO TIMES to use illustrators like you at that time?*
'Before the war RADIO TIMES was the only magazine I knew of which was prepared to take that kind of risk. There were one or two big firms like London Transport and Shell who used *avant-garde* artists, but this was certainly not true of run of the mill advertisers or magazines. So RADIO TIMES was very valuable to illustrators with something new to say.'

Both Sides of the Microphone – 1941
'Enormous fun to do'

I remember a full-colour Christmas cover, which I think was reproduced by roto gravure. What did you feel about drawing in colour for RADIO TIMES? You did quite a few like, for example, the 50th anniversary special publication.
'I was delighted to have the commissions and I enjoyed doing them but, unfortunately, I was always very disappointed by the final result, which in my opinion bore very little resemblance to my original artwork as far as colour was concerned. I always found this to be true of any colour reproduction, unless it was by the most expensive method, say by a seven colour process. I was, of course, trained as a painter, there was no such thing as a commercial art course then, and I'm very glad there wasn't. I was just taught to be an artist.'

'Au Lapin Qui Saute'

Produced by John Watt

Au Lapin Qui Saute: 1930
'A rather dashing dancing girl, slightly sexy'

DENNIS AND LARRY
INTERVIEW THE MAYOR.

THE WRECK OF THE *TOYTOWN BELLE*

THE MAYOR OF TOYTOWN'S CHRISTMAS PARTY.
In this group are Mr. Growser, the Mayor, the butler, Larry the Lamb and Dennis the Dachshund, Mrs. Goose, Captain Higgins and Ernest the Policeman. The party will be given this afternoon at 5.15.

THE BABES IN THE WOOD.

CIRCUS

Broadcasts from two big London Christmas circuses, at Olympia and the Agricultural Hall, will be given on Wednesday.

Following the lead in 'atmospheric' dressing-up, set by the Ridgeway Parade, Colonel Blood, in his Talk on Big Game Hunting in M'imbo Jimbah, finds a little local colour very stimulating.

What The Listener Family *Thinks*

Welcome to the Isle of Man !

It's Time to Laugh!

NAT
and
REG *The Studio Hounds*

You have just heard Battling Bowlegs, the former heavyweight champion, discussing his proposed come-back.

Whether he has any chance at all is, as everybody knows, extremely doubtful . . .

Oh! here he *is* coming back!

Hello, everyone ! Professor MacSkye is about to commence his excavations for buried bones . . .

The Professor has already uncovered an exciting find and there seems prospect of controversy . . .

We must apologise to listeners . . .

And here we have Slippery Sam, the Circus Sea-Lion . . .

Tell me, Sam, can you *really* keep two objects spinning on your nose ?

Oh, yes, easy. Watch!

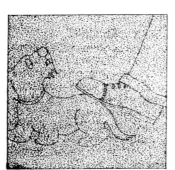

'Ow!'

'Try this, Reg.'

'Nearly as good as Nat !'

JACK *and* the BEAN- STALK

A RADIO PANTOMIME

Written and Composed by
ERNEST LONGSTAFFE.

With a selection from the season's songs by various authors and composers.

Introduction by
The Spirit of Pantomime (*a festive spook*)
Harman Grisewood

Characters (*as they appear :*)

Dame Jill (*who cannot make ends meet*)...Miriam Ferris
Son Jack (*a sheer anxiety*).........Leonard Henry
Daughter Jill (*a grave responsibility*)...Wynne Ajello
The Old Retainer (*a trusted servant*)...Philip Wade
The Prince (*a noble prisoner*) ...John Armstrong
The Giant (*24 x 12 and* all *wicked*)
Foster Richardson
The Magic Harp (*a diatonic mystery*) ...Elsie Otley

The Villagers, The Drover, The Cow, The Hen and the 'Uneatables.'

Daventry National	*London Regional*
tonight	*tomorrow*
at 7.45.	*at 7.45.*

'The Wind in the Willows'

Toad was just passing underneath the bridge when . . . !

Another Phantom Pantomime, written, composed, and produced by Ernest Longstaffe.

CURIOUS CRITTERS
by HARRY ROUNTREE
Hero No. 5, The SPECTACLED OWL

This is a real one—young, and when young they can be tamed.

Fancy taming a judge! A wise-looking bird—surely the one on which Their Worships modelled their wigs.

Above you see him as he is. On the right you see how he will be when the artist has put His Portly Worship on canvas. To be found in the town halls and country houses of old England.

A tiny little fellow who lives in the sands of Africa—this is Master Jerboa.

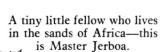

What he does with this yard of tail nobody knows—but me! He uses it to make a swing for his children

CURIOUS CRITTERS by HARRY ROUNTREE
Hero No. 1
THE SLOW LORIS

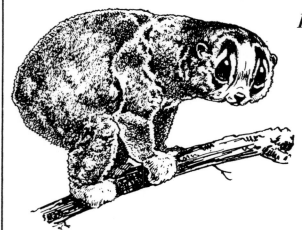

You'll find him in North India, Burma, Malaya, and Siam—and the Zoo, if you're lucky. 'Too slow to catch cold' just about describes his speed. A quaint likeable little fellow. Observe his most *pathetic* expression.

Here you see a real Slow Loris, really drawn from real life.

As a film star he would be the World's No. 1 Beggar.

The drawing on the right shows him dressed for the part. I ask you—could you refuse to pay up?

CURIOUS CRITTERS

by HARRY ROUNTREE

Hero No. 6, THE KOALA

From the Australian Bush to Civilisation.

Here he is—the teddy-bear of Australia — perfectly harmless — injures nobody and nothing, except gum leaves—very shy —cries like a baby when he is hurt.

Most attractive to look at—but that's mostly on account of his fluffy ears—and I'll prove it to you. Take his ears away—stick a bowler hat on him —dress him—and behold—'Any old iron '— standing at the corner of the street.

In many ways he behaves more like a dog—but he has a dreadfully loud ' meaow '. Comes from Siam and has black face, paws, and tail. Some people think that these cats once had a nigger minstrel troupe and they have never been able to wash off the burnt cork.

CURIOUS CRITTERS by HARRY ROUNTREE

Hero No. 2, The Meerkat

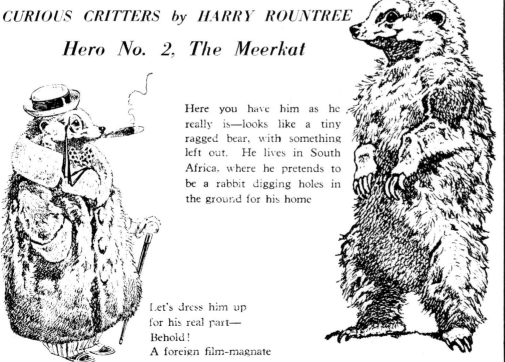

Here you have him as he really is—looks like a tiny ragged bear, with something left out. He lives in South Africa, where he pretends to be a rabbit digging holes in the ground for his home

Let's dress him up for his real part— Behold! A foreign film-magnate

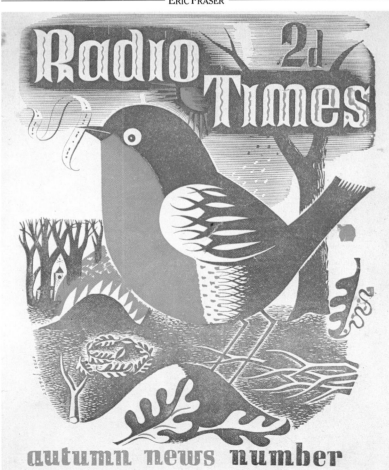

—the old lady who's sure **her** parrot could broadcast

—the one-man band who's better than Henry Hall

—the man whose flea circus would surprise them

'WE ARE NOW GOING OVER TO THE QUEEN'S HALL.'

—the inventor of a new
portable set

—the man who wants a chance
to prove the earth is flat

—and the proud mother of the
infant prodigy

—and of course, they all turn up at Broadcasting House!

THE RADIO TIMES
SUMMER NUMBER

'I wish they'd play "Just Wonderful You," George'

GOODBYE,
Messieurs

'ITHURIEL'S HOUR'. Listeners will hear an adaptation of the novel by Joanna Cannan this evening at 7.30. It is the story of how one man's all-mastering will to reach the goal he has set himself ends in tragedy.

'. . . So many gauges and knobs . . . What are they all for? . . . What a terrible position to find oneself in! . . . That must be the altimeter . . . ten thousand feet! I mustn't go any higher! Ten Thousand. And nothing below me but white clouds!' **'The Peaslake Crash', a new radio play, will be broadcast at 8.30.**

A Comedy in Three Acts by Hubert Griffith

Adapted from the German of Paul Vulpius

The action takes place in an office in the London and Metropolitan Bank. One week elapses between Acts I and II, three weeks between Acts II and III.

The story behind five items in the small print column of a newspaper will be traced in the play, 'In Small Print', tonight at 8.45.

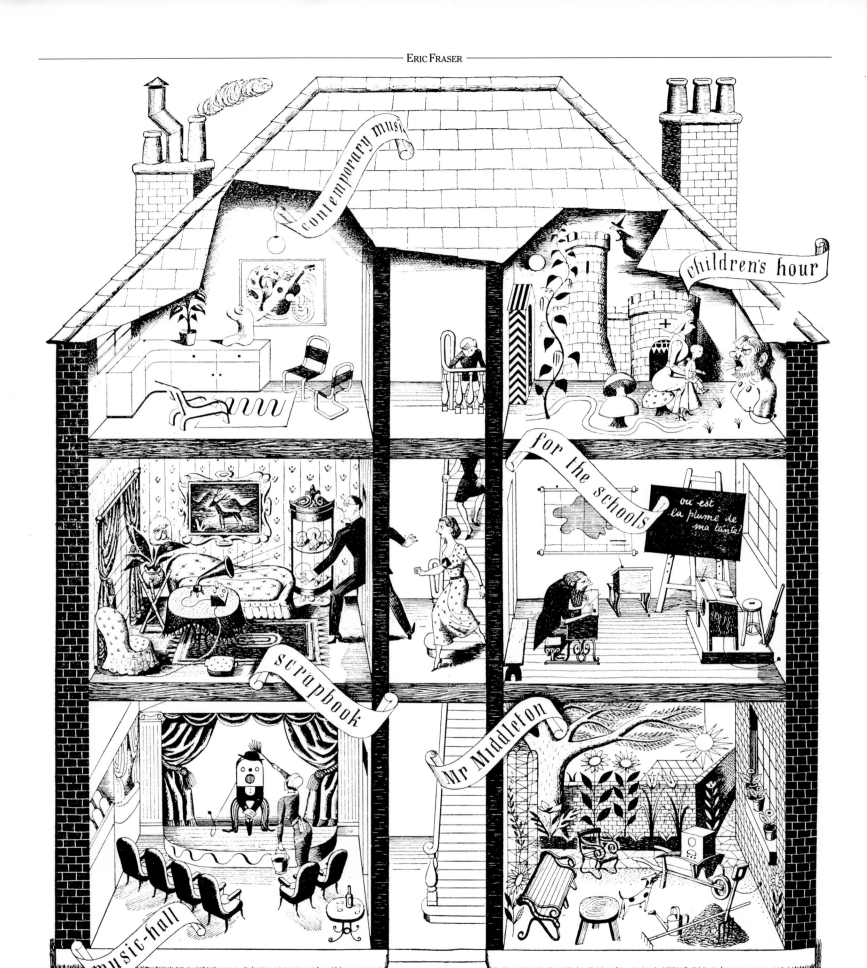

Eric Fraser designs the Complete Radio Home

I am a CONVERT to DANCE MUSIC?

AMERICAN JAM SESSION!

Tonight at 9.0 America's greatest stars of Swing come to the microphone to play to British listeners. The names of the players taking part in this informal party will be found under the programme heading on page 86.

C. Henry Warren, the writer of this article, has done a good deal of pleading for serious music in these pages. Now, however, he turns round and appeals to the musical highbrows to listen to dance music in the right spirit and see if they do not enjoy it—as he finds he does.

'SPRING TIDE', a comedy by George Billam and Peter Goldsmith, which was first produced at the Duchess Theatre in 1936, will be broadcast by the Coventry Repertory Company tonight at 9.30. It tells how some young people living in a South Kensington boarding-house struggled to make a living and, as a last resort, formed themselves into a company, with headquarters on a houseboat. Although run on unconventional lines, Consols, Limited, eventually saved the situation. The drawing shows the first meeting of the company in Mrs. Porrett's dining-room.

EDWARD ARDIZZONE WAS BORN IN TONKING IN 1900 AND EDUCATED IN ENGLAND AT A SMALL PUBLIC SCHOOL UNTIL THE AGE OF 16½. ON LEAVING SCHOOL, HE SPENT A YEAR LEARNING SHORTHAND AND TYPING, THEN HAD VARIOUS JOBS AS A CLERK WHICH HE QUITE ENJOYED. HIS LAST CLERK JOB WAS WITH THE EASTERN EXTENSION TELEGRAPH COMPANY, HIS FATHER'S OLD EMPLOYER

'I stayed with them for six years, 1920 to 1926. Then my father gave me a little money because the company had been rather generous on his retirement and I threw my job up–of course, the poor man nearly had a stroke. During the six years I was with the Telegraph Company I used to go three or four times a week, in the evening, to study life drawing under Bernard Meninsky, a great artist who ran the life class at the Westminster Art School. I met my brother-in-law there, Gabriel White, and another great friend Augustine Booth.

'The first thing I did after leaving my job was to paint a lot of little pictures, and I had a show at the Bloomsbury Gallery. I had a very good write-up in the newspapers, very exciting, although I didn't sell a single picture. This was in 1930. And then, of course, came the real struggle of making money. I got married and the children arrived, three of them: two boys and a girl or rather a girl and two boys, in that order. At about this time I turned to Maurice Gorham of RADIO TIMES. I was ready to take on any job, advertising, drawing of any kind–I felt far from "grand." '

Maurice Gorham was the first BBC Art Editor of RADIO TIMES. Where and when did you meet him?
'I'd known Maurice from the time when we were both children and I met him again in London. When I heard that he was an art editor–or rather he said so–naturally I had a shot at selling some drawings to him and he was nice enough to buy them. This was in the days when his office was at Savoy Hill, he worked there with just an underling of sorts.'

Was he a hard man to work for, did he ever throw any of your drawings back at you?
'No, he always accepted what I did. Gorham was a clever chap, because he took my early work which wasn't entirely suitable–he must have had some feeling that I was going to do much better.'

You have said yourself that at that time you regarded yourself as an amateur. How then did you develop your technique and style? A drawing by you is unmistakeable, it has a sort of integrity of line and vision which puts you quite on your own…
'I think it really came from doodling and

filling sketch-book after sketch-book. I was always drawing, very often not from life. I loved drawing trees, I have hundreds of tree drawings in my sketch-books. Shall I tell you the best way to learn? I had a Victorian book on how to draw trees, how to make the special squiggle to suggest an oak tree or whatever. That book was invaluable!'

RADIO TIMES Art Editors have always made life hard for their illustrators–a drawing was commissioned at best on Thursday afternoon, but often not until Friday morning, and the finished article had to be in the hands of the Art Editor by Monday lunchtime. How did you find that kind of pressure?
'Well, I think that pressure is very good for an artist: he's jolly well got to get on with it, it's a lesson that all artists who have to make a living must learn.'

We've just been looking at some RADIO TIMES drawings of yours, one of them an illustration of E. M. Forster's 'A Passage to India.' Had you read the book? Did you have to re-read it in the limited time available? Whichever, did you then go on to draw roughs and then have to decide: 'That's enough, I must get on with the finished drawings'?
'Nearly always I went straight for the finished drawing, but, in fact, I had to read the books of most of the jobs I was asked to do. I am fairly widely read, so that not much came quite out of the blue. As to costume, I had quite a number of reference books before I really started. A good reference library is very important to an illustrator.'

Your illustration for Trollope's novel 'Barchester Towers' must have been home territory for you?
'Absolutely. I think drawing is both enjoyable and, in my case, hard work, enjoyable hard work if you know what I mean. I'm always very pleased when it comes off. I'm never satisfied at the time with what I've done. Years later you look back at your work and you think, "My

word, I didn't think I was as good as that." That's why I always say, and to students in particular, never tear up a drawing, put it away, because it won't be as bad as you think. I've torn up too much, you see. It's very sad, what I've torn up.'

May I ask you about one of the thorniest problems with which RADIO TIMES confronts its illustrators. At the great national festivals of the year the programme pages are decorated with headings and borders. The Art Editor presents you with a rigid layout within which the programmes are to be contained. The shapes are always extremely awkward. You are essentially an illustrator, so how did you find this as a design problem?
'It was difficult, but not hopelessly so, because I think a good draughtsman is usually a good designer, you know. Shall I tell what I really think about drawing? I always think of drawing as the making of little pictures, and making little pictures you have to design them, it's a matter of composing the shapes. Mind you, I certainly found this sort of commission a challenge.'

Another of your drawings we have just been looking at is of Shakespeare's 'Falstaff' and, to me, I can never again see the fat knight any other way; it is to me the definitive drawing. How did you arrive at it?
'Before I did that drawing I had done some lithographs for a little book called "Hey Nonny Yes," in which I had to create this figure of Falstaff, not exactly the same as the one I drew for RADIO TIMES, so I'm afraid RADIO TIMES can't claim paternity rights.'

Ted, you have created some of the greatest of children's books, 'Tim and the Sea Captain,' for example. Is it a kind of work you particularly enjoy, and were you asked to travel in order to talk about them?
'Yes, I didn't find the travel and the talking very enjoyable but I've done it.

I've been to Australia and to America. The books do–thank God, because they're my income still–have an international appeal. They've been translated into most languages. The royalties go on until 50 years after you're dead, and they get reprinted–that's the whole point.'

When was it you become a Royal Academician?
'That happened in 1970 and I go up to town annually for "varnishing day." It's now just a lunch–a very good lunch, too, all the RAs. But, of course, in the old days they all came and worked on their pictures. You'll remember that Turner used to turn up with a practically blank canvas and then paint it up in bright colours to kill the painting next door.'

The young of all generations tend to view the Royal Academy as a sort of last-ditch, anachronistic and reactionary survival. What does it mean to you?
'Well, yes, I've been the same. As a young man, having shows in the West End, I belonged to the London Group. That was respectable, but not to the Academy, mainly because they hadn't asked me. Now I enjoy it.'

Ted, as an illustrator for RADIO TIMES over something like 33 years, you must have been aware of the others who were doing the same job. The glory of RADIO TIMES has been in the incomparable standard of its illustrators, were there any of them for whom you had particular respect and admiration?
'One of them was Lynton Lamb–he was a very beautiful draughtsman and he had a quality of sincerity, truthfulness and rightness. He knew his figure drawing all right, and that's the basis of it. I admired also the work of Len Rosoman. I got to know him very well when I became an RA, I've always admired his "painterly" drawings.'

I know how you have had considerable influence as a teacher, where did you do your teaching?
'First at Camberwell, and then at the Royal College of Art. At the College I was supposed to teach etching. Robin Darwin, the principal, was determined to get "names" teaching there. "My dear Ted," he said, "you must come and teach etching." But I'd never etched in my life so the students had to teach me.'

Artists and illustrators don't retire, they just go on being. What are you doing now at age 79 plus?
'The trouble is, everybody wants my little drawings and I'm always having to do more work. And, very often, today, I can't do it; I can't keep up the pace. Quite frankly, I've now got to get down to it and do a lot more. I've been tied up doing books, which takes so much time.'

A Passage to India–1955
'I had read the books of most of the jobs I was asked to do'

CONVERSATION IN THE TRAIN'
'Are Brains a Handicap?' is the subject of another railway-carriage discussion in this series which will be broadcast tonight at 8.0.

'**HORTI-MANIA**', the story of how Lady Quince Medlar and Col. Swete-Williams fought for the Marrow Championship of Catcham Green, will be broadcast tonight at 8.40. Mabel Constanduros, who plays the part of the Lady of the Manor, wrote the book, and her nephew, Denis Constanduros, was responsible for the lyrics.

Tonight at 7.40

The Old Music-Halls Favourite old-time songs sung by the singers who have made this series so popular

'COME ALONG LIZA', a show including Mabel Constanduros's Buggins family, will be broadcast tonight at 7.40. A trip down the Thames to Margate gives the Bugginses plenty to talk about.

'THE LUNATIC AT LARGE.' This exhilarating farce of the 'nineties, with Naunton Wayne as the lunatic, will be broadcast tonight at 8.0. This picture shows how the lunatic disposed of the doctor.

Regional listeners will hear another competition this afternoon at 5.0. The Under-Sevens Competition results will be broadcast on Midland at the same time.

NORTHERN CONCERT-PARTY CAVALCADE

RADIO TIMES, DECEMBER 24, 1937.

RADIO TIMES

Christmas Number 6d

Anthony Collins, the conductor, says

THEY'RE ALL EASY—

—except the French Horn!

'Unless one is bow-legged'

'. . . more of a mechanic than a musician'

LIGHT MUSIC
for the MILLION

Dan Aitken and Alan Frank survey the ever topical subject of Light Music in all its varied styles.

'. . . on anything from an outsize orchestra to a penny whistle'

Brahms's admiration for Wagner was not returned

Berlioz's harmony was disagreeable to Tchaikovsky

AMERICA'S HUMOUR

For men must Work...

A programme dedicated to tired business men; a plea for those who lead harassed lives of unending toil, broken only by morning coffee, two-hour lunches, afternoon tea, and occasional days at golf and/or the races. Tonight at 8.5.

5.8.38

THREE ASPECTS of CRICKET

This afternoon at 3.45 there will be a commentary on each of them

CLUB   VILLAGE   COUNTRY HOUSE

THE SEASIDE BANDSTAND will be the meeting place for listeners to tonight's 'Saturday at Nine-Forty'. F. H. Grisewood will be there to tell you how things are going.

BOOMERANGS !
This evening at 6.45 listeners will hear a cyclist on motorists and a motorist on cyclists.

'LADIES AND GENTLEMEN, HERE WE HAVE . . . .'
A charabanc driver will talk about holiday-makers as he sees them, in the 'Private View' series, tonight at 8.30.

AN ORCHESTRA ARRIVES AT BROADCASTING HOUSE

CORNET

SECOND VIOLIN

FIRST VIOLIN

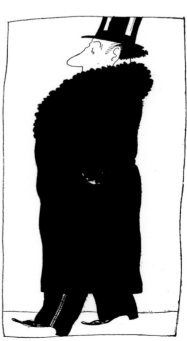

OBOE and FLUTE

TUBA and TROMBONE

TRIANGLE

'CELLO

THE CONDUCTOR

'SNAPPED IN THE STUDIO'

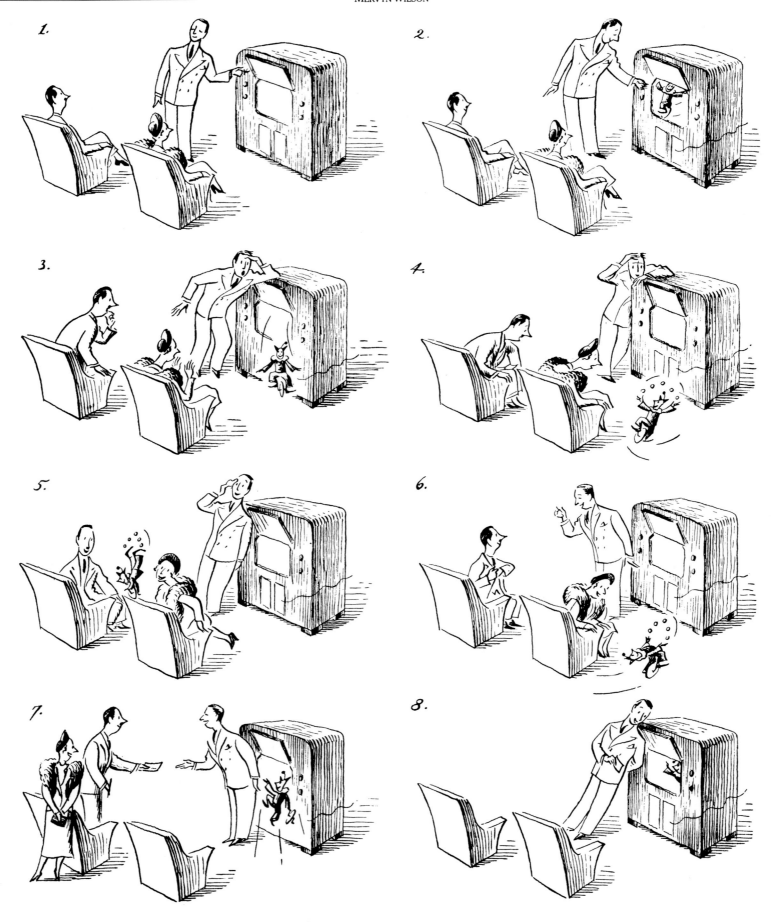

'THE SUPER SET'—a fantasy of television by Mervyn Wilson

Home Number

'GREEN FINGERS', A HUMOROUS RADIO-REVUE ON GARDENS AND GARDENERS
Dedicated to those 'who search their borders every night, and catch their slugs by candlelight', this revue, based
on the book of the same name by Reginald Arkell, will be broadcast tonight at 8.0.

A REGIONAL TOUR

LONDON REGION.

(*Left*) The new uniform worn by the Wireless Military Band

(*Right*) The giant 'effects' machine

MIDLAND REGION. Broadcast from the Pump Room of a well-known Spa. The Mayor unveils a new pump

NORTH REGION. A concert by the Lancashire Symphony Orchestra

SCOTTISH REGION.

Discussion on haggis by well-known chefs

'THE KING WHO DIDN'T MATTER'
The story of King Oswald the Negligible and how he was turned into a telegraph pole. The play will be broadcast tonight at 8.15.

Outside Broadcasting:
THE WRONG WAY!

BALLOONS
or
Squaring the Circle!

By Bruce Sievier

We have received this amusing verse from the well-known broadcaster who is now Flying-Officer R. B. B. Sievier, M.C. (R.A.F.V.R.), of the Balloon Barrage

When I was but a baby boy
In coat and pantaloon,
My nurse would wheel me in the park
Behind a toy balloon.

　　★　　★　　★　　★

When I arrived at walking stage
(An artful little mite!)
I used to buy a ball of string
And fly a baby kite.

　　★　　★　　★　　★

But now I'm virile, big and strong,
I work from noon to noon
And all day long I sit beneath
A ruddy 'big' balloon!

　　★　　★　　★　　★

The moral of this story is
Enough to drive one wild,
For those who try to wage a war
Just treat one as a child!

'DOWN,

DOWN,

DOWN

'Adolf in Blunderland', a political parody of obvious topical interest, by Max Kester and James Dyrenforth, will be broadcast this evening at 7.45

THE RADIO TIMES
Christmas Number

Principal Contents :

'The Coming of Wireless'
by the Archbishop of York

'Twilight of the Wise'—a Christmas story
by James Hilton

'This Great Family'—Christmas Day programme
explained by the Producer

'Cads at Christmas Time'
by the Western Brothers

'What Has Happened to Christmas?'
by Sir Richard Terry

'The Satire-day Magazine'—a parody
by John Dighton

'And Now What?'—by Henry Hall

Also articles by :
Leslie Baily   R. Ellis Roberts   Ashley Sterne
D. B. Wyndham Lewis   Maurice Lane-Norcott
Stephen Schofield   Filson Young   R. M. Freeman
Irene Veal   'Mac'

Full BBC programmes for Christmas week

Eight-page photogravure souvenir of 1935

HENRY HALL

'THE BIG BROADCAST'

Crooners—and others—caught by our Caricaturist

Here is a composite impression, by Sherriffs, of fifteen singers of popular melodies, the majority of whom are most likely to be heard between 10.10 p.m. and midnight. Do you recognise your favourites? Joe Crossman is seen on the extreme left (full length). The three standing high above the others are (left to right) Brian Lawrence, Elsie Carlisle, and Sam Costa. Immediately below them are the heads and shoulders of Gerrie Fitzgerald, Les Allen, Harry Bentley, and George Barclay. In front are Sam Browne, Harry Roy with his saxophone, Peggy Dell, Nat Gonella with his trumpet, and Phyllis Robbins. Girvan Dundas stands behind the microphone, and on the extreme right is Peggy Cochrane. You never hear them all at once, as Sherriffs has suggested here, but what a broadcast it would be if you did !

The Radio Times, June 7, 1935 Vol. 47 No. 610
Registered at the G.P.O. as a Newspaper.
Every Friday TWOPENCE
THE RADIO TIMES
WHITSUN HOLIDAY NUMBER

CARROLL GIBBONS

and the

SAVOY HOTEL ORPHEANS

play tonight at 8.10

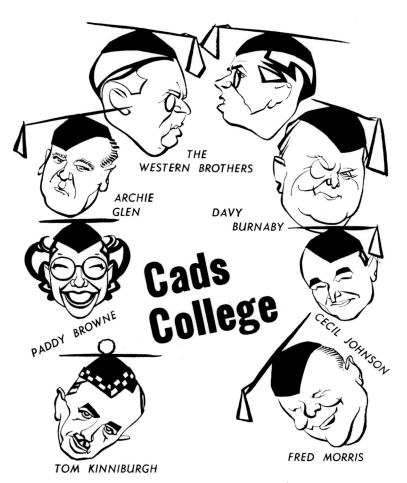

THE WESTERN BROTHERS

ARCHIE GLEN

DAVY BURNABY

Cads College

PADDY BROWNE

CECIL JOHNSON

TOM KINNIBURGH

FRED MORRIS

ROMANCE IN RHYTHM

Geraldo and his Orchestra present another of their new dance music programmes tonight at 8.30

This caricature of Geraldo was drawn by Sherriffs.

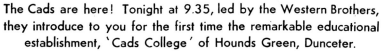

The Cads are here! Tonight at 9.35, led by the Western Brothers, they introduce to you for the first time the remarkable educational establishment, 'Cads College' of Hounds Green, Dunceter.

BOTH SIDES OF

RADIO NEWS AND GOSSIP, BY 'THE BROADCASTERS'

HIS MASTER'S MASK

A sidelight on women's perils on the Home Front reached us the other day from a girl on the BBC staff. As instructed by the latest circular from Defence Executive, she was testing her Civilian Duty respirator in the quiet of her own home and had just got it on when her Sealyham came into the room. In spite of the fact that he has been her devoted slave for years, he had no sooner seen her in the gas-mask than he flew at her and tried to bite her. Defence Executive will have to issue another circular about this.

THE MICROPHONE

RADIO TIMES, CRAMPED FOR SPACE OR NOT, DOGGEDLY CAME
OUT EVERY WEEK WITH NEWS OF RADIO'S ACTIVITIES–AND, IN
GOVERNMENT ADVERTISEMENTS, WARNED ITS READERS
ABOUT THE DANGERS OF 'CARELESS TALK'

The 1940s–the decade of danger and austerity–saw the RADIO TIMES shrink to an average of 20 pages throughout the war years, and there was precious little space for the lavish illustrations of previous times. It was found necessary to include programme material on the front cover and any illustration was limited to about a quarter of a page.

The familiar 'Both Sides of the Microphone' feature, a diary of broadcasting news and gossip, survived together with articles about serious music. Other features in the limited space available were of a morale-boosting nature in the early war years–and this tendency was also noticeable in some of the pictures–for example, 'Digging for Victory' and 'Saving the Salvage'.

War-time gave broadcasting its most vital role. With the infant television stifled at the outbreak of war, Radio was called upon to do more than ever before. Radio programmes helped to promote the home-front war effort and comedy shows like Tommy Handley's legendary *ITMA* answered the people's need for laughter–and reassurance. *ITMA*'s significance lay not exclusively in its contribution to the morale of the British people; it was also the forerunner of the BBC's illustrious line of comedy successes, all the way from *Hi, Gang*, Hancock and Horne to Steptoe and Basil Fawlty.

RADIO TIMES, cramped for space or not, doggedly came out every week with news of Radio's activities–and, in Government advertisements, warned its readers about the dangers of 'careless talk'.

Radio's Home Service was joined by the General Forces Programme which, in the main, presented a mixture of big-band music, news and variety programmes directed at the Forces–outstanding examples were *Forces' Favourites* and *Navy Mixture*. This was to set the pattern for the Light Programme, which emerged after the war. The pre-war Reithian Sunday listening pattern was soon changed, with light entertainment joining the more serious output and religious programmes.

A RADIO TIMES cover featured J. B. Priestley and his well-known 'Postscripts', which were intended as a counter to the broadcast propaganda of Nazi Germany; Gordon Stowell, who followed Maurice Gorham as Editor of RADIO TIMES, described Priestley as 'the voice of Britain'. Later, Priestley was to claim that his 'Postscripts', which ended after the second series, were killed off on the orders of Winston Churchill, who didn't like the way Priestley began to talk about the better Britain he wanted to see built after the war. Churchill's stirring war-time broadcasts ensured that he, too, like Priestley, became a RADIO TIMES cover star, as did the Queen (now the Queen Mother), who gave a special talk to the women of the nation. And in October 1940 the then Princess Elizabeth made her first broadcast during a Sunday *Children's Hour*.

The war-time Christmas covers–in black and white–made gallant attempts to emulate their illustrious forerunners. Gilroy's famous tin-hatted Father Christmas (*right*) appeared in 1940. Three years later, in 1943,

C. W. Bacon depicted a rather forlorn tin-hatted soldier holding a sprig of holly from home and labelling the scene: 'The Fifth Christmas'.

The sales of RADIO TIMES fell away during the early war years, inevitably, perhaps, at a time of such uncertainty. But, by 1943, they began to increase again and in 1944 the tuppenny-wonder passed the three-and-a-half million mark.

By the time victory in Europe was achieved in May 1945, a rather bolder black logo had emerged and this was to remain into the late 50s. A special issue was swiftly prepared to mark the victory celebrations and this appeared with a cover design by Freeman which captured the nation's joy and thankfulness in montage form.

The war was over but paper rationing–like all other rationing–persisted. Nevertheless, as austerity loosened its grip, RADIO TIMES found opportunities, albeit limited, for tried and fresh illustrators alike.

The year 1947 was a vintage one with the wedding of the then Princess Elizabeth, Queen Mary's 80th birthday and the 25th anniversary of broadcasting. Within the constraints of a broke Britain, RADIO TIMES did them all proud, as it did the silver wedding in 1948 of the King and Queen.

With the war in Europe over, full regional broadcasting returned on 29 July 1945. Listeners had the choice of a Home Service (more than one in areas where regions joined), a Light Programme (which replaced the General Forces Programme) and, from 1946, the Third Programme to cater for minority tastes and interests of cultural content. It was impossible to include all regionalised information in full in one edition–so Tom Henn, who followed Gordon Stowell as Editor, presided over the expansion of RADIO TIMES into six editions. The North and Northern Ireland shared an edition. The others were London, Midlands, West, Wales and Scotland. All carried the National programmes but presented their own area's details in emphatic style–even to the extent, on occasion, of having their own regional covers.

This, looking back, was Radio's golden age. Television had returned but only on a modified basis and would not really seize the nation's imagination until Queen Elizabeth's Coronation in 1953. The years in between would belong to Radio, whose planners and producers had the peace-time stage to themselves. Parents–who had first caught the radio bug from *Children's Hour* back in the 20s–were now encouraging their own children to tune in. Millions of listeners thrilled to the exploits of *Dick Barton–Special Agent*, who was the RADIO TIMES cover star on 31 January 1947. *Mrs Dale's Diary* was another daily date for an army of listeners. The year 1946 saw the start of *Woman's Hour* which, unlike Barton and Mrs Dale, is still very much with us.

Radio had come through the war years triumphantly. The whole nation turned to it as a trusted friend. Meanwhile, as the decade closed, the weekly sales of RADIO TIMES had approached an amazing eight million...

Radio Times, December 20, 1940   Vol. 69   No. 899   Registered at the G.P.O. as a Newspaper

PRICE TWOPENCE

PROGRAMMES FOR
December 22 — 28

RADIO TIMES

JOURNAL OF THE BRITISH BROADCASTING CORPORATION

(INCORPORATING WORLD-RADIO)

Here is the Christmas News and this is Father Christmas reading it....

'Christmas Under Fire'

Radio tour of the Empire in the front line (page 20)

'From Across the Atlantic'

Broadcasts from Canada (page 13), dance band exchange (page 21), and Hollywood greetings (page 23)

Evacuee Children

Sending greetings to their parents in three programmes (pages 20 and 23)

Pantomimes

Tour of three Northern pantos (page 16), 'The Forty Thieves' and 'The Sleeping Beauty' (page 22), 'Aladdin' (page 26)

Stars of the Week

Edith Evans, John Gielgud, and Peggy Ashcroft (page 11), Eva Turner (page 12), John McCormack, Arthur Askey, Richard Murdoch, Elsie and Doris Waters, and Jack Warner (page 21), Sir Harry Lauder (page 30)

Music

Handel's 'Messiah' (page 11)
Bach's Christmas Oratorio (page 15)
Rutland Boughton's 'Bethlehem' (page 18)

Five short plays by Berthold Brecht will be broadcast tonight at 9.40 depicting typical incidents in the lives of the ordinary German man and woman under the rule of the Nazis.

THE RAFT

Six men adrift on the Atlantic, after their ship has been torpedoed, discuss the war in Eric Linklater's new play to be broadcast this afternoon at 3.30.

Tonight at 8.30 the first of two programmes will be broadcast explaining the function of the German Secret State Police—the dreaded Gestapo, the eyes and ears and brutal right arm of the Nazi regime. Tonight's programme deals with the rise of the Gestapo inside Germany.

SCRAPBOOK FOR 1919, edited by Leslie Baily, will recall the first of the troubled years between the two World Wars, when the uneasy peace was made, and the first transatlantic flight foreshadowed the inescapable intermingling of the fortunes of mankind . . . Listen at 9.30 p.m.

' FIVE HUNDRED THOUSAND DOGS WENT TO TOWN '
The unfortunate result of a journalist's bright idea is the high spot of the eccentric comedy by H. R. Jeans to be broadcast tonight at 9.35.

'WAR AND PEACE'

A radio adaptation of the greatest novel ever written—Tolstoy's supreme achievement, the story with the Russian people as its hero and the struggle with Napoleon as its setting—will be broadcast in eight instalments, of which the first will be heard on Sunday afternoon and the second on Sunday night. The other instalments will follow in pairs on successive Sundays. Full details appear inside.

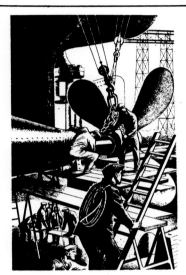

SHIPYARD WORKER
Listen to this evening's 'Professional Portrait' at 7.45

'THE FATHER'
By August Strindberg

WORLD THEATRE: AT 9.15

A GIANT AWAKES. The voice of the Tennessee Valley tells the story of man's greed and neglect—neglect that drained the very life-blood from the valley—in a programme on the vast project of the Tennessee Valley Authority tonight at 9.20. The roar of water through the sluices of great dams and the ever growing hum of giant turbines is sending new life coursing through the veins of the valley as the task of T.V.A. daily moves nearer completion.

'Information from the Enemy'

Listening to the BBC news, a German couple discover that their son is safe. The ironic situation that arises from this forbidden listening is the subject of the play tonight at 10.15.

'*I am writing this in the morning as Keetje and I wait for Uncle Pieter . . . I can't believe that mother is dead and that we shall never see her again. Mother was killed when the hospital was bombed*'.

'My Sister and I', the diary of a Dutch boy of twelve, who lived through the horror of the Nazi invasion of Holland and escaped to America, will be broadcast tonight at 8.0.

'*To build a world worthy of our faith and sacrifice*'

RADIO TIMES

'The Fifth Christmas'   Drawing by C. W. Bacon

Full programmes for Christmas Week and Christmas Day

In this fifth year of war, and at the approach of its mighty climax, the simple symbols of Christmas and of the old ideals of peace and goodwill need be none the less honoured because mankind has had to learn again that peace and goodwill must be fought for. BBC programmes during Christmas week will be found, as usual, to reflect the traditional spirit of the season, with a special thought this year for all whom the call of war has torn far from the homes they love and the kind of Christmas they like best to remember. To all in the fighting Services on Britain's battle-fronts, on land, in the air, and on the perilous seas; to the millions who toil with hand and brain in their staunch support; to all who now live in loneliness and anxiety—to all listeners, indeed, but this year to these in particular, Greetings! And may you find among these programmes many happy memories of the past and a still happier promise for the future!

BOTH SIDES OF THE MICROPHONE

'It' is crime; this new series will show how formidable are the odds against the criminal in the light of modern scientific methods of detection. The first programme, dealing with murder, will be heard tonight at 9.30

'So This is Man'

Hominidæ

TAKING STOCK

What is the future of the Middle Classes?

Speakers:

HENRY SNELL

educated at Winchester and Jesus College, Cambridge, President of the Cambridge Union Society, 1932. Worked with the London Municipal Society and the National Union of Ratepayers' Associations. Lieutenant, Second Royal Gloucestershire Hussars during 1939-45 war, and a prisoner of war for three and a half years. Now works with the Economic League

WILLIAM CORBETT

first met the Middle Classes when delivering vegetables at the age of ten. Gunner (R.F.A.) 1914-19. Unemployed when his eldest son was born in 1924. For nine years chief caretaker for the St. Pancras House Improvement Society Ltd. An electrician and meter reader

Professor DENIS BROGAN

author of ' The English People—Impressions and Observations '

Chairman:

Sir WILLIAM FYFE

Principal of the University of Aberdeen, 1936-48

TONIGHT AT 9.15

THE PLAIN MAN'S
Guide to Music

Sir Adrian Boult introduces

The Orchestra
and its Instruments

Musical illustrations, including parts of Tchaikovsky's Symphony No. 4 played by the

BBC Theatre Orchestra
(Leader, Alfred Barker)
Produced by Roger Fiske

TONIGHT AT 8.0

TAKING STOCK

The Atomic Bomb

A discussion on the international control of atomic energy between:

BERTRAND RUSSELL, F.R.S.

P. M. S. BLACKETT, F.R.S.

Langworthy Professor of Physics at the University of Manchester, and author of ' Military and Political Consequences of Atomic Energy '

RAYMOND BLACKBURN

Labour Member of Parliament for King's Norton

Lieut.-General
SIR FREDERICK MORGAN, K.C.B.
Deputy Chief of Staff to General Eisenhower, 1944-45

TONIGHT AT 9.15

RADIO'S CONCENTRATION

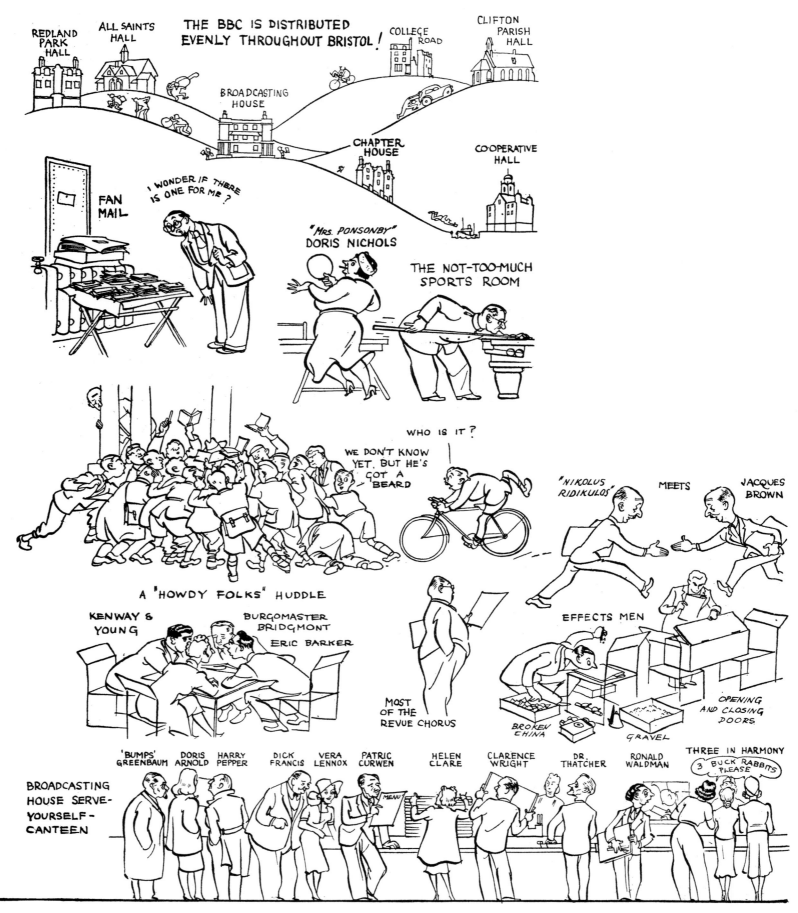

CAMP!

Jack Dunkley, popular RADIO TIMES artist, went to Bristol to see the radio stars back-stage. This is what he saw—

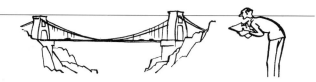

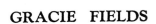

Flanagan and Allen

GRACIE FIELDS

At Rochdale tonight 'Our Gracie' will greet friends in her home town, and all over the country, in the first of her weekly parties

She will have with her—
Rochdale Festival Choir (Leader, Oscar Clifton)
Some Lancashire Lads and Lassies
Richard Valery and his Concert Orchestra

Produced by Bowker Andrews : From The Champness Hall, Rochdale

'GRACIE'S WORKING PARTY'—AT 8.30

'MERRY-GO-ROUND' FROM RADIOLYMPIA
*The two-hundredth edition will be broadcast on Friday in the Light Programme at 9.0 p.m.
To celebrate the occasion Eric Barker sends listeners a 'message' which is published, with new
pictures of the cast, on page three*

UP THE POLE!
returns at 7.30 with—
JIMMY JEWEL and BEN WARRISS

SPECIAL ARTICLES INCLUDE

Putting the Laughs into Radio
By Michael Standing, Head of BBC Variety

Brighter Broadcast Dance Music :: Meet the ' Have a Go ! ' Team
What the Radio Critics Say :: Round the Shows in Pictures
Variety's Back-Room Boys :: How Far Back Does Your Memory Go ?

☆   ☆   ☆

ALL REGULAR FEATURES and FULL PROGRAMMES FOR THE WEEK

Hi, Gang! 1949

Vic Oliver   ☆   Bebe Daniels   ☆   Ben Lyon

ERIC BARKER *returns tonight at 7.30 to* WATERLOGGED SPA

FULL PERFORMANCE IN FRENCH OF
'Les Troyens à Carthage'
Opera in four acts and five tableaux

Words and Music by HECTOR BERLIOZ

Cast, in order of singing
Dido, Queen of Carthage
................................Marisa Ferrer
Anna, sister of Dido...Yvonne Corke
Iopas, a Tyrian poet...Frans Vroons
Ascanius, son of Aeneas.Maria Braneze
Pantheus, Trojan priest...Charles Paul
Narbal, Dido's adviser.Charles Cambon
Aeneas, Trojan hero...Jean Giraudeau
Hylas, a young Phrygian sailor
................................Colin Cunningham
First soldier.................Ernest Frank
Second soldier..............Scott Joynt
Ghost of Cassandra......Yvonne Corke
Ghost of Coroebus...Charles Cambon
Ghost of Hector...........Ernest Frank
Ghost of Priam..............Scott Joynt
The god Mercury............Stearn Scott
Chorus of Carthaginians, Trojan warriors, priests, attendants, and huntsmen

Royal Philharmonic Orchestra
(Leader, Oscar Lampe)

BBC Theatre Chorus
(Chorus-Master, John Clements)

'*THE GOLDEN BRIDEGROOM*'—*the radio play at 9.15—tells the entertaining story of the trial of the silver-tongued Lucius Apuleius, philosopher and orator, who lived in the second century. He married a rich widow of Oea in Tripoli and was accused by her family of winning her affections by magic arts*

WORLD THEATRE

HUGH GRIFFITH and HUBERT GREGG in

'A NEW WAY TO PAY OLD DEBTS'

by Philip Massinger

Frank Wellborn, a prodigal
................................Hubert Gregg
Tapwell, an alehouse-keeper
................................Jack Shaw
Froth, his wife......Gladys Spencer
Tom Allworth, a young gentleman, page to Lord Lovell
................................Andrew Faulds
Steward, usher, cook, and porter to Lady Allworth:
Order.....................George Owen
Amble..................Ronald Sidney
Furnace........Andrew Churchman
Watchall..........Charles Maunsell
Lady Allworth, a rich widow
................................Rosamund Burne
Greedy, a hungry Justice of Peace
................................Arthur Ridley
Sir Giles Overreach, a cruel extortioner................Hugh Griffith
Marrall, a term-driver; a creature of Sir Giles Overreach
................................Michael Martin-Harvey
Waiting-woman......Susan Richards
Chambermaid........Betty Baskcomb
Margaret, daughter of Sir Giles Overreach................Olive Gregg
Lord Lovell...........Peter Williams
Willdo, a parson......Cyril Gardiner

Scene: the country near Nottingham
Narrator, Stanley Groome

The play arranged for broadcasting by Stanley Groome

PRODUCED BY JOHN RICHMOND

TONIGHT AT 9.15

One of the studies for a portrait of William Walton which Michael Ayrton made in Italy last summer. He will talk about Walton's Violin Concerto (written at Amalfi) when he discusses music and musicians from the painter's point of view at 6.45 tonight

Edward Elgar . . . . Spirit of England

'... he hurried past us at an unnatural speed'

'... then a door opened and in walked Father Christmas'

Catherine makes a discovery in what she romantically imagines to be a 'most mysterious cabinet'

'Northanger Abbey,'

adapted for radio by Thea Holme from Jane Austen's novel will be broadcast

AT 9.15

'A Whit Monday Picnic,' by Edward Ardizzone

Christmas Day to New Year

EIGHT DAYS PROGRAMMES IN FULL

Contributors to this Christmas Number include the Bishop of Chelmsford, who writes on the Spell of Christmas, Arthur Askey recalling his experiences as an announcer, and Laurence Gilliam, who introduces the Christmas Day World Programme 'Good Neighbours' preceding the broadcast by

HIS MAJESTY THE KING

RONALD MILLAR'S 'FRIEDA' IN THE LIGHT PROGRAMME ON WEDNESDAY

'*The Dawsons are a perfectly charming, perfectly ordinary English family, and we may assume that if Robert, the only surviving son, had not married a German nurse who helped him to escape from Oflag VIB they would have continued to be liked and respected by everyone. But Robert did; and the impact of Frieda on Denbury, a typical country town in the South of England, is the cause of a series of catastrophes*'—Stephen Williams in his drama diary on page six

'"I done another bad thing." "It don't make no difference," George said, and he fell silent again . . . from the distance came the sound of men shouting to one another.' A radio adaptation of John Steinbeck's 'Of Mice and Men' will be presented in Saturday-Night Theatre at 9.15

'One has inspirations, you know. Extraordinary inspirations—and I have one tonight!'

'ROPE'

Patrick Hamilton's play of the macabre will be broadcast at 8.0 tonight

'OLD SOLDIER'
A good-natured tribute in serious vein to that 'British institution,' the Company Sergeant-Major : at 9.15 (449.1 m.)

'RAIN' '*Sadie Thompson, you are doomed!*'—the Rev. Alfred Davidson, terrible in righteousness, wrestles for a soul. A radio adaptation of the play founded on the story by W. Somerset Maugham will be broadcast tonight at 9.15

RADIO TIMES

BBC Programmes for Christmas Week

2D

All the Home Service,
Light, and Third Programmes,
which include
'Men of Goodwill,'
the traditional Christmas afternoon
exchange of greetings preceding
H.M. THE KING
who speaks to his peoples at 3.0

Christmas Week will bring
Carols from King's College, Cambridge
Bach's 'Christmas Oratorio'
The Christmas Variety Party
Children's Party on Christmas Day
Agatha Christie's 'Ten Little Niggers'
Special editions of all
your favourite Variety Shows

'Celia'

Introducing a young lady whose ambition to make her name as a character actress leads her into a series of adventures with a private investigator. Their first case comes on the air

TONIGHT AT 9.30

'I have been the Devil's General here on Earth . . . I must go ahead and get his billets ready in Hell.' Carl Zuckmayer's play, to be broadcast at 8.0 tonight, is set in the Berlin of the winter of 1941 when the German army was still sweeping victoriously across Europe and the Nazi Party was all-powerful in the Reich

Captain Thwaite and his ship had grown old together and he took unkindly to being beached. You will hear about 'The Independence of Daniel Thwaite' in the play at 9.15

'THE SILVER BOX'

John Galsworthy's first play (see the article by Stephen Williams on page 6) will be presented in 'Saturday-Night Theatre' at 9.20

'Better ring for a doctor, 'adn't I? 'E looks pretty done up . . .'

In his time Charlie Hopkins had been an expert safe-cracker — but that was ten years ago and nothing, it seemed, could now spoil his plans for an honest future except— the unexpected . . .

'ONCE A CROOK'

AT 9.30

'If you touch me I shall jump into the water. The violent arrival of Gemma Jones, which is to have such dire consequences, disturbs the placid course of life in the McClean household in Venice. A radio version of the play by Margaret Kennedy will be presented in Saturday-Night Theatre

'ESCAPE ME NEVER' : AT 9.20

'THE ENIGMA OF THE JAPANESE' will be discussed by four ex-prisoners of war at 10.30 tonight. This drawing of a typical Japanese soldier was drawn by Ronald Searle, one of tonight's speakers, who was captured at the fall of Singapore and spent three-and-a-half years as a prisoner of the Japanese. He made a record of his captivity in a mass of drawings

RAILWAY OF DEATH—the story of thousands of Allied prisoners who slaved to build the Japanese railway through the belt of jungle that divides Siam from Burma. Another drawing by Ronald Searle illustrates the introductory article by Mark Quin, the author of the programme, on page 4. Both, as prisoners of the Japanese, were forced to work on the railway

AS THE 50S PROGRESSED, THE GATHERING INFLUENCE OF
TELEVISION BECAME EVER MORE MARKED...IN 1957, FOR THE
FIRST TIME, TELEVISION'S BILLINGS WERE PLACED AHEAD
OF RADIO'S. THE END OF AN ERA INDEED

RADIO TIMES greeted the 1950s by continuing to rewrite the record books: a new peak was reached in 1950 and then, after a slight fall, a new all-time high of a weekly average of more than eight million copies was achieved in 1955. The Coronation number of 29 May 1953 had a sale of 9,012,358; the Christmas issue in 1954 sold 9,253,025 copies.

With such an immense circulation, it was appropriate for Waterlow & Sons Limited, the printers of RADIO TIMES, to open a second factory, at the East Kilbride new town near Glasgow, in order to print northern editions of the journal.

In fact, the peak was passed. The arrival of Independent Television in 1955 saw to that. With the ending of the BBC's television monopoly, the sales of RADIO TIMES began to slide and this continued through the years until they eventually found their level around the four million mark–still enough to maintain it as Britain's biggest selling weekly journal.

In 1951 the cost was increased to three pence–the first rise since its inception in 1923 and, by the end of the decade, another old penny had been added to the cost of each copy. In March 1950 RADIO TIMES and the rest of BBC Publications were able to return to their headquarters at 35 Marylebone High Street after having been scattered by the war to Wembley and various offices adjoining Broadcasting House.

The decade began with the important internal BBC challenge between the well-established Radio network and the fast-developing Television service which received a tremendous boost from the Coronation broadcast. From 1955, the real challenge was between BBC*tv* and the commercial companies. And the BBC looked to RADIO TIMES–now Edited by Douglas Graeme Williams, who had joined the magazine as an art assistant under Maurice Gorham–for the support it was entitled to expect from the country's most successful weekly journal.

The size of the magazine was stabilised at 52 pages and the extra space available enabled the magazine to re-emphasise its role as a major source of patronage of the graphic arts in Britain. Eric Fraser was commissioned for the cover of a Whitsun number which also depicted the Trooping the Colour and it was he who drew the heraldic cover for the Coronation (*right*)–the first cover in colour since the war.

In 1956 RADIO TIMES encountered the trauma of industrial action: Waterlow's went on strike. A French businessman offered printing facilities at a factory which normally produced pornography and race cards. Douglas Williams headed for France with an editorial team of four –including Art Editor Peter Harle–and for the six weeks of the strike they produced six million copies each week.

'It was produced as one national edition', Peter Harle recalls, 'and it was broadsheet size, so it didn't look like the normal RADIO TIMES. But we could justify our proud claim that it contained all details of BBC programmes, albeit in abbreviated form.' The typesetting was done at sites all over Paris,

including a monastery. Frenchmen setting British programme listings led to some intriguing outcomes, including: 'The Nine O'Clock time signal, conducted by Sir Malcolm Sargent'.

The covers during the early 50s mainly celebrated Radio programmes during the final years of a predominant Radio era with photographs of favourites such as *The Archers*, *Mrs Dale's Diary*, *Educating Archie*, *Life with the Lyons* and a new production of the Dylan Thomas classic *Under Milk Wood*, together with traditional sporting and national events.

From 1955 Television vied weekly for cover space with Radio programmes; after 1957 the cover emphasis was on Television. This was a time when much of the population remained loyal to Radio but the gradual draw to Television, especially for evening and weekend entertainment, was attracting ever-larger audiences and, by the end of the decade, the Television era had arrived. The State Opening of Parliament by the Queen was televised for the first time in October 1958 and RADIO TIMES marked the occasion with a cover by C. W. Bacon.

The 50s produced some delightful Christmas covers following the traditional pattern–by C. Walter Hodges in 1950 and 1954, J. S. Goodall in 1953, Fritz Wegner in 1955 and James Hart in 1957 (the famous redbreasted robin). Eric Fraser and Victor Reinganum provided the 1958 and 1959 Christmas covers–examples of artistry which becomes timeless. The same was true of the regular variations on the Spring and country church themes for some effective Easter covers.

Early in the decade, in February 1952, the sudden death of King George VI necessitated widespread changes in programmes. RADIO TIMES was already on sale for that week but a special supplement was produced giving the revised schedules, and retailers were able to distribute this free to their customers.

For three years–1954, 1955 and 1956–Radio Times Annuals appeared. Ninety-six pages, with full colour on the cover and some inside pages, provided copious articles and lavish photographs on all main features of Radio and Television. The first cover showed the scenes at a popular television programme, *Café Continental*, while the following two annuals had colourful drawings on their covers–by Abram Games in 1955 and James Hart in 1956.

Another innovation, which was to last for only a year due to a new style RADIO TIMES in late 1960, was a Junior RADIO TIMES–a four-page pullout supplement. Prior to this venture a weekly column had been included for news of *Children's Hour* programmes.

As the 50s progressed, the gathering influence of Television became ever more marked. Nothing could have emphasised this more clearly than the change that occurred on the RADIO TIMES programme pages in 1957 when, for the first time, Television's billings were placed *ahead* of Radio's. The end of an era indeed.

'MARSHAL NEY'

A PLAY BY J. C. MASTERMAN
Adapted for radio by Helena Wood

Aglaé, Princess of Moscow..Joan Hart
Michel Ney..............................Howard Marion-Crawford
Louis XVIII..Gordon McLeod
The Duchess of Angoulême............................Helen Haye
The Count of Artois....................................Frank Duncan
Marshal Duras, *Court Chamberlain*......................John Garside
Batardy, *Ney's lawyer*....................................Eric Anderson
Dr. Marshall..Edward Lexy
Majordomo..Arthur Lawrence
A young usher......................................Norman Claridge
An old usher..Allan Jeayes
General Bourmont....................................William Fox
General Lecourbe......................................Jack Livesey
The Baroness de Bessonis............................Molly Rankin
Mlle. Vennier, *her housekeeper*....................Ella Milne
Dambray, *the Chancellor*............................Baliol Holloway
Berryer père, *Ney's Counsel*..........................Dennis Arundell
Duc de Broglie..Peter Assinder
The Duke of Richelieu, *Prime Minister*............Howieson Culff
Cauchy, *Secretary to the Chamber of Peers*............Cyril Shaps

WITH

T. St. John Barry, John Cazabon, Alexander Davion, Garard Green, Richard
Hart, Brian Hayes, Nan Marriott-Watson, Evelyn Moore, Nancy Nevinson,
Michael O'Halloran, Joan Clement Scott, Elsa Palmer

PRODUCTION BY PETER WATTS AT 9.15

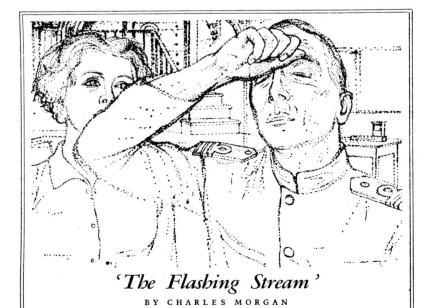

'The Flashing Stream'

BY CHARLES MORGAN

At an isolated naval station a devoted group of scientists are working to perfect
a new weapon. To them is sent the one mathematician good enough to help.
She is a woman but in singleness of mind there can be no respect of persons

at 9.15

'NOT
BY BREAD ALONE'

'Danger, Men Working'

Adapted for broadcasting by the author, J. D. STEWART

Mary Reilly, *a shorthand typist*..........................Patricia Stewart
Desmond Doherty, *general foreman*....................Joseph Tomelty
Erskine Craig, *a civil engineer*.........................Allan McClelland
Paddy Hoy, *a disabled craftsman*.............................J. G. Devlin
Gerry McMahon, *a navvy*..............................Patrick McAlinney
Charlie Quinn, *a foreman*...John McBride
Sam Toler, *a ganger*..Noel French
John Peoples, *a foreman*..Will Leighton
Fred Scanling, *a chief ganger*......................................Pat Magee
Major Trumbull, *Engineer in Charge*....................Michael Kelly

The play is set in Northern Ireland, on a site where a hospital is under construction, and it examines the impact of mass-production methods and mass-production mentality on a community of workmen accustomed to other, more personal methods

PRODUCED BY TYRONE GUTHRIE
at 9.15

'MR. GILLIE'

James Bridie's play about the village schoolmaster who 'devoted his life to opening cages and letting prisoners fly free'
SATURDAY-NIGHT THEATRE AT 9.15

AT 9.15 TWENTIETH-CENTURY THEATRE PRESENTS

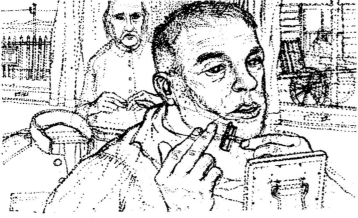

'DISTANT POINT'

It is the name of a remote and tiny station on the Trans-Siberian Railway. In Soviet Russia, as in the days of Chekhov, the life of the station staff has a peculiar and slightly melancholy charm. But suddenly it is brought into touch with the world of affairs when a general's private coach is marooned at the station for the night

'PROFESSOR BERNHARDI'

The play explores the implications, moral, political, and personal, of an incident in an Austrian hospital between the wars, when the director conscientiously refuses to allow a priest to visit a dying patient
at 9.15

Leonard Rosoman

LEONARD ROSOMAN WAS BORN IN 1913, EDUCATED AT DEACONS SCHOOL, PETERBOROUGH, AND SUBSEQUENTLY STUDIED ART AT DURHAM UNIVERSITY. AS A STUDENT HE WAS GREATLY INFLUENCED BY GAUGIN, PAUL NASH AND, PARTICULARLY, EDWARD BURRA

'I graduated in 1935. I'd made up my mind that I wanted to get back to London. So, back in London I got a job with Edward Halliday who was an ex-Rome Scholar, interested in mural painting, as I was. At that time I was also doing the odd job or two and I did a book for Dennis Cohen at the Cresset Press, an absolutely marvellous book by J. B. S. Haldane called "My Friend Mr Leaky"–an absolutely classic fairy story. Round about then I got a job teaching at The Reinmann School–I ran the life-drawing classes. The school carried on for a while at the beginning of the war. Austin Cooper even wrote postal-courses in an effort to keep going; I wrote a perspective course myself, quite a formidable thing to do as I was by then in the Fire Service.'

I remember very clearly some of the paintings you did while you were in the Fire Service. Can you tell me something of your life then?
'In the few months before war actually broke out we spent the time training very hard in Hampstead, where I lived. During 1941 and early 1942, with all the fierce activity going on, a curious body called Fireman Artists came into being. Working along with me in the Fireman Artists were Norman Hepple (who is now a colleague of mine at the Royal Academy and the Royal Portrait Society), Bernard Hailstone, Paul Desseau, E. Boye-Uden–really quite a number of very talented painters.

'In 1943 I got a letter from the War Artists Committee asking me if I would like to go to the Pacific and be attached to the fleet as a war artist. I was made a captain in the Royal Marines and sailed on a troopship to Australia. I succeeded, eventually, in getting aboard *HMS Formidable*, which had just been bombed by Kamikaze pilots off Japan, and had a whacking great hole blown in its foredeck. From the moment I got on board I started to work in real earnest, I loved the look of it and I loved the people.

'The *Formidable* was the fleet carrier with Admiral Vian in charge and he was very sympathetic and helpful to me. I had a battle station right up on the signal bridge, and I had to wear battle-gear as we steamed into an operation and the squadrons of Avengers and Corsairs took off. Thank goodness, during my stay the ship was never once hit. It was on board *Formidable* that we heard of the Japanese surrender, that was the end of the war for Leonard Rosoman.

'GOLDEN BOY'
Clifford Odets' play of a young life in which the pursuit of the prizes of the ring conflicts with an awareness of other values

at 9.15

Golden Boy–1951
'I suppose I was frightened a bit'

'Very shortly after the war I became friendly with the painter John Minton. Now, John, as well as being a wonderful artist, was one of the most generous men I've ever met. He was then teaching at Camberwell School of Art and Crafts and he rang me up one day and said, "Len, would you like to do some teaching?" So I said yes. We actually shared a class of 35 or 40 kids and Johnnie was marvellous with this noisy great mob; he used to let them go on for a bit and then roar at them very hard indeed and they would quieten down immediately while he proceeded to lash off a drawing for RADIO TIMES.

'After Camberwell, I was offered the job of running a new department of mural painting at Edinburgh College of Art; I said I would go for about two or three years. However, exciting things happened there. For example, the Diaghilev Exhibition which I mounted in the college with the help of about 20 students and which subsequently was sponsored by *The Observer* newspaper, in Forbes House by Hyde Park Corner.'

During your stay there, in 1951, you did your first drawing for RADIO TIMES, an illustration of a play by Clifford Odets, 'Golden Boy.' As a painter you made your own timetable, how did you feel about working under pressure, over the weekend for RADIO TIMES. Different way of life surely?
'Yes and no. You see, involvement in other fields has always been very important for me and illustrating for RADIO TIMES fitted in awfully well. I

suppose I was frightened a bit, but fear appears to me to be very much part of my painting and drawing. When I got a telephone call on a Friday from the Art Editor, I was usually at work on something else, I stopped dead in my tracks and said to myself, "All right, here's a story by Somerset Maugham, 'Cakes and Ale'; I read it ten years ago so I'll have to re-read it, that'll take me tonight. It's a period piece, so I must get my facts right." So it would be Saturday afternoon before I could begin drawing. This sounds pretty awful, I suppose, to anybody else, but the creation of all painting and drawing is a gamble; you never know when you start how it is going to end. Even if I'd had three weeks to do the drawing, it wouldn't have made all that much difference, because the drawing could easily have failed.'

Going back for a moment to Maugham's, 'Cakes and Ale,' there was a small history about that commission which I think we both remember. For an Art Editor one of the most wounding things to do was to have to reject a drawing.
'I was in Edinburgh when I did that drawing and the then Art Editor, R. D. Usherwood, rang me up and asked if I'd like to do it and I said that I was in the middle of a rather important painting. Then he said, in a marvellously seductive way, "I think you'll like it–it's a very interesting story." So I did the drawing, and it was a difficult one; it didn't go too well at first, but eventually, came the Monday morning, it was all right

I thought and I sent it off. Now, one of the nice things about working for RADIO TIMES was that Usherwood wrote to me about the drawing and said, "Marvellous, thank you very much, it's exactly what we wanted." So I was very happy about it.

'However, the following week, I got another letter from Usherwood of a rather different sort, I think I can almost quote it: "Doubtless you'll be very sad to hear that your drawing for 'Cakes and Ale' is, in fact, not going to be used. It went before the committee, and," he said, "it was decided that it was a little forthright for what, after all, is a family magazine." I had drawn the barmaid, Rosie, who after the pub closed had gone home with the hero and they went to bed: the story develops along those lines. The drawing was merely of Rosie, not terribly much in *déshabillée*, standing by a lace curtain, with the young man in the background tying his tie; her corsets were hanging on the bed, and that was it. When I read Usherwood's letter I felt so much of his feeling coming through–I was sad, naturally, that the drawing wasn't going to be printed, but I thought it was quite a historic moment in my career. I was very happy when, later, RADIO TIMES did publish it.'

It so happened that there was a change of Editor and hence of 'committee.' Luckily, the play was re-broadcast and so justice was eventually done. In 1960 you became an ARA and a full Academician in 1969. Did you find the Academy was, as many young painters felt at the time, an anachronistic hangover, unrepresentative of what was really going on in the world of art?
'I think what you say is absolutely true. The Royal Academy establishment in the 30s, 40s and 50s seemed to me to be a very limited, club-like set-up and the interesting painters were completely outside. Here was this wonderful gallery, right in the middle of London, at that time empty for most of the year. One or two marvellous exhibitions in the winter, and then the tremendous hotch-potch of the Summer Exhibition and that was about it. I talked about this at the Royal College and with my painter friends and we did think this was rather sad. So, in 1960 when I was asked if I would stand for election, I thought hard about it; I didn't think it would be of enormous help to me, but I thought if a number of interesting painters became elected–painters who thought rather as I did–we might change its image and enable it to act as a shop window for a much wider range of British painting, and also for young painters who might find it very difficult to get a showing in commercial galleries. So, all through the 1960s, a considerable number of us worked really hard to achieve this end.'

BETWEEN TWO WORLDS

'The Great Gatsby'

A NOVEL OF THE JAZZ AGE

by F. Scott Fitzgerald

In the raffish, disillusioned society of Long Island Nick Carraway finds he is often asked ' Do you know a man named Gatsby? ' Everyone goes to Gatsby's fabulous parties; no one knows—or wants to know—much about him. Nick comes to the heart of the man's enigma; it is unworthy but not altogether contemptible

at 9.15

'Brideshead Revisited'

EVELYN WAUGH'S novel, first published in 1945, was considered by many to be Mr. Waugh's finest book to date. Certainly although this author's famous satirical touch is amply in evidence, there is a more serious atmosphere than in his earlier novels.

The story is a rope of several strands, one being the development of Charles Ryder (who acts as narrator), and the others concern in the main his relationships with the various members of the Flyte family —Lord Marchmain who lives in Italy, his wife who lives in England, and their children, Cordelia and Julia and the pathetic, unforgettable Sebastian, whom Charles meets in early days of never-to-be-repeated happiness and freedom at Oxford. The story is set in the pre-war period, but the occasion for its telling is the unexpected wartime billeting of Ryder, now temporarily ' a middle-aged infantry officer,' at the Flytes' country seat, Brideshead Castle. *Peter Forster*

at 9.15

'A Ram in the Thicket'

A PLAY BY

Mary Frances Flack

Revised for broadcasting by the author

Shlomo Gavronsky............................Theodore Bikel
Rachel, *his wife*.......................................Lilly Kann
Moshe, *their son*...............................Leonard Sachs
Mirium Doniach.......................Catherine Willmer
Mark, *her husband*.....................Michael Hitchman
Sara, *their daughter*........................Dorothy Gordon
Deborah Youngman,
    the Gavronskys' younger daughter....Joan Miller
Daniel, *her son*...Brian Roper
Hannah Goldberg,
    Moshe's fiancée.....................Jeanette Tregarthen
Alexander (Sasha) Poushkin............Anthony Jacobs
Yacov..Charles Leno
Michael Johnson...............................Ralph Michael

PRODUCTION BY E. J. KING BULL

at 9.15

The action of the play takes place during the year 1947. The scene is Tel-Aviv

HOWARD MARION-CRAWFORD AND MARIUS GORING IN

'The Mayor'

BY HOWELL DAVIES

Adapted for broadcasting by John Richmond

CAST IN ORDER OF SPEAKING:

Lieutenant Haussman, *a German officer*...............Anton Diffring
Cook.. ....Nancy Nevinson
Lucienne, *the Mayor's housekeeper*....................Cecile Chevreau
Jacques Bonnecoeur, *the Mayor*.........Howard Marion-Crawford
Marcel, *a newspaper editor*.......................................Ivor Barnard
Guilliaume, *a doctor*...Stanley Groome
Jules, *a carpenter*..Roger Delgado
Captain Erkling, *German Commandant*..............Marius Goring
Daudet, *a schoolmaster*.......................................Wilfred Babbage
Annaury Duval...Aubrey Richards
Annette, *his wife*..Grizelda Hervey
Geneviève, *as a young girl*...Sarah Leigh
Mlle. Geneviève Hamonet, *a schoolmistress*....Violet Marquesita
A blind fiddler...Bryan Powley

PRODUCED BY HUGH STEWART

at 9.15

BREWSTER MASON IN

'The End of the Tether'

BY JOSEPH CONRAD

CURTAIN UP!

★

'A Street in Soho'

'Dr. Saunders is one of those patient, humble men who go unpretentiously about their duties and whose only immortality is the memory they leave in their neighbours' hearts'
Stephen Williams writing on page 8

★

at 8.30

SATURDAY-NIGHT THEATRE AT 9.15

'Rutherford and Son'

The play takes its name from a firm of glass manufacturers in Yorkshire, and the firm takes its name from John Rutherford. He is a dour character, proud of his work and determined not to see it come to ruin, but lonely and disappointed in the generation that will survive him

'RETURN TO TYASSI'

by Benn W. Levy

★

Rachel Kempson,
Cathleen Nesbitt
and Robert Harris
with
Michael Gough

★

Susan Hubbard..........Yvonne Mitchell
Gilbert Cotton...............Robert Harris
Mrs. Grenfell.............Cathleen Nesbitt
Martha Cotton..........Rachel Kempson
Christopher Green.......Geoffrey Dunn
Francis Hubbard..........Michael Gough
Ems............................Susan Richards

Adaptation and production by
E. J. King Bull

AT 9.15

'THE RISING SUN'

As the lights get bigger and brighter on the 'Rising Sun' stores Matthew Strong's small family shop sinks into the shadows. Dunned by his creditors and facing ruin he takes refuge in a whimsical humour which hides both his despair and courage from all but his devoted daughter

at 9.15

9.15   Alec Clunes

with Carleton Hobbs and Harold Scott in

'THE MAN FROM THERMOPYLAE'

BY ADA F. KAY

An old woman..................*Valerie Skardon*
A girl................................*Sheila Johnson*
Geron.............................*Carleton Hobbs*
Pantites................................*Alec Clunes*
Frixos...........................*John Southworth*
Melissa..................................*Joan Heath*
Iolaus..................................*Harold Scott*
Hippias..............................*Lionel Jeffries*
Helena.........................*Margaret Wedlake*
Penthesilea..........................*Jill Fenson*
Koryander.......................*Jonathan Field*
Philander............................*Jeffrey Segal*
Hermes...........................*Geoffrey Banks*
Other parts played by
Betty Alberge, Jeremy Bradbury, Leslie Moorhouse
PRODUCED BY COLIN SHAW
in the BBC's North of England studios

anthony gross

ANTHONY GROSS WAS BORN IN MARCH 1905 IN DULWICH OF A HUNGARIAN FATHER AND AN ITALIAN/IRISH MOTHER. HE WAS EDUCATED AT REPTON AND, AT THE AGE OF 17 WENT TO THE SLADE SCHOOL OF FINE ART BUT STAYED FOR ONLY TWO TERMS. HE COULDN'T AFFORD TO LIVE IN ENGLAND AND SO HE WENT TO FRANCE WHERE LIVING WAS MUCH CHEAPER AND, FOR A SHORT TIME BECAME A STUDENT AT THE ACADEMIE JULIAN AND AT THE ECOLE DES BEAUX ARTS, AND THEN MOVED ON TO MADRID. HE WAS BROUGHT UP TO BE, AND HAS ALWAYS REGARDED HIMSELF AS, A EUROPEAN

'I never had any doubts, when young, about what I wanted to do–I wanted to paint. The matter of earning a living never entered my mind. I worked mostly in oils on canvas but I filled sketch-books with water-colour drawings, working all the time. In the end I came to the conclusion that Spain was too far from the centre, so, for that reason, I came back to Paris and to the Beaux Arts.

'Eventually, I thought perhaps I'd better go home, so off I went, painting all the way to London. I suppose I was about 25 and I went back again to the Slade because somebody had said to me, "You can't draw." I got a bursary and I said I would stay at the Slade until Tonks, my tutor, said I could draw. In fact, within about a month, Tonks came to look at my work. He looked over my shoulder and said, "Now, Gross, you know how to draw but..." That was good enough for me, the next day I was off to Paris again.

'By this time I was selling some of my etchings to Deighton's in The Strand; I had a contract with him by which he agreed to pay me some ridiculous sum like £2 a week. I was a bit bronchial and my doctor had told me to go somewhere warm for the winter, so I went to Algiers and got myself a room in a brothel where I did a lot of painting. I was there for about four months, painting, painting and painting: the girls, the clients, the market and the carpet-makers– working very hard. I have always regarded drawing, particularly drawing from life, as absolutely essential, still do. Drawing for me is number one and painting number two, I draw and then I colour it in.'

When I studied life drawing under you at the Central, I was very surprised to see you using a plumb line.
'Oh, you have to use a plumb line. You see, it's like building a wall, you must have a vertical to start with. In drawing the figure, the plumb gives you a line against which the curves can be measured as variations on each side. It is an essential tool of craftsmanship in the business of learning to draw.

'My contract with Deighton was near its end and I decided that I was going to live and work in France. You could say that was the end of my student days in so far as any artist ever stops being a student. I went to live near Paris, and started painting pictures of all the country around. I took them to Paris and showed them to a dealer who liked them and bought at least one a month off me.

'This suited me beautifully and I worked steadily until about 1930–until the world slump came. My agent said to me, "Do what they do to the coffee in Brazil, go home and burn all your work, then perhaps we can start selling pictures again." That of course was a disaster for me, I'd just got married and my wife was expecting a baby.

'Then, out of the blue, a friend of mine called Hector Hoppin asked me to work with him on some film cartoons; he'd got all the equipment together and then found that he didn't know what to draw.

'I got interested and spent ten years producing cartoons with him. Perhaps the most famous cartoon we made was *The Fox Hunt.* Anyway, we were then asked to work on the Jules Verne thing *Around the World in 80 Days,* and that's what we were doing when the war broke out.

'We were in Paris at the time so I thought I'd better get back to England and get myself called-up. I left my wife, who is French, with her family in the South of France where I thought she would be safe. Anyway no one called me up. I showed my cartoons to Kenneth Clark who, luckily, had just seen a French exhibition of contemporary etchers and engravers and the work he had liked best had been mine. He welcomed me with open arms and asked if I would like to be an official war artist, so I said why not indeed. My first job was to join a troopship and make a pictorial record of the crowded life on board on the way to the Far East. It was a very good life for an artist and I really enjoyed it for the rest of the war.

'At the end of the war I flew back to England from the "forgotten army" as a "forgotten man." I think Ted Ardizzone was the first war artist to get back. I'd met him and lived in the flat over his in Cairo and we became very good friends, a friendship which lasted for years.'

So, the war was finally over, what was the outlook for you?
'Well, I got a commission to illustrate "The Forsyte Saga" for Heinemann's who paid me £500, which was a good start in being a civilian again.'

Do you regard illustrating as a separate thing, quite different to the 'fine art' thing of painting?
'Not really. I think you have to watch out that you don't get too heavily involved. To me the most important thing is painting, and I must not allow myself to be diverted from it–plus, of course, my etching and engraving. Illustration I've always done as little as possible because it becomes a profession very quickly. Ted Ardizzone and Lynton Lamb thought differently–for them illustration was just as important as their other work. I suspect Edward Bawden thought similarly. The funny thing about Bawden is that he's one of the best designer/painters living, but he has difficulty in drawing. Both Ted Ardizzone and Lynton, on the other hand, were beautiful, superb draughtsmen. I started teaching at the Central and stayed about five years from 1946, then Coldstream and Phillip James asked me if I would teach etching at the Royal College of Art, but I chose to go to the Slade.'

You know, of course, that Ted Ardizzone took that job at the Royal College, even though he always claimed that he had to learn etching from the students as he went along.
'Yes, I know, it was all a bit embarrassing

as he'd talked Darwin into offering me the job when Austin retired.

'Usherwood, the then Art Editor of RADIO TIMES, rang me up on a Friday in January 1951 and asked me if I'd do a drawing for him which he needed by Monday, and I thought I couldn't possibly do it in time. He told me that was the way it had to be, so I said, all right, I'd have a go. The drawing was for Anouilh's "Point of Departure." I knew Anouilh and his work fairly well, of course, which fitted closely with my own way of thinking.'

I remember that Ralph Usherwood had proofs of your illustrations for 'The Forsyte Saga' all over one wall of his office, and I knew that he admired them immensely.
'Yes, I think it was those that led him to ask me to draw. I discussed the job with him over the phone and it seemed to me, as a painter, that it was odd to have so little time in which to work at it. But he said again that it had to be, and that anyway, many people, if given more time, tended to get bogged down. I came to think after doing one or two that, in fact, it was a good way of working.'

If I recall correctly, the next drawing you did was for a play called 'The Beech Tree is Red'.
'That's right. It was really a straight bit of "Forsyte Saga." I still had all of the sketches I'd done for the book, and several of them were of just such London squares.'

Looking back 20-odd years, Tony, are you still pleased with the work you did for RADIO TIMES?
'With two, yes. "The Gambler," which was my next one, was perhaps a bit of a muddle. I know where it came from. It was from one of the first jobs I did after the war: it was for a book called "Old Christmases," and I did some drawings very much in the vein of "The Gambler." But "Point of Departure" is much more my line of country. I wasn't very fond of "The Seagull" which I drew in 1953, although Usherwood was kind enough to say that it caught the atmosphere of the play admirably. Of course, I'm not really a book man, I've never had much time to read; I read occasionally–which is perhaps why I'm a painter not an illustrator.'

I usually ask all the people I've interviewed about their fellow illustrators on RADIO TIMES, whether they particularly admired or respected any of them. How about you, Tony?
'Well, I've already mentioned the two I admired most–Ted Ardizzone and Lynton Lamb who produced, regularly, notable illustrations for RADIO TIMES. John Minton, too, was a considerable illustrator and I liked him very well.'

Point of Departure–1951
'I knew Anouilh and his work fairly well'

'The End of Things'

'LA FIN DES TEMPS'

A play of a woman who, late in life, saw a vision of a world
in torment and thought to come to its help

BY GABRIEL MARCEL

at 9.15

'THE BEECH TREE IS RED'

A PLAY BY MARY FRANCES FLACK

adapted for broadcasting by the author

CAST IN ORDER OF SPEAKING:

Gavin Roberts................................James Dale
Madeleine Balfour.............................Elizabeth Henson
Eve Balfour.....................................Joan Miller
Lotta Emerson...................................Avice Landone
Val Balfour.....................................Valentine Dyall
Sybil Roberts...................................Gladys Young

PRODUCED BY WILFRID GRANTHAM

at 9.15

AT 9.15 WORLD THEATRE PRESENTS

'The Seagull'

BY ANTON CHEKHOV

ADAPTED FOR BROADCASTING FROM THE TRANSLATION
BY GEORGE CALDERON

★

Madame Arcadina, *an actress*.................Fay Compton
Constantine Treplef, *her son*.....................Derek Hart
Sorin, *her brother*................................Allan Jeayes
Nina, *daughter of a rich landowner*......Ursula Howells
Shamrayef, *manager of Sorin's estate*...Hugh Manning
Pauline, *his wife*...............................Joan Sanderson
Masha, *their daughter*.......................Mary Wimbush
Trigorin, *a writer*...................................Val Gielgud
Dorn, *a doctor*...........................Leon Quartermaine
Medvedenko, *a schoolmaster*..............Norman Claridge

Guitarist .   *Narrator,*
Alexis Chesnakov   Hamilton Dyce

*The action takes place on Sorin's estate in Russia, towards the end of
the last century*

PRODUCED BY VAL GIELGUD AND DAVID H. GODFREY

Pincher Martin

Pincher Martin was a man who had
no love, no compassion, no God—a
man in whom the Divine Spirit was
hopelessly obscured in his greed for
a separate individual life.

What can such as he do at death
but refuse to be destroyed?

AT 8.0

'THE GAMBLER'

A PLAY BY NORMAN GINSBURY

Robin Jacques

ROBIN JACQUES WAS BORN IN 1920, LEFT SCHOOL AT THE AGE OF 15 AND WENT STRAIGHT TO WORK IN AN ADVERTISING AGENCY, LOOKING AFTER THE NEEDS OF THE SENIOR ARTISTS. AFTER TWO YEARS HE GOT TIRED OF IT AND WORKED AS A BARMAN FOR ABOUT NINE MONTHS IN KILBURN, NORTH LONDON

'At the end of that time I went back to advertising in an American firm called Erwin Wasey. Then the war happened and we all went our separate ways. I was just 19 and not quite ready for call-up so I found myself helping out at The Players Theatre. Then I went off to the war, which over the next four years took me to France, Holland and eventually to Germany, where I was invalided out in 1945.

'The first drawings I do remember very clearly doing for RADIO TIMES were for T. H. White's "Sword in the Stone." I loved the series because it was imaginative and different. Anyway, in 1945 I began to do quite a lot of work for RADIO TIMES. The sort of work which came my way was the C. S. Forester adventure-type serial. I began to specialise to some extent in military and costume drawings. Most of these were commissioned from my by Douglas Williams who was Art Editor at that time, and he was enormously helpful in briefing me on the background to his commissions.'

As one who has been an art editor himself, and a very good one too, for such as the Strand Magazine, would you say what you felt as an illustrator about working for RADIO TIMES. What about the pressures, and the rewards, if any, of working in this peculiar over-the-weekend manner?

'Well, the pressures are pretty scary, one has to face it; adhering to RADIO TIMES schedules is a real test of stamina and invention. One would collect the script on Friday and discuss it with the Art Editor, then trot away to collect any necessary reference material. The difficulty always was to get the final drawing right, as you had wanted it. I would do half-a-dozen roughs, perhaps more, and then select one to work on as the finished drawing; that was the test, to leave oneself just enough time to complete it. I really had to concentrate and crystallise my ideas very early on to get the drawing done in time and to please myself and to do a good job for RADIO TIMES. It became a little easier as time went on.'

I remember you doing your first 'headings and borders,' decorating the day's programmes around the margins of the pages. Did you find this a difficult commission?

'Designing those headings was a very special job one rather hoped would come one's way. They were very exciting to do and a great test of ingenuity, to try to fit the different elements around the text without them looking too bitty. Every season presented a different problem and this really kept you on your toes.

'One of the complications was that if, over the years, you did a number of them–if you were lucky enough to get them–there was a slight danger of them all looking much the same, so rather than have earlier examples beside me while doing a new one, I really made quite sure that I came to each assignment quite freshly. The content of each heading, of course, varied with the season: each has its own elements. If you think of Christmas, for example, you have quite a lot of design elements to play about with. When you get to Good Friday or Easter, the elements are severely reduced.'

The Art Editors of RADIO TIMES obviously felt that you were the right man for Shakespeare's plays, of which you illustrated many. I think the first one you illustrated for us was 'The Tempest,' for which you designed a magnificent cover and several drawings on the programme pages. What were your feelings when you received that first commission?

'"The Tempest," particulary, being given that to start with was almost like being given the marzipan before being given the cake. Of all Shakespeare's plays it has always been my favourite, it's so full of opportunities for an illustrator. The dominant figure is Prospero, and to some extent he's always a gift, although one never quite knows how to draw him. Should he be a slim, aesthetic intellectual as he is described in the play itself or should he be a more robust father figure? I rather settled for this second version, although I sometimes think I was wrong. Luckily I was given several bites at it. Looking at the drawings now, I would love to do them all again–quite differently of course.'

Before we leave 'The Tempest,' it has always seemed to me a major part of an illustrator's life to be aware of the context in which his work is to be placed. Working for RADIO TIMES, you were drawing for a magazine with a marked typographical style. Were you aware of the weight of typography that would accompany your drawing on the programme page?

'Yes, I'd grown used to the hand of the particular typographer at that time. I found it really very congenial, because the choice of type had exactly the right weight, it seemed to me, for the sort of drawing I was doing. I've always found myself drawn to typography. I'm no typographer, but I've always enjoyed lettering and doing a certain amount of my own, as is the case in the programme-page illustration for "The Tempest."'

From 'The Tempest' you went to 'As You Like It,' and from there to the great tragedy 'Julius Caesar.' What were your reactions to these two very different challenges?

'"As You Like It" is frivolous, light-hearted, full of poetry, and in the drawing I tried to match that mood of gaiety. I tried to make a space within the drawing to contain the title, which had a fairly loose, light-hearted outline to it; whereas with the later drawings with the rather more sombre "Julius Caesar," I tried for a very much grimmer, more oppressive feeling.

'The title page displaying the billing on the programme page carries a drawing which had to fit into another of these longish, shallow shapes, and I remember being exercised as to quite how to fill it. Then I think I had a real stroke of luck, I had the idea of simply drawing the prone, shrouded figure of the assassinated Caesar under the title, which in effect sums up the whole of the play. Happily, I think it worked quite well. It is more successful in its way than the larger drawing, but you will notice the same shrouded shape is picked up again in the larger drawing behind the figure of Brutus on the steps of the Capitol.'

On 10 September 1954 you were asked to illustrate a military subject, Lillian Helman's play 'Monserrat,' and very soon after that, in March 1955, an adaption of C. S. Forester's novel 'The Gun,' both of which were costume dramas by modern dramatists. Something of a departure?

'Those two plays presented me with a new and interesting challenge. They gave me a chance to start to work on the fairly gorgeous accoutrements of military uniform, the epaulettes and so on, involving a great deal of research, and that in itself is something of a problem when RADIO TIMES has given you only the weekend to come up with a finished drawing. I had to find a great deal of material which I didn't have by me. But I was glad of it, because "Monserrat" initiated a series of drawings with military backgrounds which I undertook for RADIO TIMES. "The Gun," by Forester, was a Peninsula Wars' story. I chose to draw the manhandling of the gun up the side of a mountain. In the foreground I drew a couple of soldiers, one a Portugese irregular and the other a young English officer.'

We've been talking, Robin, of costume drama–but in October 1956 you were asked to illustrate Isherwood's 'Prater Violet' and, soon after, 'Mr Norris Changes Trains.'

'I've always enjoyed the steamy, rather specialised world of Isherwood. "Prater Violet" is a story about a German-Jewish film producer working in England, having known better days on The Continent and in Hollywood, and it was a lovely little character-sketch to do. Isherwood himself comes into it in a rather more disguised way than in some of the books about himself, but it really was a chance to work using modern backgrounds. "Mr Norris Changes Trains" is essential Isherwood, of his period in the Berlin of the 30s and a little before that. Mr Norris is a marvellous character to draw: a strange, bewigged, lecherous, sexually ambivalent man in the play.

'I enjoyed this little drawing very much, because it used that 20s, 30s Berlin background which people have come to know so much better recently through such films as *Cabaret.*'

Moving a little further on, we're now into the period of the 'new theatre' and, in particular, the new theatre of Samuel Beckett and the play that mystified many people when it was first produced, 'Waiting for Godot.' It obviously didn't mystify you too much, because you produced what many people consider to be the definitive drawing for this play in RADIO TIMES.

'Well, "Waiting for Godot" was part of the general excitement in the theatre after "Look Back in Anger" broke on to the scene. "Godot" was very much central to the whole movement. I remember seeing it at The Art Theatre in London and being baffled, and I was excited to be given a chance to do a drawing for it in RADIO TIMES. I was really very pleased with the end product. The play is simply full of atmosphere and a gift to the illustrator.'

Julius Caesar–1955
'Happily, I think it worked quite well'

ON WEDNESDAY EVENING IN THE HOME SERVICE WORLD THEATRE PRESENTS
Shakespeare's 'THE TEMPEST'

'THE TEMPEST'
by William Shakespeare

The TEMPEST

BY WILLIAM SHAKESPEARE

★

John Gielgud as Prospero

AT

Jeremy Spenser
as Ariel

William Devlin
as Caliban

9.15

Leslie French
as Trinculo

Leon Quartermaine
as Gonzalo

MARGARET LEIGHTON AND
LAURENCE HARVEY IN

As You Like It

by William Shakespeare

The Tragedy of 'Julius Caesar'

Denholm Elliott and Stephen Murray in

'MONTSERRAT'

A PLAY ADAPTED BY LILIAN HELLMAN
FROM THE FRENCH OF EMMANUEL ROBLES

Cast in order of appearance
Zavala.........................*David Yates*
Antonanzas.............*Derek Sydney*
An orderly.............*Ronald Frazer*
Montserrat..........*Denholm Elliott*
Morales....................*Percy Herbert*
Izquierdo.............*Stephen Murray*
Father Coronil........*Noel Howlett*
A soldier............*Eddie Sutherland*
Salas Ina, a merchant
Wensley Pithey
Luhan, a woodcarver
Donald Pleasence
Matilde, a mother
Maureen Pryor
Salcedo, an actor.....*Peter Copley*
Felisa.........................*Clare Austin*
Ricardo......................*John Breslin*
A monk...............*Randal Kinkead*
Designer, John Clements
Produced by
STEPHEN HARRISON
at 8.35

The action takes place in an outer hall of the Spanish General's palace
in the city of Valencia in Venezuela in the year 1812

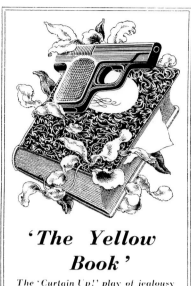

'The Yellow
Book'

*The 'Curtain Up!' play of jealousy
and murder*
AT 8.0

'THE GUN'

The armies of Napoleon have swept through the Spanish Peninsula.
Small bands of bloodthirsty and resourceful peasants fight on in the
mountains, giving to the word guerilla a new and sinister meaning. But
without artillery they cannot shake the French garrisons. Just one really
heavy gun would make all the difference; it might even make history

SATURDAY-NIGHT THEATRE

'THE HOUSE BY THE SEA'

'The Case of
SARAH CHANDLER

AN ORIGINAL PLAY FOR RADIO

'The Leader'

BY HELENA WOOD

HUGH BURDEN AND GEOFFREY SUMNER IN

'A Penny for a Song'

A COMEDY BY JOHN WHITING

William Humpage......................................*Richard Pearson*
Sir Timothy Bellboys...............................*Hugh Burden*
Samuel Breeze...*Stuart Burge*
Lamprett Bellboys...................................*John Ruddock*
Hester Bellboys.......................................*Barbara Cavan*
Dorcas Bellboys.......................................*Judith Stott*
Hallam Matthews...................................*Godfrey Kenton*
Edward Sterne..*Joseph Shaw*
Jonathan Watkins...................................*Derek Hodgson*
George Selincourt....................................*Geoffrey Sumner*
Pippin..*Joyce Chancellor*
Joseph Brotherhood................................*Alban Blakelock*
James Giddy...*Richard Wade*
Rufus Piggott...*Paddy Hayes*

Setting by Richard Wilmot

PRODUCED BY BARBARA BURNHAM

at 8.45

'THE RAPHAEL RESURRECTION'

It is the spring of 1947 and Kerr's gratuity is almost completely spent. Since nobody will buy his paintings it looks as if he will have to return to the world of 'commercial art' which he despises so vehemently. And then Talbot comes on the scene, breathlessly, and with a cunning plan. That it includes theft does not bother him in the slightest and gives Kerr only momentary qualms. What becomes far more important to Kerr the artist as the play develops is the fact that the plan involves depriving the world of a major work of art. Can he bear to do so, even for the money he needs so desperately? He ponders the question as he and Talbot get nearer and nearer to finding the missing Raphael which is to make their fortunes. The result of their search, and the course of action Kerr decides upon, tonight's performance will reveal. For while the play poses a neat problem of conscience it does so in terms of violent action which should make for exciting listening.—*Elwyn Jones*

SATURDAY-NIGHT THEATRE AT 9.15

'MELLONEY HOLTSPUR'

'SOUTH WIND'

THE NOVEL BY NORMAN DOUGLAS

adapted for radio by Stafford Byrne

THOMAS HEARD, Bishop of Bampopo	
	Deryck Guyler
MR. MUHLEN	Allan McClelland
DON FRANCESCO	Hedley Briggs
THE DUCHESS OF SAN MARTINO	Barbara Couper
DENIS PHIPPS	David Peel
MR. KEITH	Howieson Culff
ERNEST EAMES	Denis Goacher
ANGELINA	Martina Mayne
COUNT CALOVEGLIA	Leonard Sachs
MISS WILBERFORCE	Barbara Leake
MADAM STEYNLIN	Irène Prador
MRS. MEADOWS	Patricia Hilliard
FREDDIE PARKER	Richard Waring
THE PARROCO	Keith Pyott
MR. VAN KOPPEN	Stuart Nichol

Other parts played by
Christine Sheldon-Williams and Bryan Powley
*The scene is the Mediterranean island of
Nepenthe just before the first world war*

PRODUCTION BY FREDERICK BRADNUM AT 9.15

'The Celestial Onion'

A BIOGRAPHICAL PORTRAIT AND A SHADOW PLAY
Contributed on the occasion of the centenary of the birth of
ROBERT LOUIS STEVENSON
by John Keir Cross

Taking part: John Keir Cross, Henry Donald, Margaret Haslett, Carleton Hobbs,
Moultrie R. Kelsall, Moray McLaren, Maud Risdon, D. A. Clarke-Smith,
Jean Taylor Smith, David Steuart, and Meta Forrest
Produced by Robin Richardson

at 9.55

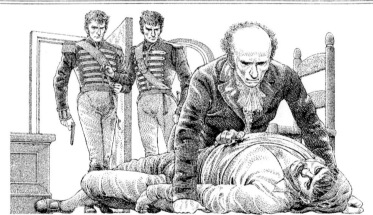

'THE ENGLISH CAPTAIN'

BY LYDIA RAGOSIN

Captain Samuel Pridie	*Stephen Murray*
Lieut. Stuart Lindsay	*Roger Delgado*
Ensign Miles Parker	*Derek Hart*
Ignacio Concha, the Alcalde	*Tony Quinn*
Juanilla, his niece	*Doreen Keogh*
Rosa Henriquez	*Maureen Pryor*
Sergeant Bray	*Manning Wilson*
Todd, the Captain's servant	*Edward Kelsey*
Father Miguel	*Edward Byrne*
El Zanquilargo	*Robert Mooney*

The action of the play takes place in a small village in the Guadarrama
mountains of Spain, October 1812

PRODUCED BY WILFRID GRANTHAM

at 9.15

'There seemed to be nothing very particular about the island—except perhaps
that it was curiously complete in itself . . though it became the most dreaded
place in the world to us.' Barrie's fantasy 'Mary Rose,' with Norman O'Neill's
music, will be presented at 2.30 this afternoon

'TREASURE ISLAND'
**Robert Louis Stevenson's classic
adventure story will be presented as a
radio play at 7.30 tonight**

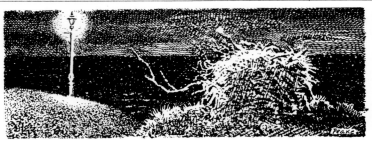

'THE BRUSHWOOD BOY'

THE STORY BY RUDYARD KIPLING
adapted for radio by Giles Cooper

★

George, *as a man*....Derek Hart   George, *as a boy*....Denise Bryer
The Girl...............Diana Maddox
Mrs. Cottar........Mary Wimbush   Colonel Cottar.........Allan Jeayes
Other parts played by
Fred Yule, Elsa Palmer, Patricia Hilliard, Frank Tickle, Geoffrey Bond, Arthur
Lawrence, Michael O'Halloran, Thelma Hughes, Nancy Nevinson, Antony
Kearey, Hugh Manning, Margaret Ward
Incidental music composed and conducted by John Hotchkis
PRODUCTION BY CLELAND FINN AT 7.30

RUMPELSTILTSKIN
*I know I'm 'orrible ter look at, but
ain't it a relief ter see me, eh?' A
new version of an old old story will be
presented at 9.30 tonight*

'For Mr. Pye—an Island'

The adventures of Mr. Pye in pursuit of the Good

The people he meets and the Island
he calls Sark have never existed;
but suppose they had . . .

A PLAY FOR RADIO BY
Mervyn Peake
based on incidents from his novel 'Mr. Pye'

MR. PYE: Oliver Burt   MISS DREDGER: Betty Hardy
Others taking part:
Wilfred Babbage   Ysanne Churchman   Hamilton Dyce   Haydn Jones
Ian Lubbock   Nan Marriott-Watson   Frank Partington   Eric Phillips
Robert Sansom   John Sharp   Mary Wimbush   Arthur Young
Music composed and conducted by Malcolm Arnold
PRODUCED BY FRANCIS DILLON

at 9.45

A fable by
ARTHUR PINERO
'The Enchanted
Cottage'
AT 2.50

AT 9.15 WORLD THEATRE PRESENTS

'The Lady from the Sea'

BY HENRIK IBSEN
IN A NEW TRANSLATION BY PETER WATTS

'Now we shall both be married to the sea—and to each other'

Dr. Wangel..*William Fox*
Ellida Wangel, his wife...*Marie Ney*
His daughters: Boletta....................................*Nancy Nevinson*
Hilda....................................*Margaret Barton*
Arnholm, a tutor...*Heron Carvic*
Lyngstrand..*Ronald Sidney*
Ballested...*John Turnbull*
A Stranger..*Valentine Dyall*

SCENE: *a small town at the head of a landlocked fjörd in Northern Norway, 1888*
PRODUCED BY PETER WATTS

CECIL TROUNCER IN

'The Judgment of Doctor Johnson'

by G. K. Chesterton

Adapted for radio and produced by
FREDERICK BRADNUM

★

CAST IN ORDER OF SPEAKING

Ian MacLean	*Duncan McIntyre*
Moira MacLean	*Isla Cameron*
John Swallow Swift	*Laurence Payne*
Mary Swift	*Mary Wimbush*
Dr. Johnson	*Cecil Trouncer*
Grant of Inverballoch	*Wyndham Milligan*
James Boswell	*James McKechnie*
Captain Draper	*Malcolm Hayes*
John Wilkes	*Howieson Culff*
Marquis de Montmarat	*Marion Jennings*
Edmund Burke	*Cyril Conway*
Lieut. Crockford	*Wyndham Milligan*

at 9.15

'The Voysey Inheritance'

BY HARLEY GRANVILLE-BARKER

The inheritance that Mr. Voysey left to his son was a burden of shame which he must either redeem openly or perpetuate in secret

Adaptation by Marianne Helweg. Production by E. J. King Bull

Peacey	James Ottaway	*Alice Maitland*	Joan Matheson
Mr. Voysey	Clive Morton	*Honor Voysey*	Joan Hart
Edward Voysey	Robert Flemyng	*Beatrice Voysey*	Mary Morris
Booth Voysey	Felix Felton	*Mrs. Voysey*	Marjorie Westbury
Denis Tregoning	Donald Gray	*Hugh Voysey*	Olaf Pooley
Mr. George Booth	John Turnbull	*Trenchard Voysey*	Eric Anderson
The Rev. Evan Colpus	Bryan Powley	*The Maids*	Marjorie Westbury
Ethel Voysey	Sarah Malcolm		Sarah Malcolm

★

FESTIVAL WORLD THEATRE AT 9.15

'Edward My Son'

BY ROBERT MORLEY
AND NOEL LANGLEY

WORLD THEATRE PRESENTS
Donald Wolfit and Miles Malleson in

'TARTUFFE'

BY MOLIERE

Freely adapted into English by
MILES MALLESON

★

MONSIEUR ORGON, *a rich merchant*........Miles Malleson
DAMIS, *his son*......................................Desmond Carrington
MARIANE, *his daughter*..............................Violet Loxley
MADAME PERNELLE, *his mother*....................May Agate
ELMIRE, *his second wife*............................Frances Rowe
CLEANTE, *Elmire's brother*....................David King-Wood
VALERE, *betrothed to Mariane*....................Robert Rietty
DORINE, *maid to Elmire*................................Jessie Evans
LOYALE, *a bailiff*..John Moffatt
A POLICE OFFICER..................................Hamilton Dyce
TARTUFFE...Donald Wolfit

SCENE
Paris 1660. The house of Monsieur Orgon, a rich merchant
Rhymed couplets by Sagittarius
Music adapted by Leslie Bridgewater from Rameau, Lully, and Campra
PRODUCED BY WILFRID GRANTHAM

at 9.15

THE SUNDAY EVENING SERIAL AT 8.30

'THE EUSTACE DIAMONDS'

BY ANTHONY TROLLOPE

'THE HOLLY AND THE IVY'

BY WYNYARD BROWNE

' The holly has a bark, As bitter as any gall '

SATURDAY-NIGHT THEATRE AT 9.15

'*The sweet birds sang*'

A COMEDY BY ROMILLY CAVAN

r.f. micklewright

BOB MICKLEWRIGHT WAS BORN IN 1923 IN WEST BROMWICH. HE WENT TO A GRAMMAR SCHOOL IN BALHAM AND, AFTER THAT, TO CROYDON SCHOOL OF ART IN 1939, WHICH CLOSED DOWN ON THE OUTBREAK OF WAR. FROM THERE HE WENT TO SUTTON AND WIMBLEDON ART SCHOOLS UNTIL HE WAS CALLED UP INTO THE RIFLE BRIGADE IN 1942

'I was in the signals section and finished up in the Northumberland Fusiliers where my company commander, incidentally, was Laurence Whistler, the glass engraver. I was far too busy and tired being a soldier to do any drawing. I saw service in Algiers, Italy and finished up in Greece helping to put down the communist attempt at a take-over. I was there until the end of the war and, apart from one spell of painting murals in a barracks canteen, I was too discouraged by the difficulties to do any more in the way of painting or drawing.

'In 1946 I went back to Wimbledon to get enough work together to get into the Royal College of Art, but I had only three months to do so, and I failed to get in. So I took my work along to the Slade where I was put on the waiting-list, and eventually got a grant and a place.

'The Slade was a "fine art" school rather geared to finding the odd genius like Augustus John, but wasn't an awful lot of use to ordinary mortals like myself. I spent my three years drawing and painting from life, practically nothing else. In 1951, while I was still at the Slade, I got married and in consequence my £3-a-week grant was doubled, and we managed moderately well on that. I was beginning, however, to feel one of the oldest students in the world, I was 28. In the late summer of 1954 I went, very nervously, to see RADIO TIMES ith some specimens I'd done specially and met the Art Editor, Usherwood. He was very charming and said I was just the man he needed to illustrate some Wednesday-night plays set in humdrum suburbia, so I went away from the office feeling very pleased with life.

'In fact, strangely enough, the first drawing I did couldn't have been less suburban, it was for the magazine programme on the Home Service on Saturdays called "In Town Tonight."

 I dropped everything and rushed up to London and, standing on the kerb at Piccadilly Circus, I did a small drawing of Eros looking up Shaftesbury Avenue. There was no flower-seller, I think they had gone years before, so I dug up a life-drawing I'd done of a rather ancient model and I dressed her up and used her in the foreground.

'It was quite terrifying in the beginning to be asked to do a finished drawing over the weekend, and I found it a terrible chore getting it down in the time–especially if I had to find references: libraries tend to shut over the weekend. It was absolutely essential to produce something by Monday, so I got down to it and hoped for the best. I used to start drawing on tracing paper and make a sort of montage jigsaw-puzzle; I'd get a figure, or part of a figure I liked and stick other bits, background etc, on to it until I'd made a complete jigsaw, then trace it on to the board I was going to use for my finished drawing. Odd things around my home would trigger me off. I remember I had to do a drawing for a Russian play and we had an old typewriter up in the loft which was just the right period, so I built the drawing around that. I always used the things around me to build up the image given me by the text. Things like anglepoise lamps and engravers' tools (which I'd never used by the way, I'm just a painter and illustrator).'

In the years you drew for RADIO TIMES, _you must have had some awareness of, and estimation for, some of your fellow illustrators. Were there any of them you held in particular regard?_
'I think foremost among them was Leonard Rosoman; I remember seeing his drawings and, in a sort of blinding flash, I suddenly knew how to do black and white drawings. I also liked Fritz Wegner and Gage who, I suspect, was also influenced by Rosoman.'

As I remember Rosoman taught him in Edinburgh. In 1957 you did a drawing which we published and which you re-drew later because it contained a technical error. It became a sort of definitive drawing for RADIO TIMES _and was used many times for chamber-music quartets._
'Actually, it started off as an illustration for a play. I put a cello leaning flat on to a

The Last Summer–1954
'We had an old typewriter up in the loft which was just the right period'

chair; it should have been with the waist of the instrument against the seat of the chair. I've still got the letter which pointed out the error of my ways which came from a clergyman on the Isle of Wight. Usherwood asked me to get it right, which I did, and it was used many times again after that–must have been one of the most useful drawings I've ever done. The chairs, actually, in the drawing were my own drawing-room chairs which I'd just bought.

'I did a drawing for you which was also pretty important for me. It was, I think, for a play called "Cruising Down the River" and was of a pleasure boat on the Thames. Two people got in touch with me as a result: Nicolas Bently of André Deutsch, and he gave me quite a lot of book-jackets to do, and the other

was Cara Strong of Saxon Artists who asked me if they could take me on and be my agent. I took her up on it and she's acted for me ever since.'

Did you ever have, for whatever reason, a drawing rejected by RADIO TIMES?
'No, it never happened to me. I only ever had to alter two other drawings. One was a fairly early one about sailing toy yachts on the Round Pond: I missed giving the central character a bald patch which the script described. So I simply scraped one on to his head. The other one was a cover. Douglas Williams, who was Editor then, asked me to strengthen the tone washes, and I had to do that in the office. It was very nerve-wracking because he was leaning over my shoulder saying, "Just a bit stronger, Bob, go on."

'I did have one other problem with a drawing. It was a single-column, full-depth-of-the-page drawing of how a television news bulletin was put together. I went to Alexandra Palace to meet the author of the feature, and we went out with a camera crew who had to cover the scene of a bank robbery, somewhere near London Airport.

'We interviewed the local police who re-enacted some finger-printing they'd been doing, but the whole story was a bit of a flop. I didn't see the resulting article, but I believe the article somewhat gave the impression that news was being manipulated. The news people were furious about this and got the article stopped. However, a small part of the drawing was eventually used for a different television programme.'

What are you doing now, Bob. Are you still involved in illustration?
'Oh, yes. I'm still at it. I've been illustrating quite a lot of non-fiction and guide books lately. Recently, too, I've done some drawings for stories in _Punch_. There are some posters that I'm doing at the moment that will keep me busy. I have also illustrated gardening books; I've learned how to grow things!'

Quartet–1957
'Usherwood asked me to get it right'

'Lies my father told me'

'FAIR MUSIC'

The day of such schools as Mrs. Millicent's is passing. Parents can no longer afford to pay for an advanced education at a small private school. But to her and to Mason, her headmaster, it is a trust, handed on from Mrs. Millicent's dead husband, a trust to which they can dedicate their lives, selflessly cultivating the growing minds given into their care. But this is an attitude that the new science master does not at first appreciate.

at 9.15

'VIRTUOSO'

by Cedric Wallis

at 9.15

Maigret, that most human of French detectives, sets out to solve the mystery surrounding the brutal murder of a girl whose body has been found in a street near the Place Pigalle in the heart of Paris

'Maigret and the Lost Life' at 8.45

'The Blood is Strong'

Life for a Highland immigrant in Cape Breton Island in the nineties is hard and strange. But if he faces the truth Murdoch MacDonald knows that the New Scotland is not so bleak and uncharitable as the old. To his dying day he will regret his native Skye, but his family has taken root in its new home; the MacDonalds have become Canadian

SATURDAY-NIGHT THEATRE AT 9.15

*The tawny owl—a woodland bird
—preys on the smaller creatures*

THE THRUSH'S ANVIL
*In Birds in Britain at 1.10 the discussion concerns the five British repre-
sentatives of the thrush family and includes an account of the way in
which the song thrush eats snails by breaking them open on a stone*

At 9.0 Field-Marshal Viscount Alanbrooke and Niall Rankin show films
of Ruffs (seen above drawn by C. F. Tunnicliffe, R.A.), and Spoonbills

L O O K : Birds of Holland

IN THE EASTER PROGRAMMES

Canterbury Cathedral
Impression in sound: Home Service on Easter Day

Michael Howard's Bank Holiday
Five broadcasts in the Light Programme

Arthur Askey and Richard Murdoch
in reminiscences of 'Band Waggon' on Easter Monday

The Lincolnshire Handicap
A commentary on Saturday

EDWARD GAGE WAS BORN ON 28 MARCH 1925 IN EAST LOTHIAN AND WAS EDUCATED AT THE ROYAL HIGH SCHOOL, EDINBURGH. IN 1942 HE BEGAN TRAINING AT THE EDINBURGH COLLEGE OF ART, WITH THE KNOWLEDGE THAT HE HAD ONLY A YEAR BEFORE HE WAS CALLED UP. HE STARTED OUT ON WHAT TURNED OUT TO BE FIVE YEARS IN THE ARMY BY JOINING THE BRIGADE OF GUARDS AND, FOR BETTER OR WORSE, NEVER HEARD A SHOT FIRED IN ANGER

'Well, the years passed and eventually I was demobbed and went straight back to the college as a second-year student on the ex-service grant. I decided to concentrate on painting and drawing as I was fascinated by colour. Len Rosoman came to the college at that time and, in him, I found standards of picture-building with forms and shapes which I totally admired. I learnt a great deal from him and became very friendly with him, as did my wife Valerie, who was a student with me.

'At the end of that year I was awarded a travelling scholarship and I couldn't think where to go. The sort of thing you were supposed to do was to go on a "grand tour" of European art galleries. I thought, "I've got the rest of my life to see the art galleries of Europe; what I really need is a couple of years of working without pressures, finding out about myself, and what sort of thing I ought to be doing as a painter." So my wife and I–I just had enough to take her with me–about £300–got permission from the college to go to Majorca. I got a little villa called the Casa Castagna near a small village. We saw practically nobody, although Robert Graves lived nearby. We became good friends with Graves. He even, when the last instalment of my grant failed to come through, offered us his guest-house next to the church, so we moved in there.'

Edward, at the end of what was obviously a delightful and fruitful year you presumably had to do something about earning a crust or two?
'That's right. I came back to Edinburgh and, through the college, I got a part-time job teaching art at Fettes. Eventually it became full-time and the job became a real pleasure to me.

'We used to drink in a pub called Scott's in Edinburgh. There was a funny little man in our group who did dreadful drawings for furniture catalogues and newspapers. He said that he'd heard that RADIO TIMES was looking for illustrators in Scotland. I went to see Iain Crawford, who was the BBC's publicity officer in Edinburgh. My commercial friend had said you must draw on scraperboard, which I'd never done before. Anyway, I did a few of what I thought were RADIO TIMES-type illustrations, and took them along. Shortly after that Usherwood rang in January 1953 and asked me to do my first illustration for RADIO TIMES. It was in the Scottish edition for a programme called "The Last Tramcar for Auchenshugall." It marked the end of the tramcars in Glasgow.'

To many young illustrators, their first drawing in RADIO TIMES was quite a landmark. What did you feel about it?
'I felt great. I thought it was the biggest break I could possibly get, it was marvellous. I knew that it was the best publicity a young illustrator could get in any circumstances, because RADIO TIMES had such a tremendous reputation in the illustrators' world.'

I remember you always dealt directly with us, not through an agent. How did that work?
'It was always by telephone. It was very simple, really. You rang me on Friday afternoons when I was usually taking a sixth-form lecture at Fettes, so I couldn't always come to the phone. Luckily my wife soon got the hang of things and you were apparently quite happy to give the details to her. Of course, if I had any queries I could ring you back.'

What about the matter of scripts, Edward–you illustrated a lot of plays and serials for us. How did we manage that enterprise?
'Well, you were pretty good at this, you always sent the script a day earlier so that it got to me on Saturday morning. Of course, I felt the pressure very heavily indeed, particularly when any research was called for on my part.'

Let's take a 'for instance,' Edward. You illustrated Dylan Thomas's 'Under Milk Wood' for us.
'Yes, I remember it well. I wasn't in Edinburgh at the time; we were staying with a wealthy stockbroker friend who lived in Little Oak Hall, in Sussex. I'd left the address with you and I did the drawing there. Luckily I knew the work very well indeed, so it was no problem and I loved doing it.'

What was your working routine from the time a script landed in your hands?
'The first requirement, of course, was to absorb the script and take the all-important decision about which part of it I wanted to illustrate. Sometimes the Art Editor would ask for a certain incident in the drama to be used which made it easy for me. The next bit was doing the research, which could take some time. Then, when all was ready, I'd work my way through various ideas. After several attempts I would quite often go back to my first idea and modify it slightly. The important thing was not to allow myself to go on too long because I had to keep up with the clock ticking away to the deadline. I tried always not to take more than about an hour-and-a-half to decide the composition, the creative, intellectual bit of the work, the exciting bit. The rest, the realisation of the drawing, was the utilisation of all the training and such talent for drawing as I possessed.

'I went on using scraperboard for many years simply because I didn't know any better. I mean, it's a long way from tramcars to the "Othello" I did for you, but I went on slaving away with tiny, fine little No. 3 sable brushes, needles and knives simply because I thought that scraper was the only thing to use for reproduction on your paper. It got me into bad ways because it was always so easy to correct any mistakes with a stroke of the knife. Eventually I got fed up with it and got myself some tough sort of paste-board and attacked it with a steel pen, something I should have done years earlier, crazy isn't it?'

One of my favourites of all the drawings

Under Milk Wood –1960
'It was no problem and I loved doing it'

you did for RADIO TIMES was for 'The Drunk Man Looks at the Thistle.'
'There's a bit of a story to that one, Peter. You rang me about it on a Thursday I remember, and you asked me if I knew Christopher Grieve because you wanted a portrait. I said that I didn't but that I would go to see him. After that rash promise I asked myself how the hell I was going to arrange it. However, I managed through a mutual friend. Christopher was the most charming man, so courteous. He asked me about Robert Graves and, as we talked, I drew him in my sketch-book. I met Christopher again only a couple of years ago and he said: "You know, of all the drawings and paintings that have been done of me, yours is the one I value most." That was very kind of him wasn't it?'

Now for a stock question. I've asked all the illustrators I've interviewed if they particularly admired or respected any of their fellow RADIO TIMES illustrators. How about you?
'Oh, yes indeed. They were people I admired from afar, people I didn't know personally. I can remember before the war the memorable signature of Eric Fraser; as a schoolboy I used to hunt for it in RADIO TIMES. To me, his drawings were always superb, so beautifully executed and formalised. He is one of the greatest working illustrators, who can turn his hand to anything and produce memorable images.

'Nearer to my own time there are others, like Micklewright. I've never met him but, for me, he never did a bad drawing. Robin Jacques was, or is, another beautiful craftsman. And then there was a woman, oh she was superb, Susan Einzig. She had a rich, voluptuous quality in her line, it rang bells all over the place for me–I always wished I could draw like that. Finally, one of the greatest illustrators I ever saw in RADIO TIMES was John Minton. I remember vividly a marvellous drawing he did of a bull-fight for Bizet's Carmen.'

Edward, as you know, in the late 60s, largely because of the dominance of Television and later because of a change of editorial direction, RADIO TIMES changed. Life has gone on since for you, what have you been doing in these last ten years?
'The central thing in my life has always been painting and I've had one-man shows every three or four years, which have been quite successful. In fact, I'm selling more and more. Also I'm senior lecturer in the Design Department of Napier College, which provides my bread and butter. Teaching industrial design and technology, I rub shoulders all the time with engineers and technicians which has broadened me considerably–which is a good thing.'

8.0 WORLD THEATRE PRESENTS **9.15**

'OTHELLO'

BY WILLIAM SHAKESPEARE

Adapted for broadcasting by Peter Watts

GIRALDI CINTHIO, *the storyteller (1565)*...............Roger Delgado
RODERIGO, *a Venetian gentleman*.......................Basil Hoskins
IAGO, *Ensign to Othello*..Frank Duncan
BRABANTIO, *a Senator of Venice*.....................Graveley Edwards
OTHELLO, *a Moor, in the service of Venice*...........Valentine Dyall
CASSIO, *his Lieutenant*....................................John Westbrook
THE DUKE OF VENICE...Howard Rose
LODOVICO, *a senator, kinsman to Brabantio*.........John Richmond
GRATIANO, *a senator, brother to Brabantio*...............Stephen Jack
DESDEMONA, *daughter to Brabantio*..........................Joan Hart
MONTANO, *late Governor of Cyprus*......................Eric Anderson
EMILIA, *wife to Iago*....................................Marjorie Westbury
BIANCA, *a courtesan*.......................................Virginia Winter

with

Garard Green   Ronald Sidney   Conrad Phillips   Peter Wigzell

PRODUCED BY PETER WATTS

'OBLOMOV'

by Ivan Goncharov

A radio version by John Coulter
of his stage play based on the novel

CAST IN ORDER OF SPEAKING

Zakhar.....................................*Frank Atkinson*
Elie Oblomov.........................*Robert Eddison*
Tarantiev...............................*Derek Birch*
Andrey Stolz...........................*Olaf Pooley*
Marya Mikhelovna...................*Barbara Couper*
Baron von Langwagen................*Jeffrey Segal*
Olga Ilynsky............................*Olive Gregg*
Filip.......................................*Ian Sadler*
Agafia Shenitsa.....................*Susan Richards*
Ivan.......................................*John Gabriel*

'THE WOODEN DISH'

★

Clara Dennison has had Pop around the house for years and she is beginning to be sorry for herself. It is time someone else in the family took a hand in looking after him. He may be Glenn's father but he is an old nuisance—why she even has to give him a wooden dish because he breaks all the china

at 9.15

'There are Crimes and Crimes'

WORLD THEATRE PRESENTS

The Shakespeare Memorial Theatre Company

STRATFORD-UPON-AVON

'Richard II'

BY WILLIAM SHAKESPEARE

8.0 and 9.15

CAST IN ORDER OF SPEAKING:

King Richard II...........................Michael Redgrave
John of Gaunt, Duke of Lancaster,
    uncle to the King.............................Hugh Griffith
Henry Bolingbroke, Duke of Hereford,
    son to Gaunt..................................Harry Andrews
Thomas Mowbray, Duke of Norfolk.....William Fox
Duke of Surrey.....................................Jack Gwillim
Duke of Aumerle,
    son to the Duke of York................Basil Hoskins
Herald to Bolingbroke................................Leo Ciceri
Herald to Mowbray..............................Ronald Hines
Friends to the King:
    Sir Henry Green.......................Michael Meacham
    Sir John Bushy..................Richard Wordsworth
    Sir William Bagot.............................Peter Jackson
Edmund Langley, Duke of York,
    uncle to the King.........................Michael Gwynn
Queen to King Richard.................Heather Stannard
Earl of Northumberland.................Alexander Gauge
Lord Ross..Philip Morant
Lord Willoughby.................................Michael Bates
Servant to York...............................Geoffrey Bayldon
Henry Percy, surnamed Hotspur,
    son to Northumberland...................Robert Hardy
Lord Berkeley....................................Brendon Barry
Earl of Salisbury....................................Peter Norris
Bishop of Carlisle....................Duncan Lamont
Sir Stephen Scroop............................Peter Williams
Ladies attending on the Queen........Marjorie Steel,
                    Rachel Roberts, Hazel Penwarden
First gardener...Godfrey Bond
Second gardener..............................Edward Atienza
Duchess of York...............................Joan Macarthur
Sir Pierce of Exton............................William Squire
Servant to Exton................................Peter Halliday
Groom...John Gay
Keeper..Reginald Marsh
Narrator..Robert Hardy

Incidental music by Leslie Bridgewater

Adapted and produced by Peter Watts

from the Memorial Theatre Company production by
ANTHONY QUAYLE

AT 9.15 WORLD THEATRE PRESENTS
Gordon Heath in
'THE EMPEROR JONES'
BY EUGENE O'NEILL

The action of the play takes place on an island as yet not self-determined by White Mariners. The form of native government is, for the time being, an Empire

SCENE 1
Audience Chamber in the Emperor's Palace

Smithers, a Cockney trader............Frank Atkinson
Old native woman..................Nan Marriott-Watson
The Emperor Jones...........................Gordon Heath

SCENE 2
Nightfall: the Forest

Jeff...Errol Hill
Convict..Errol John
Auctioneer...Eddy Reed
Congo Witch-Doctor.............................Ian Catford

SCENE 3
The Edge of the Forest

Lem..Eric Lugg

THE PLAY ADAPTED AND PRODUCED BY R. D. SMITH

SATURDAY-NIGHT THEATRE PRESENTS 'STRIFE,' A DRAMA BY JOHN GALSWORTHY
with Basil Sydney and Laidman Browne as the leaders of Capital and Labour in a conflict in which victory means more than life and compromise is defeat

Henry Wood

PROMENADE CONCERTS

★

Clifford Curzon
PIANO

BBC SYMPHONY ORCHESTRA
(LEADER, PAUL BEARD)

Conductor, Sir Malcolm Sargent

Mozart : Beethoven

Serenade : Eine kleine Nachtmusik (K.525)...*Mozart*
Piano Concerto No. 27, in B flat (K.595)......*Mozart*
Symphony No. 7, in A..........................*Beethoven*

FROM THE ROYAL ALBERT HALL, LONDON

at 7.30

Henry Wood

PROMENADE CONCERTS

Ilse Hollweg   **André Gertler**
SOPRANO   VIOLIN

LONDON PHILHARMONIC ORCHESTRA
(Led by Harold Parfitt)

Conducted by Basil Cameron

PART 1 AT 7.30

Mozart

Symphony No. 35, in D (Haffner)
(K.385)
Recit. and Rondo : Mia speranza adorata
(K.416)
Violin Concerto No. 3, in G
(K.216)
Symphony No. 40, in G minor
(K.550)

PART 2 AT 9.15

Symphony.........................*William Walton*

FROM THE ROYAL ALBERT HALL, LONDON

The
Proms
at 7.30
and 9.10

AT THE ROYAL ALBERT HALL

Henry Wood

PROMENADE CONCERTS

Hallé Orchestra
(Leader, Laurance Turner)

Conductor, Sir John Barbirolli

PART 1 at 7.30

Overture : Ruy Blas...................*Mendelssohn*
Siegfried Idyll........................*Wagner*
Symphony No. 9, in C..................*Schubert*

PART 2 at 9.15

Concerto for oboe and strings......*Geoffrey Bush*

Evelyn Rothwell
OBOE

Bacchus and Ariadne, Suite No. 2.........*Roussel*

FROM THE ROYAL ALBERT HALL, LONDON

RADIO TIMES

EASTER NUMBER

Easter Day speakers include the Bishop of Bristol and Canon
C. E. Raven. The Bishop of Rochester writes on page three

LORD BEVERIDGE
with the 51 Society **(Tuesday)**

DONALD WOLFIT
in 'Henry IV' Part 1 **(Sun. and Fri.)**

MAX BYGRAVES
in his new show **(Tuesday, Light)**

ANDRE KOSTELANETZ
'The Conductor Speaks' **(Mon., TV)**

MORECAMBE & WISE
Running wild in Television
(Wednesday)

EASTER PARADE
*Television Variety from England,
Scotland, and Wales* **(Monday)**

Rugby League Cup Final: Warrington v. Halifax
(Saturday)

Susan Einzig

SUSAN EINZIG WAS BORN OF JEWISH PARENTS ON 16 NOVEMBER 1922 in BERLIN. SHE WAS EDUCATED AT THE GERTRAUDEN LYCEUM BUT WAS FORCED TO LEAVE AT THE AGE OF 15 BY THE INCREASING PERSECUTION BY THE NAZIS. IN 1939 SHE WAS AMONG THE LAST JEWISH CHILDREN TO BE EVACUATED FROM GERMANY AND CAME TO ENGLAND, WHERE SHE WAS TO STAY FOR A YEAR BEFORE GOING TO THE USA. HOWEVER, WAR INTERVENED AND SHE HAS REMAINED HERE EVER SINCE

'When I got to England I managed to get into the Central School of Arts and Crafts in London. In 1940 the whole school was evacuated to Northampton and I spent the next two years studying there. Eventually, with my age group, I was "called-up" but, being an alien, I wasn't given much choice so I opted to go into a factory. I was miserable and lonely but I did manage to keep my own work going.

'I illustrated my first book at that time, "Mary Belinda and the Ten Aunts," a piece of great good fortune as it turned out to be an enormous success. I was working at the factory from six in the morning until eight in the evening, and working at night on the book. I received no fee for the book but I was given a small royalty which, on the first edition, brought me £25. However, the book sold, I think, six editions, all of which went very well, so in the end I made more than £200 which, in 1945, was a small fortune. It also won a gold medal as the best children's book of the year.

'I was invalided out of my war service just three days before the atom bomb was dropped on Hiroshima. I met Robert Harling who gave me my first regular freelance commission (he helped so many young artists this way), and I also managed to get several magazine jobs for *Everetts* and that was the real beginning for me.'

Most young illustrators go through the difficult, and to some, embarrassing business of toting 'folios of work around the circuit of advertising agencies and art directors. Did you do this, Susan, and did you find it difficult?
'Not only did I do it, I'm doing it to this day. Never in my life have I been fortunate enough to have people beating their way to my door. I enjoyed the challenge of going to see editors. The trouble is, once I'd got a job and taken it home I always felt unfitted to do it, and that has remained with me to this day. Every drawing I have done is like a first drawing in which I have to discover how to do it–it's so difficult that I sometimes wonder how I've stuck at it.'

Do you remember bearding the Art Editor of RADIO TIMES *in his den and doing your first drawing for him?*
'No, frankly I don't but RADIO TIMES was one of the easiest clients to work for that I've ever had. I've no memory of ever having a drawing rejected by RADIO TIMES. I think it must have helped that they always put me on the spot, in that I would be given a manuscript on Thursday and, by the Monday, the agony had to be over. I do remember that the first Art Editor I met at RADIO TIMES was Douglas Williams, a very nice, portly, pleasant sort of chap who used to take me out for drinks at lunchtime after I'd delivered my drawings. Incidentally, that must have been in 1948 or 1949, because I remember soon after that Mr Usherwood left and you took over that job.'

You illustrated a great number of plays for us, involving a lot of script reading and probably research, finishing the drawing and getting it to us–and you had only three days in which to do all this. Did you find that a tyranny?
'I think it was wonderful. You see, I'm incurably forced to explore every avenue of possibility in a drawing and consequently I can never make up my mind about the final product. Since I couldn't do that with a RADIO TIMES job, I was really almost grateful for the tyranny.

'When I got a drawing for RADIO TIMES everything else had to stop for the weekend. By that time I had a child who had to be parked with a friend, then I'd lock myself away with the script: reading and re-reading it. Then, on Friday afternoon, I'd start rushing around the libraries looking for reference for period costume and so on. On Saturday I would start working on my roughs and usually by the evening I would be getting hysterically convinced that I couldn't do it. Then, on Sunday, I would grit my teeth and say, "This is it, I've got to do it and get on with it." Quite often on Monday morning when a messenger called for it, or I had to leap into a taxi and deliver it, the ink was still wet. I have even still been working on it in the taxi on the way to your offices in Marylebone High Street!'

Could you tell me a little more, technically, about how you went about producing a drawing?
'There are many artists who draw quickly and directly but, unfortunately, that's not me. I always draw with a pencil or pen and I always work with one drawing pushing it around until it's right. My drawings were always so thick with white paint and alterations and bits of paper cut out, glued over, that they became almost low-relief sculpture. I tried for years and years to cut down the preparatory work because the trouble with me is that I would work away in pencil until, in fact, I'd done the finished drawing, so that the pen drawing was just a matter of going over it in ink which was liable to produce something very dead and dull. So I tried to work as directly as possible with a pen and do the fighting with that, but it was only when the drawing was nearly there that I could really draw freely with a pen.'

Most of the illustrators I've known have been obsessive readers, so that reading play scripts came very naturally to them, is that so with you?
'Reading has been my whole life; I've lived more in books than I have in real life. When I read I've a very literal imagination; in my mind I always set the characters on a stage and imagine them in the context of their surroundings. It's a bit dangerous being so literal-minded –that, too, can produce dull drawings.'

Would you say, remembering the drawings you did for RADIO TIMES, *that we gave you the right sort of subjects to illustrate?*
'I think I actually asked the Art Editor for the sort of subjects that I wanted to draw. Some art editors type cast an artist and force a kind of specialisation that the artist might not want at all. But, in answer to your question, yes, I got the sort of jobs that I really wanted. The sad side of that was that the more I wanted and loved a subject quite often the worse the drawing was. I adored Chekhov and if I looked at the drawing I did for the "The Seagull," a play I loved, it's by no means my favourite drawing.'

Do you remember the drawing you did for a play called 'The Trial of Marie Lafarge'?
'Now that was a drawing which, for some reason, I determined would be a masterpiece. I know that's a pompous word to apply to a small, black and white line drawing. It was made more difficult for me because the name part was played by Yvonne Mitchell, and I very much wanted to get a likeness of her into the drawing.'

Susan, I ask all the illustrators I'm interviewing if they particularly admired, or were influenced by, any of their fellow artists drawing for RADIO TIMES.
'I've always had, and I think have retained to this day, a belief that painters make the best illustrators. The people I adored and admired were people like Anthony Gross, who was primarily a painter and engraver. I think if I saw all his work, and I really do hope that somebody soon will organise a retrospective exhibition of it, I would find that some of the things I would like best would be his illustrations. Leonard Rosoman is another one such. Heather Standring, who drew quite a lot for you at one time, was so gifted but I think, like me, drawing was always hard work for her, though her vision was always big– almost monumental in conception. Of course Ted Ardizzone was a wonderful artist and such a nice man, as was Lynton Lamb. Those are the people I shall always remember with gratitude and affection.'

Did you, in retrospect, enjoy your time as a RADIO TIMES *illustrator?*
'Of course. The wonderful thing about drawing for RADIO TIMES was the immediacy of it. I would hand in my drawing on the Monday and the next week there it was on the bookstalls and in people's homes. It was seen by so many people, too. RADIO TIMES had an enormous circulation in those days. It was altogether one of the perks, one of the joys of my work as an illustrator and, of course, it was a marvellous shop window for any artist's work to be in.'

The Trial of Marie Lafarge–1957
'A drawing I determined would be a masterpiece'

FAY COMPTON IN
'The Tragedy of Nan'
BY JOHN MASEFIELD

Jenny Pargetter..........Betty Linton
Mrs. Pargetter.Nan Marriott-Watson
Mr. Pargetter..........Hugh Manning
Nan Hardwick............Fay Compton
Dick Gurvil.................Brian Wilde
Gaffer Pearce.........Patrick Wymark
Artie Pearce...................Bob Arnold
The Rev. Mr. Drew.Leigh Crutchley
Captain Dixon............John Dearth

OTHER PARTS PLAYED BY
*Bernard Hepton, Peter Wilde
and Emma Young*

PRODUCED BY R. D. SMITH
in the BBC's Birmingham studios

at 9.15

The tragic story of the orphaned girl Nan Hardwick is set in a west-country farmhouse in the year 1810.

WORLD THEATRE
'The Seagull'
BY ANTON CHEKHOV
★
STARRING
**Coral Browne
Stephen Murray**
WITH
**Vanessa Redgrave
and Alan Bates**
AT 8.30

At 8.0 Curtain Up! presents Lilly Kann in
'THE GOLDEN DOOR'
BY SYLVIA REGAN
Adapted for broadcasting by Mollie Greenhalgh

Fanny Felderman...................Elizabeth Goodman
Becky Felderman.....................Lilly Kann
Aaron Greenspan...............................David Hurst
Esther Felderman..........................Miriam Karlin
Harry Engel...............................Leonard Sachs
Hymie Felderman, as a boy........Malcolm Knight
Sadie Felderman...........................Stella Richman
Irving Tashman............................Alan Tilvern
Benjamin Brownstein.....................David Kossoff
Myron Engel................................Arnold Diamond
Hymie Felderman, as a man...........Robert Rietty
Hymie Tashman.......................Malcolm Knight
Pansy...Golda Casimir

PRODUCED BY WILFRID GRANTHAM

'The Aspern Papers'
*Adapted as a play from
the story by*
HENRY JAMES
at 2.30

Coral Browne in
'The Second Mrs. Tanqueray'
BY ARTHUR WING PINERO

Adapted for broadcasting by
Muriel Pratt and Archie Campbell
CAST
Aubrey Tanqueray.....Brewster Mason
Paula............................Coral Browne
Ellean Tanqueray........Hilda Schroder
Cayley Drummle.......Denys Blakelock
Captain Hugh Ardale...John Humphry
Gordon Vayne, M.D.........Philip Morant
Frank Misquith.................Derek Birch
Sir George Orreyed, Bt..Hugh Dickson
Lady Orreyed.................Freda Dowie
Mrs. Cortelyon................Mary Hinton
Morse............................George Hagan
William.....................Nicholas Edmett

PRODUCED BY CEDRIC MESSINA

AT 9.15

One night Aubrey Tanqueray tells his friends that he is going to marry again. It is not going to be a marriage which conforms to the social conventions of the day, for Paula has been known to society for some years and not accepted as a member of it. Will marriage make her acceptable to her husband's friends or will her past be with her for ever?

At 9.15 World Theatre Presents

'THE ALCHEMIST'
by BEN JONSON

Adapted for radio by Frank Hauser
Face, the housekeeper..................Donald Wolfit
Subtle, the alchemist..................Cecil Trouncer
Dol Common, their colleague.........Betty Baskcomb

SATURDAY-NIGHT THEATRE AT 9.15

'Arsenic and Old Lace'

Abby and Martha Brewster are living reminders to the people of Brooklyn of a more spacious and dignified age. They have, however, discovered a cure for loneliness. It is a somewhat eccentric cure and one which is liable to be misunderstood, but it is certainly effective

THIRD PROGRAMME AT 7.55

Cleo Laine and Errol John in
'The Barren One'

The play 'Yerma' by Federico Garcia Lorca transposed to a West Indian setting by Sylvia Wynter

PRODUCED BY R. D SMITH

Irma.........................Cleo Laine
John.........................Errol John
Mary...................Nadia Cattouse
Victor...............Gordon Woolford
Mother Macey........Pearl Nunez
Dolores...........Pauline Henriques
Devil Woman.........Sylvia Wynter
Devil Man..........George Browne
First Girl................Sheila Clarke
Second Girl...........Ethlyn Brown
Old Woman...........Pearl Prescod
Villagers and washerwomen:
Tommy Eytle, James Clark, Aloysius Ganda, A. L. Lloyd, Andrew Salkey, John Harrison, Diana Olsson, Jane Jordan Rogers, and members of the BBC Drama Repertory Company
Traditional West Indian tunes played by Fitzroy Coleman (guitar) and Emmanuel Myers (drums)

'Heart of Darkness'

'A TAINT of imbecile rapacity blows through it all like a whiff from a corpse. . . . And outside the silent wilderness—great and invincible like evil or truth—waiting patiently for the passing away of this fantastic invasion. The word ivory rings in the air, is whispered, sighed. You would think they were praying to it.' JOSEPH CONRAD tells a haunting story of a young seaman who took command of a river vessel for a Tropical Trading Company in Africa at the turn of the century

at 9.15

'A DOG'S LIFE'

Some aspects of life in the canine world
WRITTEN BY GWEN PLUMB
Narrator, Duncan McIntyre
PROGRAMME PRODUCED BY JOHN BRIDGES
at 7.30

PART 1
7.45
WORLD THEATRE PRESENTS JOHN GIELGUD IN
PART 2
9.15

'King Lear'

BY WILLIAM SHAKESPEARE

The Duke of Kent.................................Deryck Guyler
The Earl of Gloucester........................Ernest Thesiger
Edmund, *his bastard son*................Patrick Troughton
Lear, *King of Britain*.............................John Gielgud
His daughters: Goneril..................Catherine Lacey
       Regan...........................Frances Rowe
       Cordelia............................Joan Hart
The Duke of Burgundy.............................Alan Judd
The King of France...........................Godfrey Kenton

Edgar, *son to Gloucester*........................Robert Harris
Oswald, *Goneril's steward*........................John Moffatt
A Knight attending on the King....Stanley van Beers
A Fool...John Carol
The Duke of Albany, *husband to Goneril*
       Brewster Mason
The Duke of Cornwall, *husband to Regan*
       Paul Hardwick
The Chronicler.............................Alan MacNaughtan

with Frank Atkinson, William Hutchinson, Eric Lugg, Hugh Moxey, and Ralph de Rohan
PRODUCED BY PETER WATTS

Radio Times

FULL COLOUR COVERS WERE RESUMED ON OCCASION
BUT, WITH THE ARRIVAL OF COLOUR TELEVISION IN 1967, RADIO
TIMES PROVIDED FULL COLOUR AS A REGULAR INGREDIENT
BOTH ON THE COVER AND INSIDE THE MAGAZINE

Throughout most of Britain's 'swinging sixties' Douglas Graeme Williams, who had been with RADIO TIMES since the 1930s, remained at the magazine's helm. But as the 60s ended RADIO TIMES had a new Editor–the 29-year-old Geoffrey Cannon, who came to BBC Publications with the declared intention of standing RADIO TIMES on its head...

But ahead of the Geoffrey Cannon-inspired RADIO TIMES revolution there came exciting developments on the wider front of the BBC itself. First, 1964 saw the launch of BBC2. Then, in 1967, came the first Television transmissions in colour. Radio, too, saw dramatic changes: in 1967 the long-established pattern of Home, Light and Third was replaced by the format we still have today, Radios 1, 2, 3 and 4.

Douglas Graeme Williams saw to it that these vast developments were mirrored in RADIO TIMES. But in early 1968 he retired through ill health and was replaced as Editor by Campbell Nairne, who stepped up from his role as Deputy and Literary Editor. Nairne was himself close to retirement so his Editorship was for less than two years.

RADIO TIMES began the decade as a 62-page journal costing 5d. By 1969 the average pagination was more than 80 pages and the price 9d. The issue which celebrated the opening of the Mexico Olympic Games in October 1968 contained 104 pages for just eight old pence!

The early 1960s saw RADIO TIMES covers reflecting programmes which are now recognised as truly seminal to the development of BBCtv–the daily magazine, *Tonight*, presented by Cliff Michelmore, *Z Cars*, Simenon's *Maigret*, *Hancock's Half-Hour*–as popular on Television as he had been on Radio–and the soap opera *Compact*.

Mini-skirts, the 'permissive society' and the era of The Beatles were mirrored by the BBC. Sir Hugh Greene, as Director General, presided over a BBC which saw David Frost's TW3 turn satire into a national pastime and allowed nudity on television and four-letter words to be broadcast. Not so in RADIO TIMES. It wasn't until the arrival of Geoffrey Cannon that RADIO TIMES was prepared to try to reflect this new liberalisation of BBC's broadcast material. Until Cannon, RADIO TIMES would give the gravest consideration to even the mention of divorce.

In 1962 the RADIO TIMES logo which was to be used through to the closing months of 1969 was introduced–first with a colour background and from October with coloured lettering on a white background.

The 25th birthday of BBCtv took place in 1961 with a week of special shows and an appropriate cover design by Victor Reinganum. The latter also designed the front cover when the BBC celebrated 40 years of broadcasting in November 1962, as he did again when BBC2 was launched on 20 April 1964.

In October 1960 a 'new look' RADIO TIMES arrived at the bookstalls: the weeks programmes were, for the first time, presented from Saturday to Friday, rather than from Sunday to Saturday. Eric Fraser's Christmas cover of that year *(right)* incorporated the new-style logo to great effect.

Two memorable covers appeared in April and October 1964. Eric Fraser produced yet another masterpiece for Shakespeare's 400th birthday programmes; and in October came the famous cover depicting a soldier in the trenches to herald the BBC2 series on *The Great War*, 50 years after the outbreak and in 26 weekly episodes.

National events were all given full coverage. The massive Outside Broadcast for Sir Winston Churchill's funeral in January 1965 was fully documented and happier occasions included three royal weddings–Princess Margaret in 1960, The Duke of Kent in 1962 and Princess Alexandra in 1963. Indeed, the perennially popular Royal Family had, even by their standards, something of a field day in the 60s. The BBC–and RADIO TIMES–joined in with their usual enthusiastic support. The Prince of Wales was 18 in 1966 and Eric Fraser designed an appropriate cover to accompany *Panorama*'s assessment of the Monarchy at that period. The much-proclaimed film, *Royal Family*, by Richard Cawston was first shown in June 1969 with RADIO TIMES carrying an informal cover picture of the Queen and Prince Charles. This was followed the next week by the Investiture Ceremony of the Prince of Wales at Caernarvon Castle, an event which RADIO TIMES marked with a commemorative issue.

Full colour covers–the first since C. Walter Hodges' Christmas design in 1938–were resumed on an occasional basis from September 1964. But, with the arrival of colour Television in 1967, RADIO TIMES provided full colour as a regular ingredient both on the cover and inside the magazine.

Eric Fraser produced his first full colour cover since 1939 for a BBC production on *The Wars of the Roses* in his tone heraldic style in April 1965, while the 26-part serialisation of Galsworthy's *Forsyte Saga* was featured in January 1967. Eric Fraser's traditional covers at Christmas during the early part of the decade were followed by four covers of a futuristic nature in 64, 65, 67 and 68.

BBC2 opened their colour transmission on 625 lines on 1 July 1967 but it was not until 15 November 1969 that colour was extended on 625 lines to the main BBC1 network. BBC2 coverage was launched at Wimbledon's centre court.

Apart from the emergence of Radios 1, 2, 3 and 4, another important development loomed on the Radio front–the arrival of BBC Local Radio. RADIO TIMES, committed as ever to carry details of every aspect of BBC broadcasting, ended the decade preparing to accommodate a surge in the number of editions printed to an unprecedented 25–the number still being produced today. The editorial staff and printers pondered together about what on earth they could do when the number of BBC Local Radio stations expanded from the first 20 to the then-projected 40!

For the BBC, the 1960s was a decade of experiment and then consolidation. For RADIO TIMES the fireworks were just beginning...

eric fraser

HURRICANE

Henry of Navarre

Tamburlaine The Great

The Big Hewer

DON JUAN

1940

The story of a fateful
year as recalled by
J. B. Priestley
●
SUNDAY: BBC-2

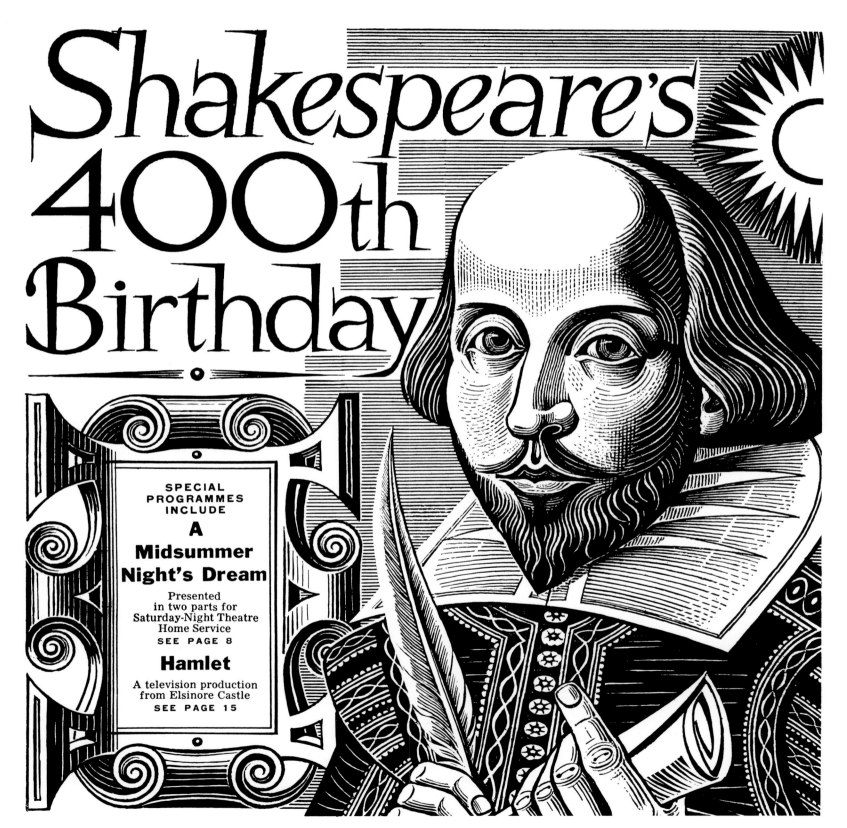

Shakespeare's
400th
Birthday

SPECIAL
PROGRAMMES
INCLUDE

**A
Midsummer
Night's Dream**

Presented
in two parts for
Saturday-Night Theatre
Home Service
SEE PAGE 8

Hamlet

A television production
from Elsinore Castle
SEE PAGE 15

Forty Years of Broadcasting

November the fourteenth is the birthday of the BBC. On that day forty years ago, the British Broadcasting Company began daily transmissions and broadcasting was established as a public service

THE BODY-BLOW

A radio ballad of the battle with polio fought by **Norma Smith, Paul Bates Jean Hagger, Heather Ruffell** and **'Dutchy' Holland** told by them and set to the singing of **Ewan MacColl and Peggy Seeger** with **Bryan Daley** (guitar) **Alfie Kahn** (clarinet) **Alf Edwards** (concertina) **PRODUCED BY CHARLES PARKER AT 9.0**

Marlowe Quatercentenary

Doctor Faustus

''Tis magic, magic, that hath ravish'd me'

•

AT 8.30 TONIGHT

Hedda Gabler

FROM THE FIFTIES : A play by John Whiting

Saint's Day

ERIC FRASER

Christ and Disorder

A Man's House

This play by John Drinkwater is set in Jerusalem at the time of Christ's crucifixion

SATURDAY-NIGHT THEATRE AT 8.30

A MAN'S HOUSE

Hugh Stewart introduces tonight's play by John Drinkwater

SMALL WORLD

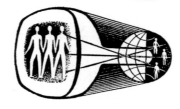

RADIO TIMES

5d

Christmas Number

NATIONAL THEATRE OF THE AIR AT 8.30

Touchstone Mildred Quicksilver Security Gertrude Sir Petronel Flash

Donald Wolfit, Charles Leno, June Tobin, and John Slater in

EASTWARD HO!

By John Marston, George Chapman, and Ben Jonson

Music by Christopher Whelen

Touchstone, a tradesman of Goldsmith's Row, Cheapside..............DONALD WOLFIT

His apprentices:
Quicksilver.....CHARLES LENO
Golding.........HUGH DICKSON

His daughters:
Gertrude...........JUNE TOBIN
Mildred..........FREDA DOWIE

Sir Petronel Flash
HERON CARVIC

Mistress Touchstone
MARJORIE WESTBURY

Security, a usurer
JOHN SLATER

Winnifrid, his wife
NERYS KERFOOT

Sindefy, a punk
JANETTE RICHER

Bramble, a lawyer
CHARLES SIMON

Captain Seagull
MICHAEL TURNER

A Drawer at the Blue Anchor Tavern by Billingsgate
KEITH WILLIAMS

Slitgut, a butcher's apprentice
MICHAEL BATES

Master Wolf, keeper of the prison...LAWRENCE BASKCOMB

Holdfast, a turnkey
TOM WATSON

Other parts played by members of the BBC Drama Repertory Company

A section of the NEW SYMPHONY ORCHESTRA Conducted by the composer

Scene: London and Thameside, 1605

ADAPTED FOR BROADCASTING AND PRODUCED BY RAYMOND RAIKES

The Confederacy

AT 1.30
PERSPECTIVE
ON
handwriting

Experts can tell a lot about a person by the way he writes; and it is this individuality in handwriting which is the subject of this afternoon's edition of 'Perspective.' Among those taking part will be a graphologist and an expert who is often consulted in cases of forgery

TO DIE A KING

Butterfly in the Snow

Education at Home

*This week the BBC launches an important new venture in television—six series designed
by experts for people who wish to build up their knowledge or skill in a chosen subject*

Italian
for Beginners

**EVERY SATURDAY
FROM OCTOBER 5**

AT 12.30

Repeated Thursday 11.10 p.m.

Home Dressmaking

*how to get a
couture finish*

**EVERY SUNDAY
FROM OCTOBER 6**

AT 11.45 a.m.

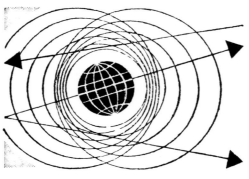

$E=mc^2$

*an introduction
to relativity*

**EVERY SATURDAY
FROM OCTOBER 5**

AT 12.0

Repeated Monday 11.0 p.m.

The Painter
and His World

**EVERY SUNDAY
FROM OCTOBER 6**

AT 12.0

THE STORM
by August Strindberg

Wuthering Heights

KIM: Friend of All the World

What Every Woman Knows

Robert Harris, Hermione Baddeley, and Susannah York
I N
'*The Richest Man in the World*'
B Y
WARNER LAW

Cast in order of appearance:

M. Bordet	GERTAN KLAUBER	Edward Barranca	MICHAEL WARD
Lucien Morelle	DAVID COLE	Dr. Saville	ERIC ELLIOTT
Mme. Bordet	JOAN YOUNG	Paul	WALTER HORSBRUGH
Martine Herrault	SUSANNAH YORK	Barranca	ROBERT HARRIS
Yvonne Dupont	HERMIONE BADDELEY	Miss Haskins	GRACE ALLARDYCE
Philippe Dupont	GEORGE PRAVDA	Mr. Fontanne	RONALD IBBS
Contessa Luisa Barranca Baldocchi			
	BETTY STOCKFIELD		

DESIGNER, REECE PEMBERTON

Produced by George R. Foa

The play is set in the south of France where Martine, a pretty young girl
who twists men round her little finger, is fascinated to hear of a new
neighbour—' the richest man in the world '

══AT 9.0══

The Sacred Flame

ALICE OR THE SERVANT PROBLEM

8.30 SATURDAY-NIGHT THEATRE

Bohemian Scenes

NOVEMBER DAY

In this play, set in Bolton in 1933, Bill Naughton creates the image of a young husband who, after months of unemployment, gets a day's job as a coal-bagger . . .

AT 8.40

IN OUR TIME

The Changing Village

AN ACCOUNT OF SOME OF THE WAYS IN WHICH VILLAGE LIFE HAS CHANGED

AT 9.0

THE COUNTRYSIDE IN JULY

The programme this month includes an account of fruit picking in Kent

AT 1.10

THE ARCHERS

FALSTAFF

Verdi's comic opera from
COVENT GARDEN
AT 7.30

Below Stairs

Servants in the days of our
parents and grand-parents were
often a closely knit community of
proud people. This afternoon's
programme pieces together a
picture of the social structure
below stairs and its place in
relation to the people it served

at 4.0

Scarfe

LAURENCE SCARFE WAS BORN IN BRADFORD IN 1914, WHERE IN THE EARLY 1930s HE BEGAN HIS FORMAL ART EDUCATION. AFTER COMPLETING A GENERAL DRAWING COURSE HE WENT TO THE ROYAL COLLEGE OF ART IN SOUTH KENSINGTON, WHERE HE STAYED FOR FOUR YEARS. AT THE RCA IN THOSE DAYS THE SYSTEM WAS BLISSFULLY UNRESTRAINED-SELF-HELP WAS THE RULE, SUPPLEMENTED BY FORMAL COURSES IN BASIC ARCHITECTURE AND CALLIGRAPHY. AT THE COLLEGE, SCARFE SPECIALISED IN MURAL PAINTING AND HIS EARLIEST JOB WAS ASSISTING EDWARD BAWDEN ON A MURAL PAINTING FOR HIS PARIS EXHIBITION. HE SPENT HIS WAR. YEARS IN CIVIL DEFENCE IN CHELSEA AND IN 1945, HE JOINED THE BOOK PRODUCTION DEPARTMENT OF THE CENTRAL SCHOOL OF ARTS AND CRAFTS

'The interesting thing about teaching at that time was that the students were arriving fresh from war service and were very mature. They were enthusiastic and, although they'd had an interrupted training, their maturity helped to make the place a most lively one as far as the students were concerned.'

In 1947 you did your first drawing for RADIO TIMES, *and frankly I'd have been a little pushed to recognise it as yours.*
'Yes, it's a wonder I was employed to do any others after that, looking at it now. I met the Art Editor Douglas Williams at a party and he asked me to do this job. A few days later I produced this very inhibited, tin-like drawing of a horrid little girl and a horrible looking mother in the wings. I was obviously a bit scared when I drew it and was trying too hard. The next drawing I did was of a great steamroller smashing over a bridge, which was far more interesting.'

There were already a considerable number of distinguished illustrators drawing for RADIO TIMES, *were you pleased at being in that company?*
'Oh yes, to draw for RADIO TIMES was one of the things to do. People watched out for one's drawings and it was something everybody saw all over England. Opportunities for illustration were few in those days, and the link with radio broadcasting made it important.'

In your first year you started drawing fairly regularly for RADIO TIMES...
'I should say about eight or ten a year, which I suppose could be regarded as regular. I was asked to draw a cover for Easter, 1947; it was considered to be a large drawing by RADIO TIMES, even though it was only about five inches wide by four inches. One had to approach a cover drawing in a circumspect manner; as RADIO TIMES went into every household in the country one had to be very careful not to offend. So, artistically, one was a bit inhibited.'

RADIO TIMES *always commissioned drawings on Thursday afternoon or even Friday morning and the finished artwork had to be in the Art Editor's hand by Monday midday. This always seemed pretty tyrannical, how did it strike you at the receiving end?*
'It used to wreck every weekend when it happened. Apart from having to read a script and quite possibly do some research, as, for example, with the Shakespearian illustrations I did-costume research, furniture, background, architecture and so on. All this had to be done, literally, in a matter of hours and then the drawing completed and submitted by Monday morning. It was a surrealistic kind of occupation; dreaming up imaginary pictures and sending them in and, before you knew where you were, they arrived on your own breakfast table a week later almost like a strange thing coming from nowhere.'

We gave you quite a few drawings in those days which demanded a knowledge of Italy. Did you do a fair amount of travelling then?
'Yes, I did. In 1950 I produced a book of my own on Rome, an illustrated travel book, and then in 1952 a much bigger one on Venice, so I began to get numerous Italian-flavoured jobs from all directions. The work I did for RADIO TIMES was a very small proportion of my activities which included mural painting and work for publishers, as well as weekly visits to the Central School...a busy time.'

We asked you quite early on to design the headings and borders for the programme pages with which RADIO TIMES *marks the festivals of the year, they are quite a design problem...*
'I found them the most difficult of the lot. The long strips of ornament and illus-tration were not easy, especially as they have a sort of picture content; it wasn't just decoration. The one I designed for Boxing Day 1952 I enjoyed because I could put funny figures into it, doing absurd things! I was never very happy though, in general, with those jobs. Far and away the easiest part of it was designing the letter forms to go with them.'

In 1953 we asked you to illustrate 'A Midsummer Night's Dream,' to me an utterly enjoyable and captivating drawing, and after that you went on to 'Othello.' What sort of a problem were they were to you?
'Well, I think the Shakespearian drawings were perhaps the things I enjoyed most in drawing for RADIO TIMES. I was less interested in drawing contemporary figures and costumes, I don't know why. But when it came to imaginative subjects like the "Dream," a marvellous subject anyway, I was off into an exciting fantasy world. There was always the problem of reduction; I like to work as big as possible, so I did sometimes turn in pretty hefty originals. I liked to draw with a fountain pen and black ink, bearing in mind, of course, all the time, how it would reproduce when reduced. When I look at my drawings for Shakespeare now I realise how closely they were connected to my interest in wood engraving-they would have made good engravings.'

In view of what you said just now about drawing contemporary scenes, you yet succeeded admirably in doing a drawing for us of Graham Greene's 'Brighton Rock.'
'Yes, I actually came down to Brighton to do it. I sat on the pier and drew the people playing with the punch-ball machine and getting all the details right of the people you would find there.'

May I ask you how, technically, you set about doing a drawing over the weekend for RADIO TIMES?
'Script reading was important because, unless I was moved at a certain point, no images would come. So I had to pick out a passage to illustrate, sort out the characters, decide what they were dressed in and what they looked like and then decide the particular "ambience," the background to set them in. This usually meant looking up references for architecture, furniture, and so the whole thing would come together in a series of rough sketches. Of course, with the Shakespearian drawings, it quite often meant going to the Victoria & Albert Museum or the Chelsea Reference Library.'

I remember from my Art Editorial days on RADIO TIMES *that there were occasions, with even the most distinguished of our illustrators, when for whatever reason, the Art Editor had to say this is wrong or you haven't done what we asked you to do. Did this ever happen to you?*
'Not very often, but on one famous occasion I was hauled up on a drawing a week or two after it had been published-it was for "Dido, Queen of Carthage." I thoroughly enjoyed this drawing; it was great fun, but at the very last moment I got a bit fed up with it. Among the classical architecture at the back I put a television aerial on one of the roofs, very small and with hatching behind it so that it was camouflaged and not easily spotted. After it was published and discovered I was given a ticking off, I think by you, and told this must never happen again. I don't think I was given another drawing for a year.'

If I remember, it weighed fairly heavily when we got about 300 sarcastic letters after publication: Art Editors tend to lose their normal happy sense of humour under that kind of fire...The radio age was a golden period for the illustrator in that you were creating visual images of the sounds people were hearing from their radios-it was a really helpful service that the artist supplied to a mass audience. Do you agree?
'Yes, it was a latterday survival of Victorian popular-book illustration in black and white-pictures sandwiched among programme lists, all of them in black and white.'

Laurence, did you hold in particularly high regard any of your illustrator colleagues who were drawing for RADIO TIMES *in your time?*
'I was pleased to be in good company. We all felt, I think, a sort of corporate growth of contemporary style and feelings. I also met many of them weekly at the Central School, like John Minton and Keith Vaughan; we all got on well.'

Romeo and Juliet–1954
'The Shakespearian drawings were perhaps the things I enjoyed most'

IN THE THIRD PROGRAMME AT 8.0

'Waiting for Godot'

A tragi-comedy by
SAMUEL BECKETT

★

'He should be here'
'He didn't say for sure he'd come'
'And if he doesn't come?'
'We'll come back to-morrow'
'And then the day after tomorrow'
'Possibly'
'And so on'
'The point is ——'
'Until he comes'

(See page 8)

THE SIGN
OF THE FOUR

Caramel for Carlota

BRIGHT SHADOW
by J. B. Priestley

PROFESSIONAL PORTRAIT AT 9.0
ARMY OFFICER

*Paul Daneman
and Leslie Dwyer
with John Westbrook in*
'The Move Up Country'

BY SIMON RAVEN

A Company stationed in East Africa is due to move up country. There are difficulties of many kinds—practical, domestic, and emotional as well as military—for Captain Symonds to sort out before everything is ready for the move.

Capt. Mark Symonds...*Paul Daneman*
C.S.M. Williams..........*Leslie Dwyer*
Serjeant Johns.............*George Hagan*
Corporal Fletcher......*Keith Williams*
Colour Sjt. Burns....*Michael Brennan*
Smithson...................*Gareth Morgan*
Lt.-Colonel Osborne......*Basil Dignam*
Lt. Courtfield...... ...*Charles Hodgson*
Capt. Hargreaves......*John Westbrook*
Major Riding..............*Duncan Carse*
Major Jamieson..........*Charles Simon*
R.S.M. Clarke............*Julian Somers*

PRODUCED BY NESTA PAIN

' SIR. *On the night of June the eighteenth, being orderly Serjeant, I went as was my duty to the Corporals' Canteen. . . .*'

The Scapegoat

THREE SISTERS

THE KING'S GENERAL

A Farewell to Arms

HEDGEHOG

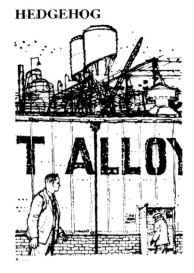

THE MURDERER

'The four of us, boxed in on all sides by Hungarian soldiers, are marched down the railway track.'

'The Razor's Edge'

BY SOMERSET MAUGHAM

The novel from which this play is adapted deals with the fascinating and eternal problem of what are the basic values of life. Yet it is anything but portentous; it is a witty and perceptive account of the author's observation of two young Americans whom he meets in Paris.

at 9.15

(See page 7)

Why is Frances Strannack so nervous and unsettled? Why is Alec so anxious to conceal his address and telephone number? His doctor has some advice to give and so has his lawyer, but Alec is driven by desperation to take drastic measures of his own—at 8.15 this evening

'MARRIAGE SETTLEMENT'

THREE SISTERS

In the boredom of provincial life Moscow seems to each of the three sisters an escape to happiness. Chekhov calls the play neither a tragedy nor a comedy, but 'a drama'

AT 8.10

A KIND OF LOVING

adapted from his novel

by Stan Barstow

'I suppose it really begins with the wedding—the Boxing Day Chris got married—because that was the day I decided to do something about Ingrid Rothwell—besides gawp after her like a lovesick cow or something'

●

AT 8.30 TONIGHT

THE ENTERTAINER

'The music-hall is dying, and with it a significant part of England. Some of the heart of England has gone; something that once belonged to everyone, for this was truly a folk art.' Thus John Osborne tells us why he used the technique of the music-hall in giving a portrait of England in the middle fifties. The fate of one particular family who belonged to the world of music-hall may have more than particular and individual importance for us all

★

at 8.30 tonight

THE THUNDERBOLT
by
Arthur Wing Pinero

The problems that arise when a rich man with an illegitimate daughter and several grasping relations dies leaving a considerable amount of money and no will

SATURDAY-NIGHT THEATRE AT 8.30

A NEW SEASON OF PROMS

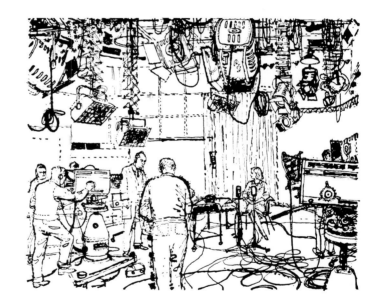

TERMINUS

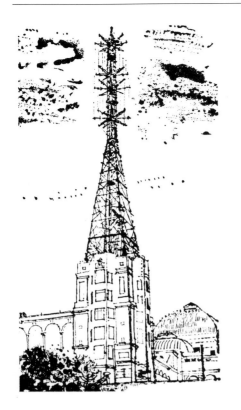

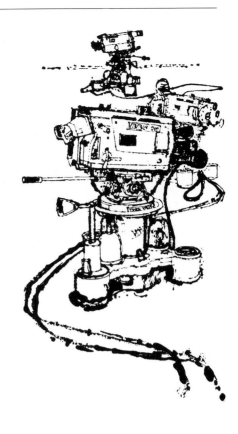

BBC TELEVISION TODAY

VAL BIRO WAS BORN IN BUDAPEST, HUNGARY, IN 1921. HIS FATHER WAS A LAWYER ATTACHED TO THE BRITISH LEGATION. HE WAS BILINGUAL IN HUNGARIAN AND GERMAN AND AT 14 WAS TAUGHT ENGLISH BY AN EXPATRIATE ENGLISH ARMY CAPTAIN. AT THE AGE OF 18, HAVING DECIDED THAT HE WANTED TO TRAIN EITHER AS AN ILLUSTRATOR OR AS A CARTOONIST, HE WAS SENT BY HIS FATHER TO THE CENTRAL SCHOOL OF ARTS AND CRAFTS IN LONDON, WHERE HE ARRIVED IN JULY 1939

'When war broke out I wrote to my father asking whether I should go home, but he wrote back instructing me to stay in England. Luckily my father had deposited enough money with an English firm to provide me with £15-a-month to live on. My father died of natural causes during the war, one day before the Gestapo called to arrest him. My sister and mother survived and were re-united with me in this country after the war. I joined the Commercial Art Department at the Central under a splendid chap, Jesse Collins, who was an inspiring teacher and I also studied life-drawing, lithography, illustration, lettering, photography and a bit of printing. Oh, and I did a bit of fabric design and lino-cutting.'

The Central, as its name implies, was in central London, so things must have got pretty difficult in September 1940, didn't you find that?
'Too difficult: the school and students were evacuated to Northampton and started again in the local technical school there.'

You must have been very aware of the war going on but, at an art school in Northampton, was it a problem?
'Yes it was, very, specially as my fellow students were being called-up. As an "enemy alien" I wasn't able to do anything about it until I left the school and came back to London in 1942. During my last year or so I'd been approaching publishers and Charles Rosna offered me a job at £3-a-week. I lived at Toc H, for 24-shillings-a-week, and the £3 went quite a long way in those days. Then I joined the Auxiliary Fire Service at Sloane Square. Every night I turned up there attending all sorts of 'incidents' and in the morning turned up to work.

'I continued on until the end of the war in the Fire Service and, looking back on it, throughly enjoyed it. By 1945, having been in the Fire Service, I got my naturalisation papers quite easily and when I left the service they presented me with my axe and helmet which I have to this day.'

In 1950 you did your first drawing for RADIO TIMES, *do you remember how that came about?*
'Very clearly. I'd been along several times to RADIO TIMES, always without success, and I'd begun to think that perhaps I just wasn't good enough to join the select band of those who drew for it. But, in 1950 Ralph Usherwood, then the Art Editor, rang me to say that he remembered my work for Odhams where he'd been an art editor, and would I care to draw for him. Of course, I said. He commissioned me to draw a little decorative angel about three-quarters-of-an-inch deep – it was a great ambition fulfilled.'

You were known to us primarily as a designer, a decorator whose work married very happily with the style of typography in the paper in those days. How did you feel about this?
'One of my interests at that time was the kind of decoration that one of my great heroes Rex Whistler used to do. Where that interest broadened out for me with RADIO TIMES was that my drawings were to be reproduced on newsprint: a very different proposition from the fine-line sort of work one did for books. So I developed a new technique using white scraperboard, which I found worked marvellously. It loosened up my work; Usherwood encouraged me to do so.'

Strangely enough, as you were of Hungarian birth, you were very strongly in the great tradition of English steel-engravers or, even more, of wood-engravers like Bewick.
'Well, you see, my art training in Hungary had been too brief to leave any sort of national imprint on me, and all my main training was done over here.'

You designed two what might be called decorative swelled rules for a programme called 'The Blue and the Grey' which were used in the text of the programme, each about one-and-three-quarter-inches wide by about half-an-inch deep, and yet the scale conveyed by them is big and strong. How did you find the pressure of drawing such things over the weekend?
'In my case it was always a stimulus. I work much better under pressure. If I get some work from a publisher with no deadline I tend to relax and say, "Well, I don't need to start on that yet awhile."'

What about getting reference for a job like 'The Blue and the Grey': American Civil War uniforms and impedimenta?
'I always felt that, as an illustrator, the subject matter was of crucial importance and that accuracy of detail was essential. You can't invent accuracy, you have to research it. I've built up a pretty comprehensive reference library of my own, and I've always had a good connection with my local libraries; they're nearly always very helpful.'

You've covered the need for accuracy, for getting it right. Having done that, how did you start work?
'I used to doodle away, doing roughs in proportion to the required size given me. I never worked too big because drastic things can happen to a drawing when it is very much reduced, so I usually drew a quarter- or, at most, a half-up. Having got all the elements together and sorted out the design I then called on whatever ability I had for decorative invention.'

You designed many headings for RADIO TIMES *– they're very different. How frightening was it to have as a commission?*
'Not really frightening, other than that every commission is a bit frightening because when you first see it you can't for the life of you see how you're going to solve it. It was a great help that your briefs were always so clear. It was a joy to get a design of this magnitude right across the top and down the sides of a double-spread of pages. In the case of Christmas Eve, with my Catholic education and background I treated it, of course, as a serious religious festival, so my baroque and rococo designing

was in the great tradition of the German churches which I have always adored, like the marvellous plaster angels, putti and cherubs and so on. That Christmas Eve heading was for television in 1955 and must have been among the first to mark the emerging supremacy of TV over radio.'

You drew quite a number of covers for RADIO TIMES, *like the one for the 1959 Edinburgh Festival. Do you remember designing it?*
'I remember it very well. I'd recently been to Edinburgh on holiday and, whenever I go on holiday, I take my sketch-book with me. The view I used on that cover, looking down from Castle Hill, was already in my sketch-book, so I used it and framed it with a fairly rich but formal decoration symbolising music and drama, plus the coat of arms of Edinburgh.'

In 1960 you did some New Year's Eve headings for us (with the obligatory 'Hogmanay' variation for the Scottish edition) which are very different from the other ones.
'Lettering by then had become very stereotyped with the advent of the self-adhesive Letraset sheets, because there were then only two or three dozen faces to choose from and everybody was using them. So I decided to have a lot of fun with my lettering, mix it up a bit and get away from the mechanical Letraset idea. I hope the jollity of the lettering gave it a New Year's Eve sort of feeling. Again I was going back to a Victorian tradition of decorated capital letters, the sort of thing any Victorian printer's catalogue would contain.'

You illustrated 'The Barber of Baghdad', an opera, and became our opera man for a while, in a very different tradition of straight illustration.
'I was delighted by that because, when I was a boy in Budapest, I had a season ticket for the opera for several years and saw virtually the whole of the repertoire. Opera became very much a part of my cultural background, so when a commission came along for an opera, the likelihood was that I already knew it, that I had a ready-made background. By the end I think I'd illustrated practically every opera broadcast, the whole of the repertoire.'

MARLBOROUGH

**BITTER
WATERS**

**Fury in
Petticoats**

HENRY IV

Dr. Faustus

'The Tragedy of Macbeth'

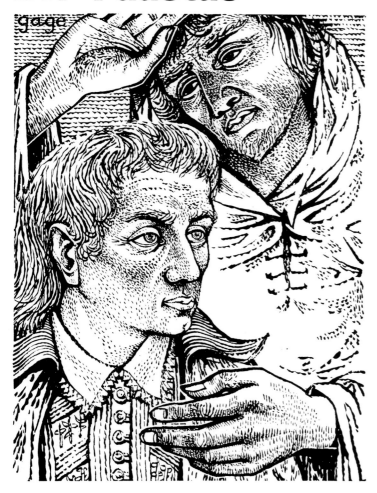

Ibsen's Rosmersholm

'I stared in bewilderment at the slip of paper'

Dr. Latimer thrust the appointments book under the startled woman's nose

The Snake Is Living Yet

Liane Craufurd went to Tangier to get away from a broken marriage—and found herself at the heart of a mystery that was to end in violence and death . . . .

at 8.30 tonight

Ken was soon swinging approvingly . . .

Latimer grabbed him by the lapels. 'What the hell do you know about Laura?'

9.30 AFTER
THE LAST LAMP
by Henry Livings

SATURDAY-NIGHT
THEATRE

Dynamite

Ginger Woods soon finds himself in trouble with Dr. Trump

Children of the Archbishop
*a dramatised version of the novel by Norman Collins
in ten parts*

Part 1, 'The New Warden,' TONIGHT AT 9.0

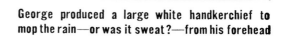

George produced a large white handkerchief to mop the rain—or was it sweat?—from his forehead

The Acknowledgement

TERENCE GREER WAS BORN IN 1929 IN SURBITON SURREY, AND WAS EDUCATED IN PRIVATE SCHOOLS IN KEW AND RICHMOND. HE SPENT A YEAR AT TWICKENHAM SCHOOL OF ART AND THEN WAS CALLED UP INTO THE RAF IN 1947 FOR TWO-AND-A-HALF YEARS

'However, I came out eventually, and went to St Martin's School of Art in London on an ex-serviceman's grant. I found it rather dull and thought that painting was a more worthwhile thing, so I moved to Twickenham School of Art–I was living at home in Twickenham anyway.

'I found the teaching tedious and limited, but I worked away at my painting, and started educating myself. The biggest visual influence on me has always been the cinema; my mother had a passion for it and took me with her from a very young age. Being plunged into the world of James Cagney and the 30s American dreamworld strongly affected the way I saw things.

'I sat for the National Diploma in Design as a painter and failed twice. It began to weigh on me a bit that I was soon going to need to make a living and I didn't feel I had the equipment to make it, so I applied to, and was accepted by, the Royal Academy School. I stayed there for three years and, towards the end, it seemed to me there were two directions open to me. One, to earn my living as a painter, but although I'd improved a lot I felt far too green and I still wasn't sure what kind of a painter I was, I'd been too busy just learning how to paint. Two, I could become a teacher, possibly of illustration, carrying on with my painting at the same time. I'd no thought of becoming a professional illustrator, however.

'Around this time I took some drawings and sketches around to Saxon Artists, an artists' agent, and Cara Strong took me on.

'I think she thought I could be of use in some way, but I had no personal style in my work. I earned just about £200 in 1953–which was hardly getting rich quickly. It picked up a bit after that but I was still doing nondescript work with no style.

'I thought I had to do something about it, so I moved to a cheap flat near Victoria Station and worked like mad at giving myself a personal style of drawing which would allow me to do the sort of thing I wanted to do. After about six months I took the results to my agents and they were very pleased. But, although they liked my style very much and were very enthusiastic about my work, they doubted if I would get any work and for three months I didn't. I nearly gave up, but suddenly work started coming in and within six months I was making more money than most of the other illustrators in the agency.'

Do you remember your first drawing for RADIO TIMES?
'Well, I'd always wanted to draw for RADIO TIMES and I liked the people who drew for it very much. When the chance came I was in fear and trembling because I thought if I blew it they would never want me again. I was given a French play to illustrate. I can't remember the name of it, but I remember I drew a French woman plucking a chicken. It was only about two-and-a-quarter inches square but I took a devil of a time doing it, tearing up drawing after drawing because I was so nervous. The finished drawing was, to say the least, cautious. However, it was accepted which was great, as I felt I was joining a very exclusive club with distinguished members.

'Working for RADIO TIMES, although an honour, was quite a sweat–drawing over the weekend. I always read the script immediately I got it on Friday morning and I used to worry at it like a terrier with a rat. If references were needed I rushed around getting them. I often waited until late Sunday night before staring the finished drawing. You see, if you put down a drawing on paper too early it fixes the idea and it doesn't grow, so I'd wait and wait until everything superfluous fell away, leaving me with only the essentials. I often found that my subconscious had been working on it overnight and I was much clearer about it in the morning. For me, it was a good thing to have a short deadline on a job otherwise I might never have finally committed myself to the finished drawing'.

In your early days you were asked to do action drawings of American epics, Highway-Patrol cars, flashing lights and so on. Do you think that this was a pay off for your early cinema-going habits?
'Undoubtedly, because I'd never been to the States. I was still going to the cinema a great deal and I collected a lot of film magazines, among other things, as reference and I was very attracted to "Americana." I don't know why, I just knew I found it exciting. I almost lived it.'

I remember a small drawing you did for us for 'High Noon' on a television

programme page in which you drew the famous shoot-out.

High Noon–1959
'I had to really get down to essentials'

'One of the things I didn't want to do was to draw a portrait of Gary Cooper because he was to be seen on the screen, and if that was what was wanted you'd probably have used a photograph. So the way I drew it was to convey a feeling rather than anything explicit. It's an example again of paring away everything superfluous, so I just got down to the gunbelt on the hips and the small figure in the distance. It was a very small drawing and I had to really get down to essentials. I remember once doing a drawing of a woman in a hospital bed with a doctor standing by and I condensed that to the woman's head turned towards you, the doctor's hand with a stethoscope, the top part of a nurse and some circles in the air to represent the lights *(below)*. It was a sort of graphic shorthand, taking away absolutely everything except the absolutely necessary.'

May I ask you about your technique? As Art Editors we would only tell you what we wanted a drawing for, not how you should draw it.
'I always used a pen, never a brush. For a drawing to be reproduced at the size of "High Noon" I used to draw three times larger than actual size; I'm not happy drawing small so I always drew as large as possible. I always found it difficult to control things in pen-and-ink because, when you put pen to paper, you are committed, so I used to draw

first in pencil and then place blotting paper to one side of it. When I started drawing in ink, I'd press the blotting paper to it and get an image in reverse on the blotter. This meant I could control the drawing; if I drew a foot and it looked good I could transfer it to the blotting paper. This gave me a more sympathetic line because, for me, a pen on paper was always very harsh. So my drawings always finished up in reverse.

'There was also a sort of conventional thing amongst illustrators that you should never draw a figure with a gesture which suggested that it was about to move. I didn't agree with that at all. I always drew people just about to move and got away with it. I used to get into trouble over my use of broad areas of solid black tones in my drawings because technically they weren't too easy to print, it was thought that they would "ink-up" or that they would fade into grey, but RADIO TIMES always did excellently with line reproduction.'

Terry, we were talking earlier of your pleasure in joining the company of RADIO TIMES *illustrators. Which of them gave you the most pleasure, or for whom did you have the greatest respect?*
'Well, I certainly had a great deal of respect for the work of Eric Fraser and in the same way for Reinganum, but they didn't influence or help me because I was off on another tack. I was very impressed by people like Johnnie Minton and Susan Einzig, but I tried to drive a wedge between their work and mine. I wanted my own style and I think this got more extreme as I got older; no way was I going to become just a second-rate Minton, no point in that.'

We're talking of something like 12 or so years ago. You've gone on, of course, since then and your career has changed.
'I got to a point where, having done several thousand drawings, there was no way I could push my work further; I would have to move, so I've tried my hand at writing plays.'

'YEOMAN'S HOSPITAL'

It is not a big hospital but for the senior staff it has been a life's work and the newcomers must be worthy of its traditions

Adapted for radio by Jonquil Antony from the novel by HELEN ASHTON

7.30
WELLS FARGO

Philip Marlowe
Private Eye

PUGWASH AHOY!

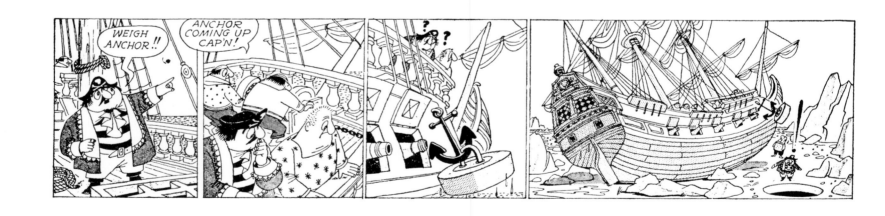

RadioTimes

THE ELEMENT OF SURPRISE, EXPECTANCY AND VARYING
PATTERNS GAVE EACH ISSUE ITS OWN SPECIAL IDENTITY. NEW
ARTISTS AND DESIGNERS WERE COMMISSIONED TO AUGMENT
THE WORK OF LONG-ESTABLISHED EXPERTS...

Geoffrey Cannon, who was to edit RADIO TIMES throughout the 70s, came to the magazine convinced that it was in need of radical change. The circulation was a little under four million when he arrived and he boldly declared that if getting RADIO TIMES right meant losing some circulation, then so be it. It lost about a quarter-of-a-million. Later in his editorship the magazine was again to reach a circulation of about four million but, when he resigned to join *The Sunday Times* in 1979, he left behind a RADIO TIMES that was selling about 150,000 copies a week less than the one he inherited.

In his early months he undoubtedly shocked some readers into giving up RADIO TIMES – he offended many with an illustration of Jesus Christ on the cover and others with a photograph of Jimmy Savile sticking his tongue out. But other factors were at work during his editorship to cost journals their circulations – not least, economic ones. In January 1970 RADIO TIMES was nine old pence a copy; ten years later, after a decade of soaring production and paper costs, it was 15 new pence – that's an increase of more than 300 per cent – and still rising sharply.

Few would deny that the magazine Geoffrey Cannon took over was in need of change. In the 60s it had, at times, begun to give an impression of being less than certain about how to deal with the rapid and extensive changes affecting Britain in general and broadcasting in particular. Cannon arrived, backed by a young and talented staff – notably Art Editor David Driver and Features Editor Peter Gillman – and the changes he made were the most far-reaching ever to be introduced in RADIO TIMES. Wholesale alterations were made to content, design and typography. Artwork, however, was still central to the magazine's main thrust and here there was much experimentation in style, colour and drawn work. The element of surprise, expectancy and varying patterns gave each issue its own special identity. New artists and designers were commissioned to augment the work of many long-established experts such as Eric Fraser and Robin Jacques. Of the new illustrators perhaps the work of Peter Brookes achieved the widest acclaim. Whether it was a Christmas cover (1976), a new approach to the Spring theme, a Russian or Chinese Week (*right*), the Fireside cat on its chair (1976), the Proms illustration (1978) or *The Americans* (1978), his drawings were always meticulous, thought-provoking and memorable.

Cannon's RADIO TIMES unveiled a new logo with the R and T much larger than the rest of the words; this was changed to a bolder, but still fundamentally the same, style in 1972. From 1972 until the end of 1976 the logo remained boldly in a white box at the top of the page. In January 1977 the logo was incorporated within the cover illustration.

The 70s saw the dawn of ecological awareness. More and more BBC programmes – particularly the respected *Horizon* and *The World About Us*, both on BBC2 – returned to the theme of a world squandering its resources. Peter Brookes caught this with his devastatingly effective cover which showed the world being wrung dry by a pair of giant hands.

As the 70s unwound, superb photographic work was achieved by a host of truly creative photographers, including Tony Evans, Dmitri Kasterine and John Timbers. Covers and articles rang the changes.

Performers adorned the Christmas covers – artists like Morcambe and Wise, the two Ronnies and Michael Crawford – but in 1975 David Driver revived the earlier tradition of regarding the cover as 'the RADIO TIMES Christmas card to its readers'. In that year Owen Wood evoked a beautiful Victorian Christmas and Pauline Ellison produced artistry of a very high quality for Christmas 1977.

The 70s saw the establishment of another innovation – the Christmas and New Year double number, two weeks' programme details in one issue. Jubilee Year in 1977 involved covers and features on every aspect of Royalty. Supremely, Candace Bahouth's tapestry cover introducing the Souvenir Issue was a work of genius.

During the mid 70s previews of programmes by invited writers were included as were reviews by well-known critics and broadcasters. More space was allocated to a wide range of readers' letters, with their accompanying cartoons. These pages grew in stature as a respected forum for a genuine exchange of views between readers and the programme makers. Variations on the earlier 'Both Sides of the Microphone' feature appeared under various headings such as 'Radio Times People'. A weekly film preview, contributed by writers like Philip Jenkinson, Bryan Forbes and Sheridan Morley, became an established favourite with readers. The major sports events – in particular, the 72 and 76 Olympics and the 70, 74 and 78 World Cups – were all covered in special, highly-detailed, lavishly-illustrated issues.

Meanwhile, BBC*tv* and Radio consolidated the pattern established at the end of the 60s as a clearer form of viewing and listening habits emerged. The English regions became centres for network productions with, for example, Bristol consolidating its role as the BBC's main source of major wildlife programmes – notably David Attenborough's *Life on Earth*. The three national regions – Wales, Scotland and Northern Ireland – increased their autonomy and, with the massive wavelength changes in November 1978, were able to extend their own Radio services.

At the end of the 1970s, as RADIO TIMES entered its seventh decade, it was still Britain's largest and most successful weekly magazine. It began the 80s with a new Editor, Brian Gearing, and facing a decade as full of challenge as any of the previous six. Broadcasting is expanding into cable and satellite to give the viewer and listener an ever-wider and even a world-wide choice. RADIO TIMES will need to change, to develop, to grow in order properly to reflect that choice. What is certain is that the full range of illustration will retain its essential role as RADIO TIMES guides its readers through the adventure of broadcasting.

Peter Brookes

PETER BROOKES WAS BORN IN LIVERPOOL IN 1943. HIS FATHER WAS A CAREER RAF MAN WHICH LED TO PETER BEING EDUCATED IN PIECEMEAL FASHION ALL OVER THE UK. AT THE AGE OF 19, FOLLOWING IN HIS FATHER'S FOOTSTEPS, HE JOINED THE RAF AND STARTED A THREE-YEAR PILOT'S COURSE AT CRANWELL, FROM WHICH HE WAS 'EJECTED' IN HIS FINAL YEAR. DURING THAT TIME HE TOOK AN EXTRA-MURAL DEGREE

'The year after getting my degree I went to Manchester College of Art on a pre-diploma course. After a year, in 1966, I came down to the Central School of Arts and Crafts in London and joined the Graphic Design Department. I very much wanted to come down to London, I had the idea then all of life happened there. I was living on next to nothing, like the other students, but there was even a certain amount of glamour in that. My main course was in graphic design, I did very little pure drawing with illustration as an end in view. Looking back on it now I have some regrets, you were encouraged to think – but you didn't learn to draw, draw as an end in itself. As an illustrator I feel that was a bit sad.'

Three years sounds a long while in the abstract but if flashes by when you're a student. Towards the end were you getting anxious about earning a living?
Yes, I was anxious, I'm always anxious anyway. But at the Central the policy was to encourage students to take on the odd freelance thing, so I did a few design jobs and bits and pieces for *New Society*, which I followed up as soon as I left with my diploma. I spent a year working for Brian Boyle, a visiting lecturer at the Central, who ran a small design studio doing things like designing paperbacks. Over the years my drawing has changed, my approach has changed but my thinking is very much as it was formed during that year. I'd always thought that I'd like to illustrate in RADIO TIMES so I went to see Sue Maxwell who was then Assistant Art Editor and she gave me my first job. I was very flattered to have got it and I remember it very well. I was asked to do it at the end of the week and I was in a huge panic because it had to be delivered by the Monday morning and I was very green.'

How did you go about it, Peter?
'I picked up the script from the office, nothing much was discussed, I was told it was all there in the script. I read the script very thoroughly and then sorted it in my mind to get the right idea for it; it's always very much a case with me that I have to get the point I'm going to make crystal clear in my mind. But then, of course, you have to put it down on paper, so I do lots of scribbles in a little book which I carry around with me. By

the time I get around to the finished thing I've got a pretty detailed rough drawing. I always leave myself as little time for drawing as possible to give me more time for the thinking.

'Sometimes the finished drawing actually suffers because I've left myself insufficient time. I think this is caused by my earlier lack of grounding in drawing. I've always had to worry about my style; I've been happy enough about the individuality of my ideas, but I'd always thought that the way I put them on to paper could have been done by anybody. Of course, lacking a marked personal style does help me with my drawings because I deliberately use pastiche, wood engravings and various techniques as a basis of ideas, so it doesn't worry me now that I haven't got an imprint which says "Peter Brookes" from a distance of 100 yards. To sum it up, I've always drawn in a laboured sort of way, I find it very hard work; the ideas not so, but when the two things do come together it gives me an enormous fillip.'

To get back to RADIO TIMES, before long you were asked to draw a cover. It was to illustrate a radio programme about the National Health Service and I remember thinking at the time that what you produced was a fairly tough representation of the subject.
'I got a call from the Art Editor, David Driver, who asked me to come in to discuss the problems involved and to brief me on the subject. This particular one was an oddity in that I had very little time to do it in, which was a bit

frightening. The subject was closely related to drawings I'd been doing for *New Society* so I didn't balk at being fairly hard-hitting in this instance. It didn't even worry me all that much that it was a cover for RADIO TIMES, which is something special again. When I talked with David the writer of the feature was there, so, as always with David, I was given all the information I needed: it's the great thing about RADIO TIMES always. This examination of the NHS on radio went throughout the week, so I did illustrations for the programme pages as well, some of which were even more gruesome.'

A year later, in 1975, you designed a totally different cover, a sort of Hokusai-based drawing to mark the 30th anniversary of the bombing of Hiroshima.
'Yes, I used Japanese calligraphy as well. As I recall, it read "Remember Hiroshima." I felt it a bit of a cop-out when I'd done it, it was a very hard subject. I couldn't really say anything about the pain and the agony, so I used the idea of the Hokusai wave symbolically – I really wanted to say something stronger but I couldn't.'

In 1977 you drew another cover under the headline 'Spring to life,' in the week the clocks went forward. You drew a sheep unravelling its own wool and knitting baby clothes because the secondary purpose of that cover was to project a programme about birth.
'Well, it was handed to me on a plate really. This being for the Spring and the

fact that it had to bring in the idea of birth was very helpful – it gave me a theme to work on.'

To mention just one more cover, you designed a 'Prom' cover for us under the heading 'Summer music.' A very clever idea again of a bouquet of woodwind instruments nestling in the bell mouth of a tuba. Are you a keen listener to music?
'Yes I am intensely interested in music and the "Proms" is an absolute gift, but that interest doesn't save me if the idea I come up with is pedestrian or slightly vulgar. That cover I had clearly in mind as an idea but it just didn't come. What I wanted to do was much more the Dutch flower painting sort of thing, something much more luxuriant. I thought that, in using the clarinets in the way I did, that would get it because clarinets are black and beautifully intricate things, marvellous to draw, and that on the cover they would stand out from a distance of, say, ten yards. Well, the clarinets do that all right, but as flowers they are slightly indelicate, so that the end product was a pretty-much vulgarised version of what I had in my mind.'

To come to your 'Brookes on…' drawings, Peter, you at times lean very heavily on visual puns…
'This is exactly what I'm heavily interested in. The drawings I'm doing in that series are examples of the way I really think. I love puns and I love things like *The Guardian* headlines – the more outrageous the better. Visual puns have always intrigued me and amused me, a lot of what I do for the "Brookes on…" drawings relates to coming up with a good headline idea. The idea, basically, is that once a week I'm asked to comment on an aspect of broadcasting. At my Friday afternoon meeting with Brian Thomas, the new Art Editor, Rodger Woddis and Features Editor David Driver, we decide on a subject for that and forthcoming weeks.'

May I ask you the same question that I've asked all the artists I've interviewed? Who among the illustrators of RADIO TIMES do you particularly admire or respect?
'I've always loved and admired the work of Robin Jacques and Eric Fraser. They go a long way back, but you can't think of RADIO TIMES as a formative influence without thinking of those two. But I think it was the overall artistic wealth of RADIO TIMES that was so impressive; pick up any issue and it is full of drawings. I remember when I left the Air Force getting a little book out of the library called "Drawing for Radio Times" by R. D. Usherwood and loving it. So I'd say that rather than specific illustrators it was this wealth of drawings which influenced me so much, and if I wanted to be part of anything I wanted to be part of that company. I'm glad it came about.'

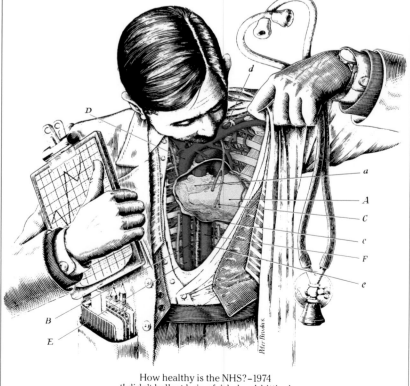

How healthy is the NHS? – 1974
'I didn't balk at being fairly hard-hitting'

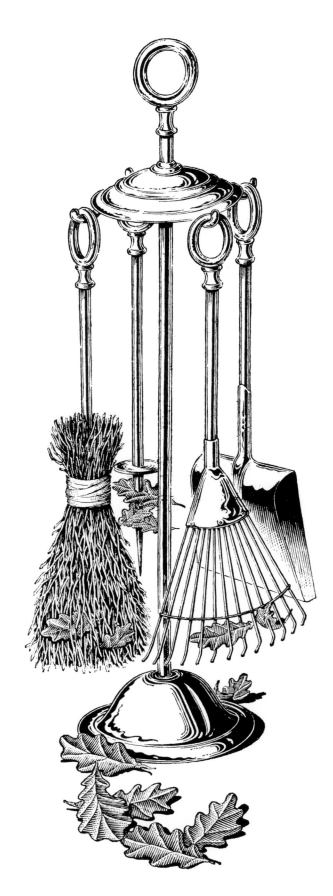

Time eat

Washoe is a chimpanzee who talks — in sign language. She uses it to question, and comment on her world to her scientist companions — not least to tell them when it is time to eat. Horizon: 9.25 pm

Muhammad Ali: 'I think about Joe Frazier all the time'

Do you think that extra vitamins will give you a boost?
Or that old people don't need more? Don't believe everything you hear about vitamins... You and Yours: 12.2 pm

Industrial espionage and counter-espionage: 6.15 pm

'For men must work and women must weep.' The words are those of
Charles Kingsley – who died almost a century ago. Must men still
work? Should women still be weeping? Your Witness, tonight: 9.25

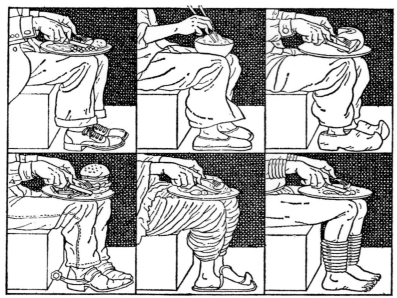

The World in a Box – tonight Festival 40 departs from the nostalgia of the past in a programme which looks at television worldwide: 8.15

D. H. Lawrence's The Daughter-in-Law: 8.30 pm

The Eventful Deaths of Mr Fruin: 8.30. Another play by Don Haworth on Friday, Radio 3

'. . . October's a good month to do a certain amount of pro-pagation . . .'

'. . . fallen leaves must be swept up to add to compost . . .'

'. . . in the kitchen garden this is the moment to harvest your late veg. Onions can be stored in old stockings . . .'

'. . . it's a time for planting, par-ticularly if you have bulbs which flower in early spring . . .'

Your relationship with your doctor is crucial to successful treatment. But does your doctor know what you want – or behave like a stranger? It's Your Line: 7.30 pm

Can we afford the luxury of a hand-reared carrot?: 8.0

Doting mums may be surprised to learn that a day-old baby can perceive clearly enough to have preferences – especially what it looks at. Child development: 11.30 am

Panorama joins the millions on the Mediterranean: 8.0

Mrs Jordan: 'Cooped in behind that wire grille all day – it must be almost like being . . . well – like being *in a cage!*' In The Cage, *tonight's Monday Play: 8.0 pm*

'These trouble the mind and make men mad.' – Robert Burton, *on garlic and onions. Frank Muir explores the dry humour behind* The Anatomy of Melancholy: *10.15 tonight*

. . . *Twice Round the Gasworks: 7.40 pm*

When The Red Cockerel Crows *tonight, certain things come to light . . . like a raging conflagration: 7.30 pm*

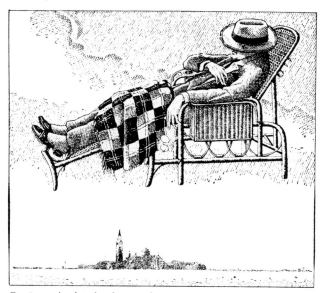

Gustave Aschenbach was the poet-spokesman of all those who labour at the edge of exhaustion: of the over-burdened. Paul Scofield reads Death in Venice: *9.10 pm*

'I know precisely what I'm doing . . . It is simply research work – in a slightly unusual form.' More than a natural interest in crime in The Amazing Dr Clitterhouse: *8.30 pm*

The Barrier – an Invention by Christopher Holme: 9.10

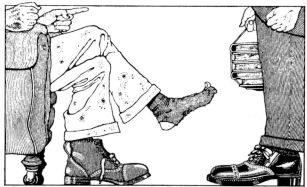

A Collier's Friday Night by D. H. Lawrence: 8.30 pm

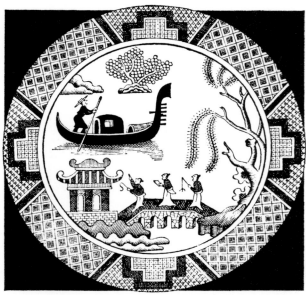

'I arrived in Cathay. I opened my eyes. I speak of that.'
And Marco Polo opened the eyes of medieval Europe
with tales of his Travels in the Far World: 8.30 pm

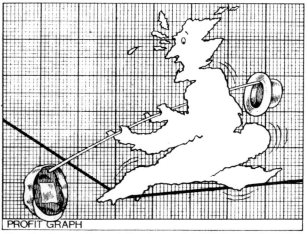

Profit – the smile and the frown on the faces of capital-
ism. How desirable is profit for our society – and the
social divisiveness associated with it? Analysis: 8.45 pm

'These cliffs are basaltic, and therefore plutonic. An
area, as large as perhaps Sussex, has been lifted en
bloc, with all its living contents.' The Lost World: 9.3

Welcome Abroad . . . to what? Make sure of a good holiday: 8.30

Save or spend? The 'traditional' and 'new' members of the middle classes face the same problems, but are not always able to arrive at the same answers. Tonight The Money Programme *investigates: 8.15*

There's rebellion and anarchy in your local primary school . . . and according to some it's behind the doors of the staff room. Horizon *looks at the controversy between teaching methods old and new: 9.50 pm*

Nader raiding: 8.10

Animal Farm begins in Story Time: 4.30 pm

The applecart upsetter

'Eustacia . . . that lonesome dark-eyed creature up there that some say is a witch. Call a fine young woman such a name . . .' The Return of the Native: 9.3 pm

Alice's Adventures in Wonderland *begin when she follows the White Rabbit. Carroll's classic – with music: 7.20 pm*

The man who killed time. The Thirteen Clocks: *3.5 pm*

'Monty sighed sentimentally. "Well, well, well," he said. "The old lad doesn't seem to have changed much since . . . Good Lord!" P. G. Wodehouse's Heavy Weather: 4.35 pm

The young Minister of Woodilee was ready to wrestle with the Devil – but he hardly expected to find his Kirk elders worshipping Satan in the Witch Wood: 8.30

The Fixed Smile

What ho! P. G. Wodehouse and The Book Programme tonight: 7.45

A respectable town in pre-war Scotland – that's Baikie. Until the local paper reveals the shocking scandal of the Provost and a wee dog. Storm in a Teacup: 8.30 pm

'Silas has most of the rank, being a man of immense Will. Will he called by his magical name: Jonas. Two men in one white head, one black woman . . .': 9.50 pm

The
power
of the
atom

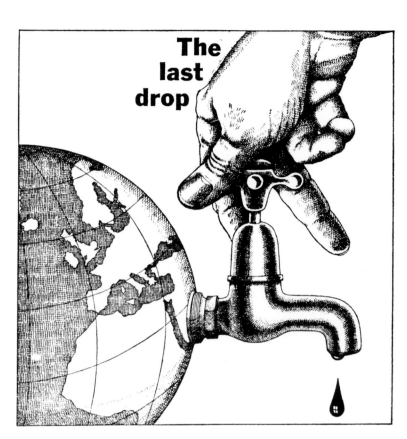

The
last
drop

Here
comes the sun

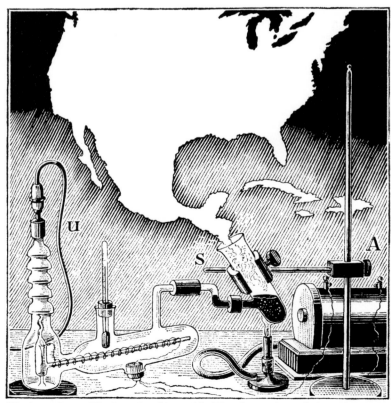

It's ingenious, it's breath-taking, it's The Inventing of America: 7.30

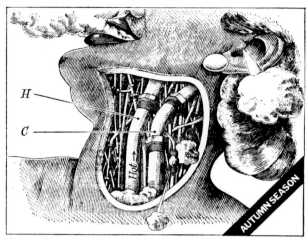

Hot flushes, sweats, tension: all symptoms experienced by 25 per cent of middle-aged women. But even substantial menopausal disturbances can be treated: 1.45 pm

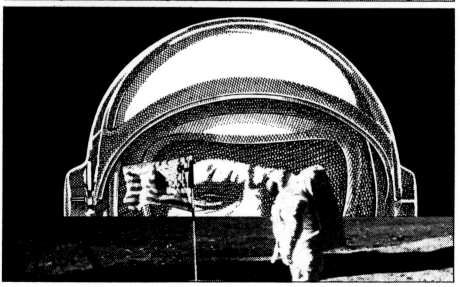

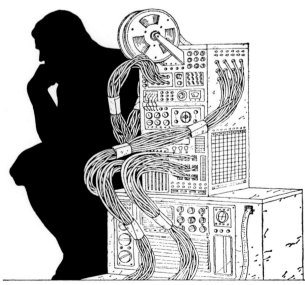

Is imaginative thinking the exclusive property of humans, or could the next generation of computers develop this faculty and become truly Machines that Think? 9.15 pm

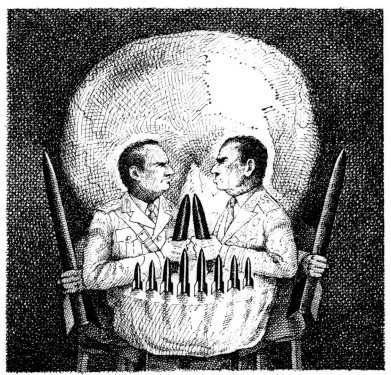

(*Panorama – The Next Deterrent, Monday 8.10 BBC1*)

Kissinger appears on 'Parkinson', Wednesday 11.2 BBC1

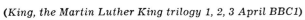
(*King, the Martin Luther King trilogy 1, 2, 3 April BBC1*)

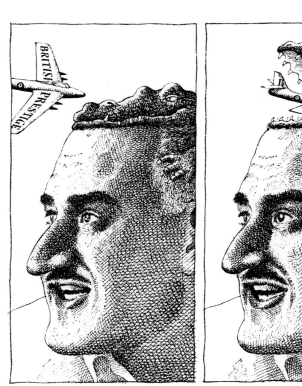

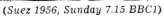
(*Suez 1956, Sunday 7.15 BBC1*)

(Today Live from Peking, Friday 6.30 am Radio 4UK)

(Horizon – A Mediterranean Prospect, 9 April BBC2)

Circuit Eleven Miami, 25, 26 and 27 October BBC2

(Women at Arms, Friday 9.25 BBC2)

FORGERY ~ totally worthless

GENUINE ~ totally worthless

(In the Post, Monday 7.45 BBC2)

(Island of the Dodo, Tuesday 20 February BBC1)

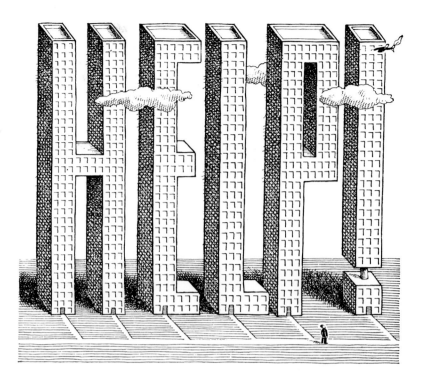

(The Devolution Debate, 9.35 Wednesday 28 February BBC2)

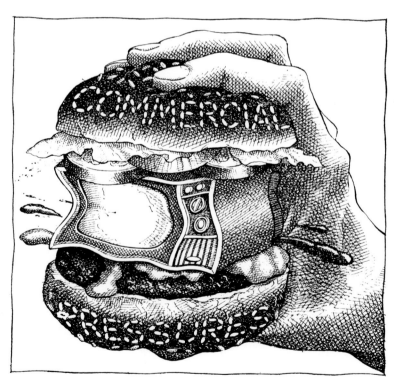

(Television World – The Ratings Business, Friday 8.10 BBC2)

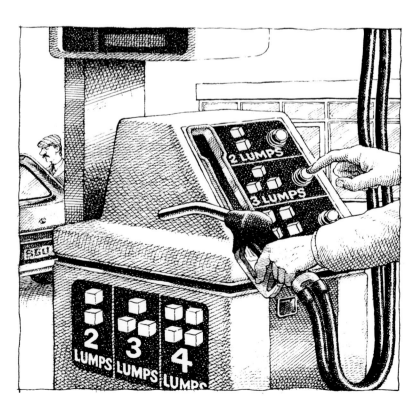

Australia v England, The First Test, BBC1, BBC2, Radio 2 and Radio 3

*(A Fistful of Dynamite, Thursday 9.20 BBC2,
first of a season of Spaghetti Westerns)*

An arresting Constable

An arresting Constable

(*Inside Story – Tom Keating: Portrait of a Master Faker, Monday BBC2*)

(*BBCtv's look at advertising – The Persuaders, Thursdays 8.30 BBC1*)

(*Antiques Roadshow, 5.20 BBC1 (not Wales), last in the present series*)

(*The final episode of Tinker, Tailor, Soldier, Spy, Monday 9.0 BBC2*)

SOME CARTOON DOGS..

..WORK UNSOCIAL HOURS..

..WITH NO INCENTIVE..

..AND FOR **PEANUTS**

(*Crufts, Sunday 3.50 BBC1*)

(Royal Ascot, from Tuesday BBC1, BBC2 and Radio 2)

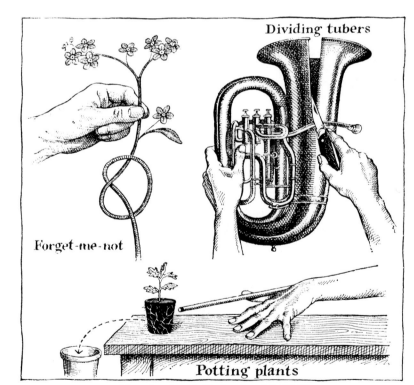

Dividing tubers

Forget-me-not

Potting plants

(Growing for Gold, Sunday 8.5 BBC2;
Chelsea Flower Show, Wednesday 9.45 BBC2)

The problem Down Under...

...is you keep falling off

(*Panorama – What Kind of Society?, Thursday 8 February BBC1*)

(*Mastermind, Wednesday 8.0 BBC1*)

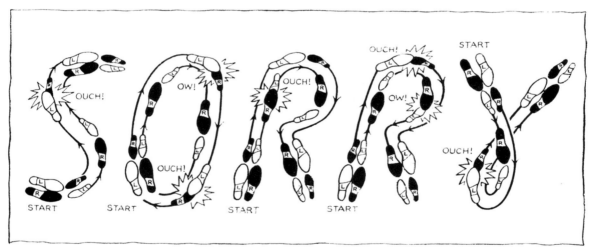

(*Come Dancing, Wednesday 10.10 BBC1*)

(*The Editors, Sunday 10.55 BBC1*)

＊Q. Can you supply the missing invective?

Fellini's Roma, Friday 11.20 BBC2

(*The Archers, weekdays 1.40, 7.5; Omnibus edition now Sunday 10.15 am Radio 4UK*)

(*An 80th Birthday Tribute to Hitchcock: The Thirty-nine Steps, Sunday 1.55 BBC1;
To Catch a Thief, Sunday 8.5 BBC1; Psycho, Sunday 11.0 BBC2*)

Nigel Holmes (signature)

NIGEL HOLMES WAS BORN IN 1942 IN YORKSHIRE AND EDUCATED AT A PREP SCHOOL IN THE SOUTH OF ENGLAND AND THEN CHARTERHOUSE WHERE HE EDITED THE UNDERGROUND SCHOOL MAGAZINE *THE GREYFRIAR*. HE LEFT AT 18 WITH TEN O-LEVELS AND TWO A-LEVELS IN MODERN LANGUAGES, SPANISH AND FRENCH. ON LEAVING CHARTERHOUSE, HE TRIED FOR THE ROYAL COLLEGE OF ART BUT WAS ADVISED TO GET SOME TRAINING IN A PROVINCIAL ART SCHOOL. SO HE WENT TO HULL ART SCHOOL, NEAR HIS HOME, WHERE HE GOT THE INTERMEDIATE EXAM BUT NEVER SAT FOR THE NATIONAL DIPLOMA OF DESIGN BECAUSE HE LEFT EARLY AFTER ONLY TWO YEARS

'I came down to London in 1962 for another interview at the Royal College of Art and this time I got in with no trouble at all. The value of being at the Royal College of Art was that I actually was in London.

'In the February of my last year I won a scholarship to go to the United States and I'm afraid, with that under my belt, I rather let the college down because I went for more and more freelance work. I did two huge jobs for Brian Haynes and Clive Irving of *Woman's Mirror*. One was a design showing the whole of the Buckingham Palace staff, all drawn–it included the facade of the palace as well as the people. The other was of Wimbledon showing the whole of the set-up during the tournament. I did all this work, of course, at weekends; I was still studying at the College. Anyway, I went to the States in August 1966 and stayed there until November. I bought a 99 dollar ticket on the Greyhound bus which gave me 99 days' travel all over the USA. When I came back to this country, I moved to a small flat in Gloucester Road and started out to be a freelance–I knew it was a gamble but I didn't need much to live on. However, Brian Haynes gave me some jobs for *The Observer* where he now worked, this was in conjunction with David Driver.

'Clive Irving had left *Woman's Mirror* and was setting up a small organisation attached to the Cornmarket Press, so in 1967 I was invited to become a part of that as a freelance with David. We worked really ridiculous hours through the nights. It was there that I first met Geoffrey Cannon.

'I decided to strike out for myself again when I started getting some drawings for *New Society*. It was a letterpress magazine and I was doing a lot of drawings, at least one a week for about a year, and I found that I very much liked working to a weekly deadline. By this time, October 1969, Geoffrey Cannon had become Editor of RADIO TIMES and David Driver his Art Editor, and they got in touch with me again to draw for RADIO TIMES. The RADIO TIMES deadlines suited me very

well; as a freelance I'd never had a nine-to-five job and it never seemed odd to me to work at any time of the day or at the weekend.'

Drawing for RADIO TIMES *involves a very close, almost intimate working relationship, was it a help that you knew David Driver well and had worked with him?*
'Undeniably that is so. David knew exactly how I worked and vice-versa, so we could immediately get on a wavelength without any preliminaries, which was a tremendous help. He allowed me right from the start to be involved with the copy: most of the work I've done for RADIO TIMES has been explanatory, involving usually quite a bit of copy. I worked hand in glove with the programme makers and David, but eventually he trusted me enough to let me work just with the programme people. I watched a lot of previews of programmes which was primarily useful in helping me avoid duplicating anything in the programme; to make my drawing complementary to, rather than merely illustrative of, the programme.'

I remember particularly a series you did for the 1972 Munich Olympic Games. How much research did you have to do for that? I know that you're not particularly interested in sport, so did you find it a difficult proposition?
'It was an absolutely fantastic job–I really loved it. There was one illustration for each day on each

programme page for two weeks and I worked with Ron Pickering, the athletics expert, who was a splendid chap to work with. I would say to him for example, "How much is the heavyweight lifter lifting, can you give me a visual equivalent?" He would say, "Well, he's lifting the equivalent of a racehorse plus a jockey, whereas ten years before he'd have been lifting a child's pony." He was clever at that sort of visual analogy and, as well, he knew everything about athletics and if he didn't, he certainly knew how to find out.'

Nigel, you did a great number of feature-article drawings for us in colour and you had the very difficult job of creating a design which would begin on a left-hand letterpress page in black and white and continue across to the next page in colour on gravure paper, was that a difficult problem?
'The main problem as far as I was concerned was that, because of the difference in the press dates (the colour went to press weeks before the black and white), I'd race around to get the colour done and then tend to forget about the black and white even though it was, in effect, one drawing, so that I had to re-educate myself back into the feeling of the bit that had gone to press five weeks ago. I remember particularly a series I did in collaboration with Peter Brookes called "Behind the Scenes." We did, I think, six of those which we conceived and wrote ourselves and

which won several awards, particularly the Gold Award of Design and Art Directors' Association. Perhaps the best of them was for the Apollo/Soyuz space mission for which we did a cover, a feature and the programme page illustrations.

'We actually interviewed the American astronauts by telephone link from my house. There are phones in every room, so Jane Wellesley, our RADIO TIMES researcher, did most of the talking while one of us listened in and took notes. On a third phone we recorded it, while on a fourth phone we put the questions we wanted to ask to Jane. From our joint interview we had enough to do the cover, symbol and programme page illustrations.'

What was the working process in designing that Apollo/Soyuz cover?
'We wanted to use the symbol of a link–the link between the Americans and the Russians, hands across space, a joining of East and West, so I scribbled lots of roughs to the right size and showed them to David Driver. I wanted to show the earth from space with linking orbital lines coming from behind it and meeting in space. It was David's suggestion that we should maximise on the hardware and bend it around a bit. So that is what I did. I had about three weeks to work on it but, of course, there were the article and programme page drawings to be done as well with Peter. I used a set of templates of elliptical curves and, when I did the tracings for the cover, I noted the numbers of each part of the curves so that when I came to draw it there was nothing to be worked out except the finished artwork itself. It's a sort of painting by numbers system really. I used the actual colours of the space vehicles with a bit of added reflection.'

You designed a great number of the small symbols used in RADIO TIMES *to identify continuing series of programmes. I always thought those postage-stamp-sized designs were quite a problem for a designer.*
'Yes, I did four series of sports symbols–probably about 200 of them in all–and I loved doing them, finding new ways of symbolising golf, tennis or soccer. I knew that, every week, I would get a rush order to design a symbol for some sport or another, so in 1977 I designed a basic shape of a symbol which I knew would work for all sports as a framework in conjunction with a matchstick figure. I said to Brian Thomas that I would get a list of the sporting events of the year and design symbols for the lot in one go, and then forget about them. So we did that and I designed the symbols and delivered them all in January, they are the symbols which are still being used to this day.'

Continuing programme symbols–1970s
'Probably about 200 of them in all'

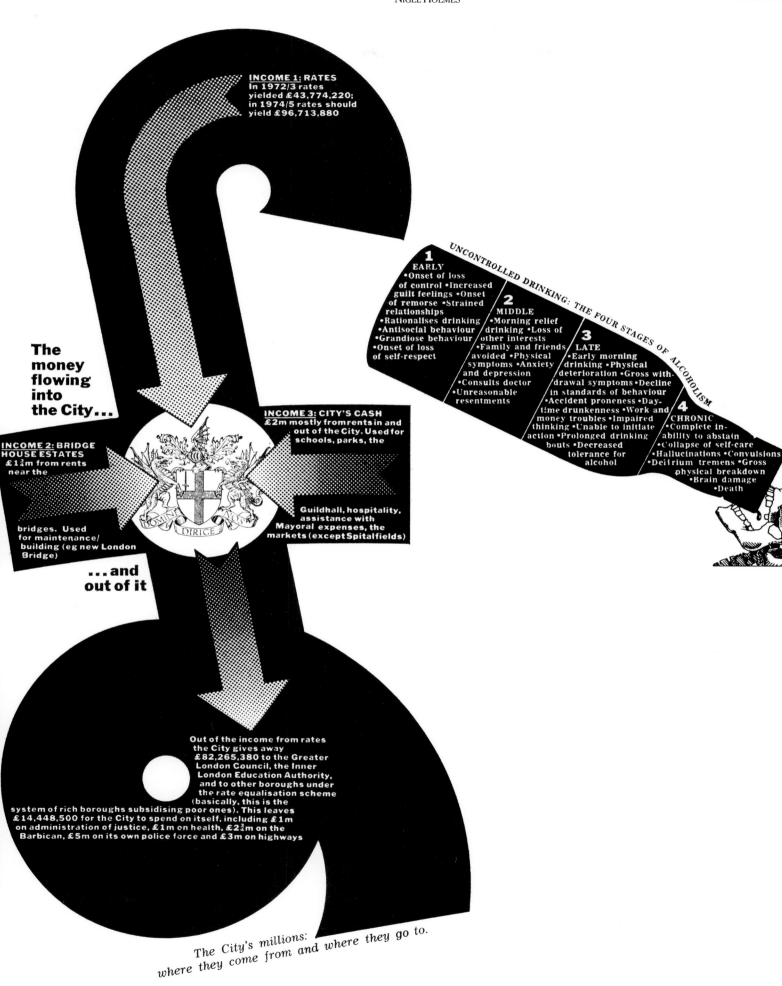

Wimbledon

BILL THRELFALL says: 'Bjorn Borg, idolised by the crowd especially the younger girls, remains unmoved, polite and always in a good temper. In the final of the 1973 World Championships, on a covered court, he was not far off beating Newcombe and on a hard court he was the winner at this year's Italian and French Championships. What will he do on grass at Wimbledon? At only just 18, he must win some day. Like Connors, Nastase, and Rosewall he goes for everything, covering the court with a great deal of action…

… in direct contrast to tall players like Smith, Newcombe or Drysdale whose long reach enables them to cover the court with less apparent effort. Stan Smith's fantastic serve is so powerful that most returns are defensive, giving him the chance to push away winning volleys. Like Borg he has a good temperament, but sometimes seems too nice a guy to keep on winning, and has had a disappointing season so far '

Borg runs for everything, appearing suddenly in all parts of the court

Smith's long reach seems to bring the whole of the court into play

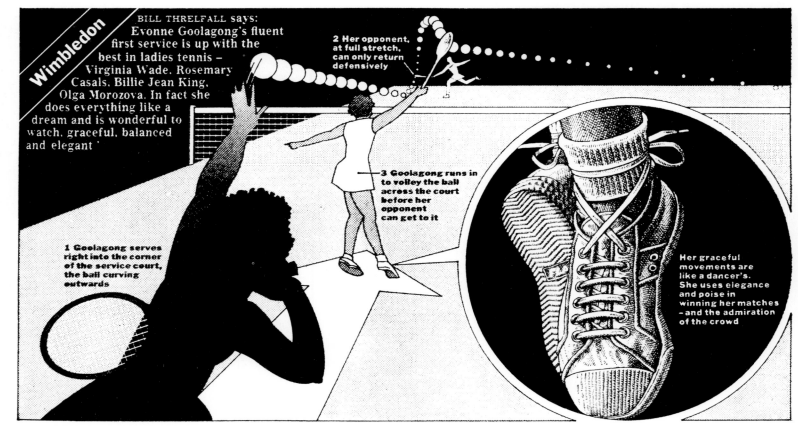

Wimbledon

BILL THRELFALL says: Evonne Goolagong's fluent first service is up with the best in ladies tennis – Virginia Wade. Rosemary Casals, Billie Jean King, Olga Morozova. In fact she does everything like a dream and is wonderful to watch, graceful, balanced and elegant '

2 Her opponent, at full stretch, can only return defensively

3 Goolagong runs in to volley the ball across the court before her opponent can get to it

1 Goolagong serves right into the corner of the service court, the ball curving outwards

Her graceful movements are like a dancer's. She uses elegance and poise in winning her matches – and the admiration of the crowd

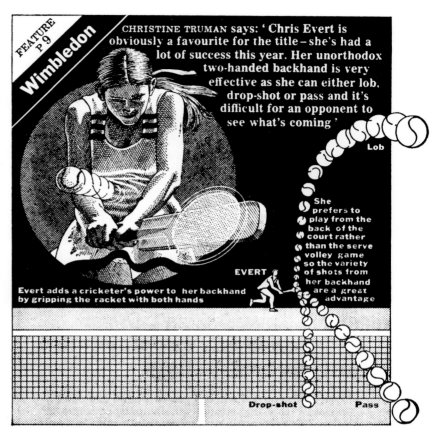

FEATURE P 9

Wimbledon

CHRISTINE TRUMAN says: 'Chris Evert is obviously a favourite for the title – she's had a lot of success this year. Her unorthodox two-handed backhand is very effective as she can either lob, drop-shot or pass and it's difficult for an opponent to see what's coming'

Lob

She prefers to play from the back of the court rather than the serve volley game so the variety of shots from her backhand are a great advantage

EVERT

Evert adds a cricketer's power to her backhand by gripping the racket with both hands

Drop-shot   Pass

Wimbledon

CHRISTINE TRUMAN says: 'John Newcombe's powerful all-round game is as good as ever and he is keen to come back to Wimbledon and win for the fourth time. He has no weaknesses or eccentricities and there couldn't be a less gimmicky player – in fact it is his machine-like consistency that must make him a favourite again this year for the men's title'

The consistent all-rounder

High proportion of first serves go in

Powerful forehand

Accurate backhand

Good volley

Wimbledon

BILL THRELFALL says: 'What went wrong for Nastase on that year? All his year? All his on the Centre or was on No 2, away eye. His concentration heard the cheers from courts. He was beaten

first Saturday last matches had been No 1 Court. Now he from the public slipped as he the main not only by a better man on the day, but by himself and his temperament – the star away from the centre of the stage'

Centre Court

No 1 Court

No 2 Court : a good shot from Alex Mayer beats an inattentive Nastase

World Cup

JACK ROLLIN says:
'The apparent casual elegance of Franz Beckenbauer who is equally at home breaking up attacks or initiating them masks a sharp footballing brain which often reads the game several moves ahead of opponents and colleagues alike. He can move in to cover an opponent in possession, whip the ball away from his feet at the precise moment and then switch quickly to the offensive. Then he is the calming influence when all around is frenzied movement, audaciously considering his next move'

1 BECKENBAUER intercepts at the split second when his opponent loses even the slightest control

Attacker pushes ball slightly too far ahead

2 BECKENBAUER

3 Beckenbauer sends a long, sweeping pass out to the wing, or makes ground himself into attack

BECKENBAUER

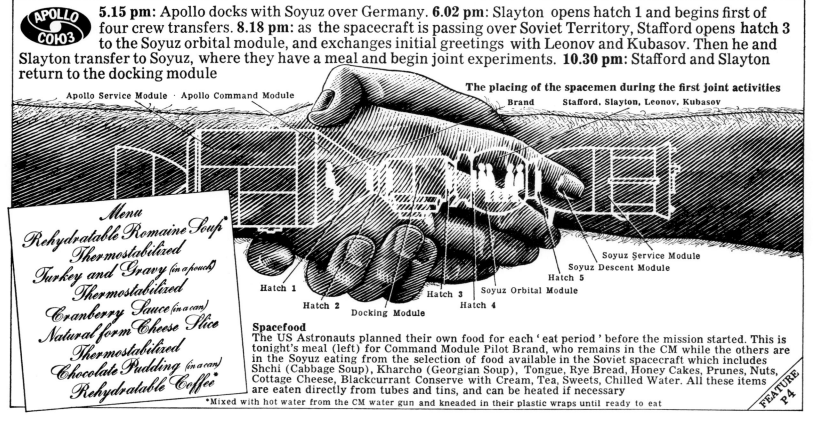

5.15 pm: Apollo docks with Soyuz over Germany. **6.02 pm:** Slayton opens hatch 1 and begins first of four crew transfers. **8.18 pm:** as the spacecraft is passing over Soviet Territory, Stafford opens hatch 3 to the Soyuz orbital module, and exchanges initial greetings with Leonov and Kubasov. Then he and Slayton transfer to Soyuz, where they have a meal and begin joint experiments. **10.30 pm:** Stafford and Slayton return to the docking module

Apollo Service Module · Apollo Command Module

The placing of the spacemen during the first joint activities

Brand   Stafford, Slayton, Leonov, Kubasov

Soyuz Service Module

Soyuz Descent Module

Hatch 5

Soyuz Orbital Module

Hatch 4

Hatch 3

Docking Module

Hatch 2

Hatch 1

Menu
*Rehydratable Romaine Soup**
Thermostabilized
Turkey and Gravy (in a pouch)
Thermostabilized
Cranberry Sauce (in a can)
Natural form Cheese Slice
Thermostabilized
Chocolate Pudding (in a can)
*Rehydratable Coffee**

Spacefood
The US Astronauts planned their own food for each 'eat period' before the mission started. This is tonight's meal (left) for Command Module Pilot Brand, who remains in the CM while the others are in the Soyuz eating from the selection of food available in the Soviet spacecraft which includes Shchi (Cabbage Soup), Kharcho (Georgian Soup), Tongue, Rye Bread, Honey Cakes, Prunes, Nuts, Cottage Cheese, Blackcurrant Conserve with Cream, Tea, Sweets, Chilled Water. All these items are eaten directly from tubes and tins, and can be heated if necessary

*Mixed with hot water from the CM water gun and kneaded in their plastic wraps until ready to eat

FEATURE P4

1st Test England v India

JIM LAKER says: 'A host of slow left-arm bowlers can bowl a length and line, and spin from leg to off, but Bedi's greatness stems from his ability to combine these simpler facets with the difficult and subtler arts of flight and pace variations'

Bedi varies the flight and therefore the pace of the ball by releasing it at slightly different times

Problem for the batsman: how quickly can he spot the pace variations?

1 o'clock
12 o'clock
11 o'clock
?

British Open Golf

PETER ALLISS says: 'Bob Charles, the elegant New Zealand left-hander, is regarded by his fellow professionals as the world's finest putter. More than one golf pro has been quoted as saying: "If my life depended on someone sinking a putt, I'd get Bob Charles to play the shot." And Charles has a fine record at Lytham. He won when the Open was held there in 1963 and was runner-up when Tony Jacklin took the Championship at Lytham in 1969'

Charles 'thinking' the putt
Intense concentration enables him to read the line that the putt must take

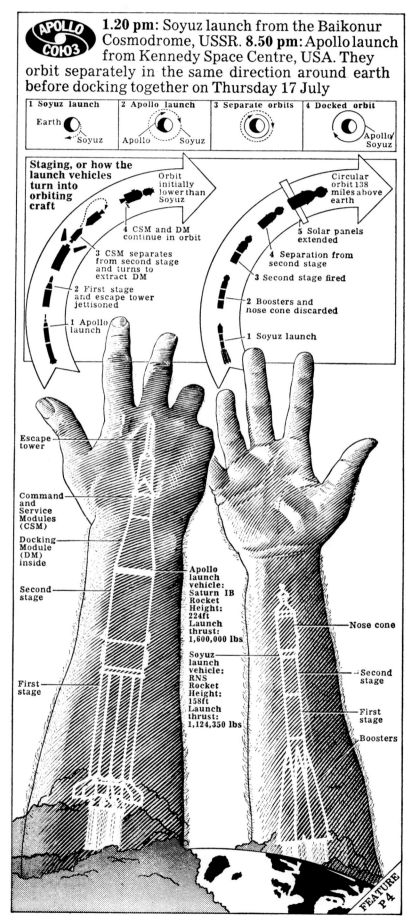

APOLLO COIO3

1.20 pm: Soyuz launch from the Baikonur Cosmodrome, USSR. **8.50 pm**: Apollo launch from Kennedy Space Centre, USA. They orbit separately in the same direction around earth before docking together on Thursday 17 July

1 Soyuz launch	2 Apollo launch	3 Separate orbits	4 Docked orbit
Earth / Soyuz	Apollo / Soyuz		Apollo / Soyuz

Staging, or how the launch vehicles turn into orbiting craft

Orbit initially lower than Soyuz

4 CSM and DM continue in orbit

3 CSM separates from second stage and turns to extract DM

2 First stage and escape tower jettisoned

1 Apollo launch

Circular orbit 138 miles above earth

5 Solar panels extended

4 Separation from second stage

3 Second stage fired

2 Boosters and nose cone discarded

1 Soyuz launch

Escape tower

Command and Service Modules (CSM)

Docking Module (DM) inside

Second stage

First stage

Apollo launch vehicle: Saturn IB Rocket Height: 224ft Launch thrust: 1,600,000 lbs

Soyuz launch vehicle: RNS Rocket Height: 158ft Launch thrust: 1,124,350 lbs

Nose cone

Second stage

First stage

Boosters

FEATURE P4

-- 215 --

World Cup

JACK ROLLIN says: 'Sir Alf Ramsey once said that Gerd Muller was the most dangerous striker in the world. Certainly his record of more than 300 goals in the last nine seasons at club and international level underlines his ability. With short muscular legs and a low centre of gravity, he has the knack of staying on his feet at all times'

A difficult player to mark, Muller keeps on the move always, taking up intelligent positions and anticipating where a goal chance will come

World Cup 74; Australia v W. Germany live at 3.55, highlights at 6.55 and 10.30. Today's other big match, Scotland v Brazil, live at 7.20

World Cup

JACK ROLLIN says: 'The world's most expensive footballer Johan Cruyff cost £922,300 when he was transferred from Ajax to Barcelona last year. Here he demonstrates just why he is valued so highly as a striker, using his ability to pick up the ball from a deep-lying position, and with a bewildering acceleration and change of pace gives the impression that he is going through opponents rather than round them, because of his remarkable control'

CRUYFF   CRUYFF

Cruyff lays off a pass . . . runs into position for the return . . . and whips in a shot at goal

World Cup Match of the Day, Uruguay v Holland live at 3.50; action highlights from the four big clashes in Groups 3 and 4 today: 10.25

World Cup

JOHN MOTSON says: 'Where there is a chance of scoring from a free kick, watch for the classic "banana" shot, created by the South Americans, and of which Rivelino is the master'

JAIRZINHO

JAIRZINHO

Jairzinho ducks out of wall at the last moment

RIVELINO →

To achieve the necessary velocity, Rivelino starts on a long run to the right of the ball, moving in an arc to swerve it left-footed round or through the defensive wall and beat the goalkeeper with pace, direction and spin

Banana bends round the wall...

...or passes through space left by Jairzinho

Left foot strikes outer edge of ball to spin it

World Cup 1974 from 2.30 pm. The Opening Ceremony at 3.0 and the first match Brazil v Yugoslavia live at 4.50. Highlights at 10.15

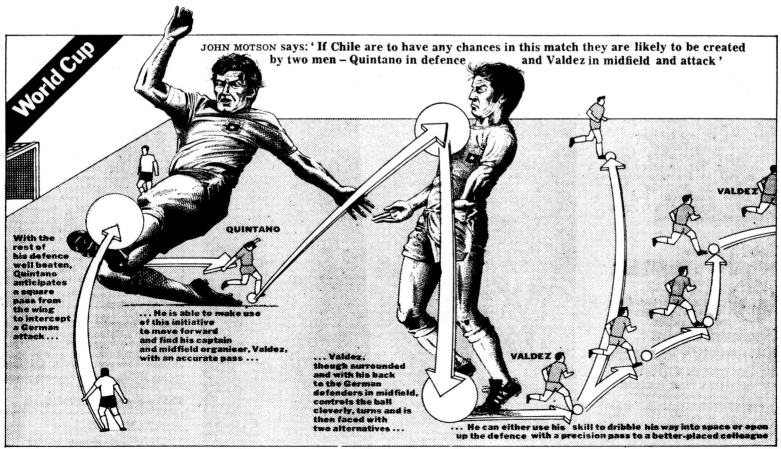

World Cup

JOHN MOTSON says: 'If Chile are to have any chances in this match they are likely to be created by two men – Quintano in defence and Valdez in midfield and attack'

With the rest of his defence well beaten, Quintano anticipates a square pass from the wing to intercept a German attack...

QUINTANO

...He is able to make use of this initiative to move forward and find his captain and midfield organiser, Valdez, with an accurate pass...

...Valdez, though surrounded and with his back to the German defenders in midfield, controls the ball cleverly, turns and is then faced with two alternatives...

VALDEZ

VALDEZ

...He can either use his skill to dribble his way into space or open up the defence with a precision pass to a better-placed colleague

World Cup 1974. The West Germany v Chile match live at 3.50. Also Scotland's first match live at 7.20. Highlights of both from 10.45

World Cup

JACK ROLLIN says: ' Once given a free transfer by modest Swansea, Giorgio Chinaglia has been rediscovered as Italy's most talked about centre forward for years. Oddly enough he is a typical broad-shouldered English style forward of the old school who cuts out the frills and goes straight and accurately for goal '

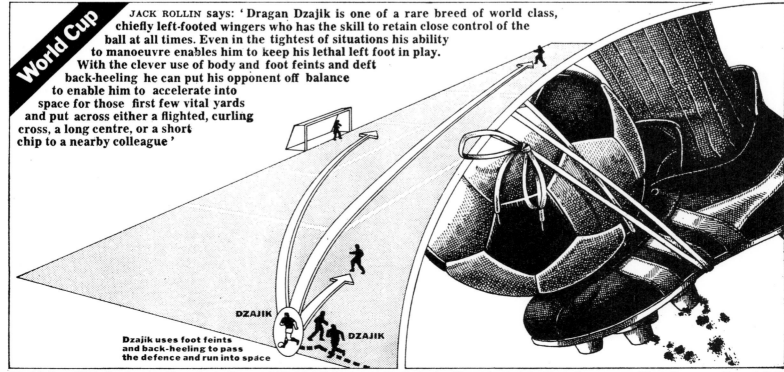

World Cup

JACK ROLLIN says: ' Dragan Dzajik is one of a rare breed of world class, chiefly left-footed wingers who has the skill to retain close control of the ball at all times. Even in the tightest of situations his ability to manoeuvre enables him to keep his lethal left foot in play. With the clever use of body and foot feints and deft back-heeling he can put his opponent off balance to enable him to accelerate into space for those first few vital yards and put across either a flighted, curling cross, a long centre, or a short chip to a nearby colleague '

DZAJIK

DZAJIK

Dzajik uses foot feints and back-heeling to pass the defence and run into space

World Cup 1974; Scotland v Yugoslavia live at 3.50, highlights at 11.50. Today's other big match, East Germany v West Germany live at 7.15

GO The oldest game in the world

The object of this 4,000-year-old game is to enclose as many free intersections on the field as possible, either by 'railing-off' space with chains of stones, or by surrounding and capturing an opponent's stones. The players continue (alternately) until the gaps in their chains and the vacant intersections separating their two chains are filled. The intersections *within* the players' chains are then counted. The player who has the most enclosed intersections is the winner

Capturing an opponent's stones is done by occupying all intersections adjacent to those stones, thus surrounding them.

The correct way to hold the stone is to grasp it lightly between the middle and index finger of the right hand

The board is usually 17½in x 16in x 8in deep. It has 19 vertical lines and 19 horizontal lines forming 361 intersections. The 180 white and 181 black stones are placed on the intersections, *not* in the spaces. Once placed they can't be removed, except when captured.

The stones are shaped like a convex lens

How to see Van Morrison with two eyes and hear him with both ears.

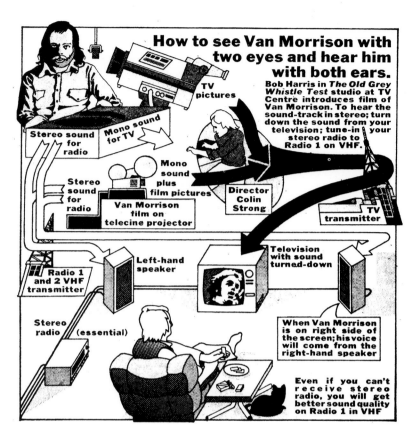

Bob Harris in *The Old Grey Whistle Test* studio at TV Centre introduces film of Van Morrison. To hear the sound-track in stereo; turn down the sound from your television; tune-in your stereo radio to Radio 1 on VHF.

TV pictures

Stereo sound for radio

Mono sound for TV

Stereo sound for radio

Mono sound plus film pictures

Van Morrison film on telecine projector

Director Colin Strong

TV transmitter

Radio 1 and 2 VHF transmitter

Left-hand speaker

Television with sound turned-down

Stereo radio (essential)

When Van Morrison is on right side of the screen; his voice will come from the right-hand speaker

Even if you can't receive stereo radio, you will get better sound quality on Radio 1 in VHF

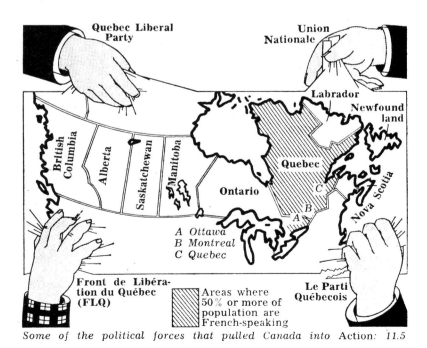

Quebec Liberal Party

Union Nationale

Labrador

Newfoundland

British Columbia

Alberta

Saskatchewan

Manitoba

Quebec

Ontario

Nova Scotia

A Ottawa
B Montreal
C Quebec

Front de Libération du Québec (FLQ)

Le Parti Québecois

Areas where 50% or more of population are French-speaking

Some of the political forces that pulled Canada into Action: 11.5

The Hawker Siddeley Hawk

is specifically designed for high reliability, long fatigue life and easy ground servicing and provides an aircraft tailored for the dual roles of training and ground attack

With 'command-ejection' in operation the instructor can operate **both** ejector seats

For its basic/advanced training role the Hawk has good handling characteristics (slow approach and landing speeds, plus high air speed)

Length 11.96m

Rolls-Royce 172-06 Adour turbo fan giving speed of 600 mph.

Fuselage tank 818 litres
Wing tank 795 litres

Wingspan 9.4m

Tandem-seat configuration (rear seat raised) provides excellent vision for both crew members

In its ground attack role, the Hawk is capable of carrying a 5,000 lb weapon load. There are 18 combinations of weapons available, such as nine 230 litre fire bombs or two missiles

Farnborough International 1974

The Hawker Siddeley Hawk has been selected by the RAF to replace the Gnat, the Hunter, and ultimately the Jet Provost. In addition to its use for instruction, the Hawk will be used by the RAF for weapon training. The first of the 175 aircraft being produced under a Ministry of Defence contract will enter service at the end of 1976. See the Hawk and more aviation know-how this afternoon: 2.0

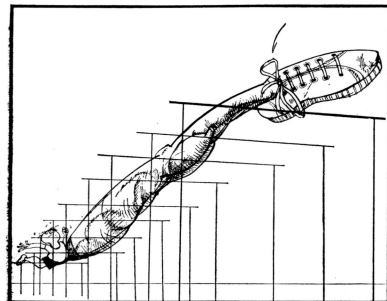

Aussie
with his
cricket
equipment
Ralph STEADman 17.3.17.

Zolder Grand Prix of Belgium. Formula 1 Glory Machine   Ralph STEADman 4.5.18

Formula 1 Guns
look things over

Ralph STEADman 18

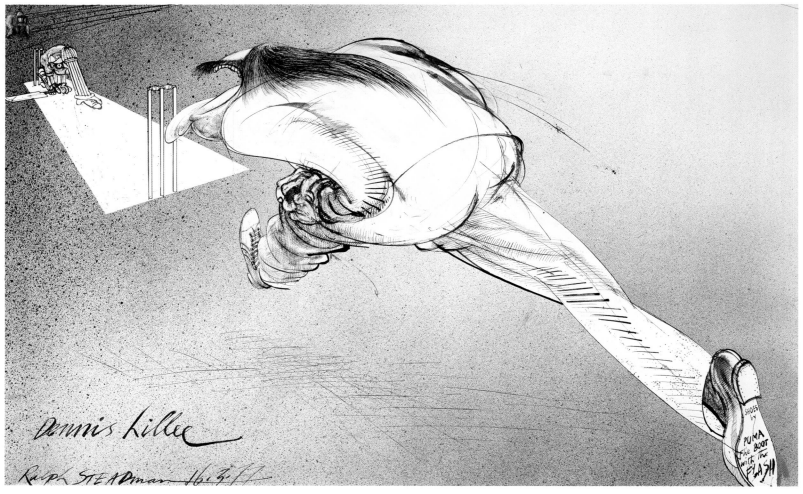

RALPH STEADMAN WAS BORN IN WALLASEY, CHESHIRE, AND EDUCATED AT ABERGELE GRAMMAR SCHOOL IN NORTH WALES, LEAVING AT THE AGE OF 16 IN 1952. HE JOINED THE DE HAVILLAND AIRCRAFT COMPANY AS AN APPRENTICE – A STRANGE START TO A DISTINGUISHED ARTISTIC CAREER. ONLY ONE USEFUL THING CAME OUT OF HIS APPRENTICESHIP, HE DID A SPELL IN A DRAWING OFFICE; IT WAS THERE THAT HE FIRST DEVELOPED HIS TECHNIQUE OF USING STRAIGHT RULED LINES COMBINED WITH FREE DRAWING. AFTER LEAVING DE HAVILLAND HE HAD A SHORT CAREER AS A TRAINEE MANAGER IN WOOLWORTHS AND THEN BECAME THE 'BOY' IN AN ADVERTISING AGENCY IN COLWYN BAY. IT WAS THERE THAT HE SAW A PRESS ADVERTISEMENT FOR PERCY V. BRADSHAW'S COURSE IN DRAWING

'I decided to have a go at that. My mother and father paid for it, £17 for 18 lessons. There were 12 basic lessons on the techniques of drawing and the last six were cartooning. So I took a further course on that while I was in the RAF doing my National Service in 1954.

'I was a bit miserable in the RAF, and having the course to do was a great relief. I did the course religiously every month and wrote letters to old Percy Bradshaw complaining about how old-fashioned his course was. He noticed that in my drawings in pubs – I used to do drawings for pints – I had an eye for character so he told me to pursue that line of drawing, saying that the more I did the more it would help me when I got to cartooning. I sent a lot of drawings to *The Sunday Chronicle*, *The Empire News* and all the Kemsley newspapers. I was offered a job in their Northern group at £10-a -week, I couldn't believe it.

'I realised very much that I still needed to learn a lot about drawing so I went to live in East Ham and joined the East Ham Technical College evening classes. I did five a week and also on Saturday morning, all in the life class. Life-drawing is to me the basis of all composition and rhythm, it gives you everything.

'The one supremely important thing that drawing does is that it forces you to look: if you're not drawing you never really see things and make decisions and judgments about them. When I do a drawing I'm making some very primal marks on paper, rather like a caveman. I am exorcising my fears, I am trying to come to terms with the world I am looking at. It is a basic impulse in me to respond like that to what surrounds me.

'I spent three years at Kemsley's until Thomson came and I got the sack – well, not exactly the sack; I was offered a job as the crossword-puzzle artist, drawing up the blanks, so I decided it was time for me to go freelance. My first wife was more or less keeping me while I was

trying to make a living earning the odd seven guineas here and there.

'This went on until I got my first drawing into *Punch*, this was about 1958. In the next two or three years I started getting my drawings in fairly regularly but, in 1961, *Private Eye* started and I was getting very bored doing gags for *Punch*, so I decided to try one of my rejected *Punch* drawings on them. I was beginning to get a bit of an edge to my drawings and I got a cheque from Richard Ingrams after a few days plus a note saying more power to your elbow, that was a beginning of something.

'At about that time I met Gerald Scarfe and he said, "I've seen your drawings in *Punch*, I'd like to come and talk to you." So he came over one day. He hadn't really started then. We became close friends for about 18 months, working together at the V&A, drawing from The Antique, studying things like the Trajan column, learning how to draw and developing our powers of observation. In 1967 I did *Alice in Wonderland* which won a prize for the best-illustrated book of the last five years, or something like that.

'In 1969 my marriage broke up and I decided to go to America for a couple of months to see if I could get any work in New York. Before I'd left, all my *Private Eye* cartoons of the 60s were published

under the title "Still Life with Raspberries," and that book somehow wrapped up the whole of the 60s for me as well.

'So I went to America in April 1970, almost with a feeling of starting again. I'd been there a week when I met a man called Goddard who was editor of a rather scurrilous paper called *Scanlon's*. I saw his art editor, J.C. Swarez, who said would I like to go to Kentucky and do a story on the Kentucky Derby? I had an absolutely crazy week which was really the beginning of finding myself again. I produced a series of drawings for an article which eventually got into Tom Wolfe's book *New Journalism*. It's also now in an anthology of Hunter's called *The Great Shark Hunt* – and has become a sort of classic.'

So you had a well established career before you had your first drawing in RADIO TIMES. *When did that happen, and were you surprised that an 'establishment' magazine like* RADIO TIMES *should want to use you?*

'In about 1974 David Driver of RADIO TIMES got in touch with me to ask if I would like to draw for them so I said yes, of course. A bit later Bob Priest, his deputy, rang me up and asked me to do a drawing of the film *Bonnie and Clyde*, this was, I think, because David and Bob had seen my American drawings.

'Then David Driver put a thought to me: he asked me if I would fancy going to Australia. He laid on another job in Hong Kong which justified the whole fare so far as RADIO TIMES was concerned.

'So I went to Australia to look at cricket. The first thing I did was to get hold of all the Aussie papers, knowing nothing about cricket, and devoured all the sports pages. I saw how badly the English were doing and then Randall went in and scored 174 in the Centenary match and my whole concept of the game changed. I suddenly realised what it was all about. It was like chess, something more than hitting a ball around and cheering. I also, for the first time, saw the violence in the game, I thought that ball is a missile, if it hit you you were finished. As he ran up to bowl, the people in the cheap stand were chanting Lillee, Lillee, Lillee: it was a sort of death ritual. There is always a stillness as the ball leaves the bowler's hand, people waiting, and then if the ball is hit the seagulls around the pitch take off like the souls of the dead in an Aztec sacrifice. That moment was the one I had to get, that moment of hushed violence.

'I carry a small sketch-book, about 8 x 10, stuck down the back of my trousers so that I can whip it out like a gun when need be, and I also carry a camera for detail, the sort of thing I would never be able to get down in time. I had to get down what it was that was different about the game in Australia, the sort of thing that would never happen at Lord's – the ice-cold Fosters, all that, all the Aussie totems. What I was drawing would probably cause me great trouble, because they were not sports drawings in the ordinary sense, they were pretty strong social comments.'

What about Hong Kong, Ralph, what were you asked to do there?

'David asked me to do some illustrations about a series the BBC were planning to do on the Hong Kong police. So I thought I'd go around Hong Kong and make my own mind up. I saw Hong Kong as a sort of luxuriant growth arising out of a bed of poverty.

'The next thing I did for RADIO TIMES was the Belgian Grand Prix. I remember that there were photographers everywhere taking detailed photographs of everything in sight – nuts, bolts, industrial espionage really. I sat down with my 8 x 10 sketch-book, with a can of beer by my side in the midday sun, behind a car and started doing a drawing of a man in effect being the body of the car, a sort of sexual thing. A guy came up and said, "What are you doing, bud? Who do you work for?" I told him I was there for RADIO TIMES. "I see, so why are you drawing the back axle, what gives?" Anyway, I got the bum's rush from there.'

Test Cricket – 1977
'The people in the cheap stand were chanting Lillee, Lillee, Lillee'

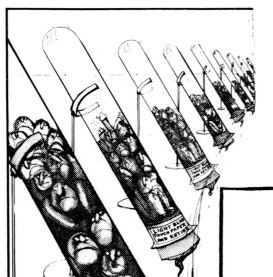

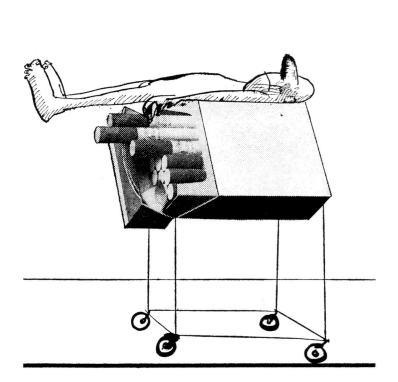

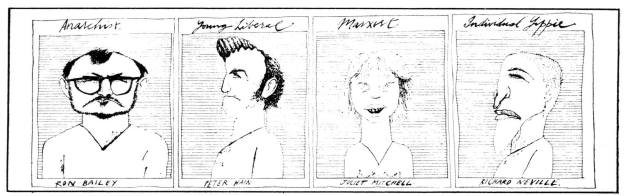

Kenneth Allsop talks to some of the New Radicals. Do they agree? 9.0 pm

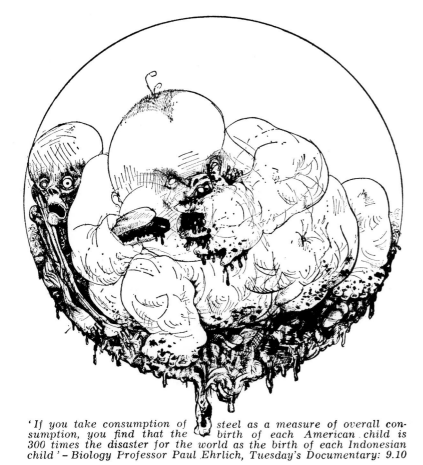

'If you take consumption of steel as a measure of overall consumption, you find that the birth of each American child is 300 times the disaster for the world as the birth of each Indonesian child' – Biology Professor Paul Ehrlich, Tuesday's Documentary: 9.10

Be fruitful and multiply and replenish the earth.
Because otherwise tomorrow may never happen: 9.20

Is it possible to duplicate a human being in a laboratory? It's an intriguing claim made by writer David Rorvik. The Clone Affair: 9.55

'Jonathan Milner did wilfully remain silent and by maintaining this silence he did knowingly inflict mental and physical suffering . . .' The War Crime: 3.5 pm

Is anyone immune to the professional opinion former? How persuasive are they and what are they trying to achieve? The Manipulators: 10.15 pm

Pawn Takes Pawn – 'just another ending in another game' for Levin, but at the World Championship there is always more at stake: 7.45 pm

Life can be difficult for a country whose nearest neighbour is the USSR, which shares a frontier with a potential enemy, or with a forceful friend. **The Bear Next Door** (10.15 Tuesday) begins a new BBC1 series of half-hour documentaries which look at four different countries – both Western and Eastern – and at how they respond to the presence next door of this unpredictable world superpower.

1 JULY 1944
FIELD MARSHALL KEITEL, CHIEF OF HIGH COMMAND, GERMAN ARMED FORCES—
'WHAT SHALL WE DO, WHAT SHALL WE DO?'
FIELD MARSHALL RUNDSTEDT, COMMANDER-IN-CHIEF, WEST—
'MAKE PEACE, YOU FOOLS! WHAT ELSE CAN YOU DO?'

WASHINGTON
0915 EASTERN STANDARD
      TIME (0315 PACIFIC TIME)
      —MESSAGE DECODED:
      JAPANESE ATTACK IMMINENT
1200 EST (0600 PACIFIC TIME)
      WARNING SENT TO HONOLULU
HONOLULU
0733 PACIFIC TIME (1313 EST)
      WARNING RECEIVED
0749 PACIFIC TIME (1349 EST)
      JAPANESE ATTACK PEARL
      HARBOUR
1458 PACIFIC TIME (2058 EST)
      PEARL HARBOUR FINALLY
      RECEIVES WARNING FROM
      HONOLULU

Then came the BOMB... now all was changed.
                                Michael Howard
                      Studies in War and Peace

DAWN FRIDAY MAY 10: THE GERMAN WESTERN OFFENSIVE OPENS. AT DUSK ON MAY 20 THEY HAD REACHED THE COAST ABOVE ABBEVILLE

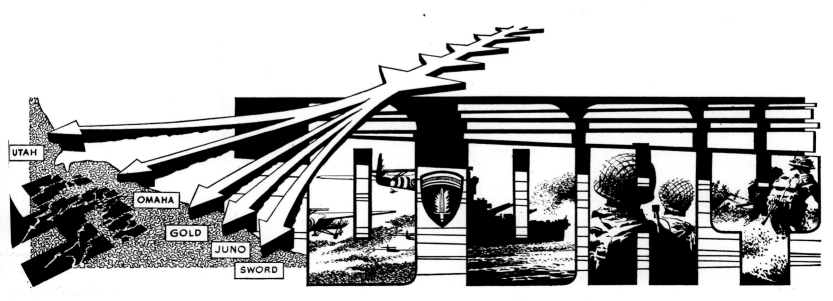

THE WHOLE PLACE
WILL GO UP IN
APPROXIMATELY
TEN MINUTES
ENJOY YOUR
REVENGE !

WHAT
IS IT ?

A tartan touch for Dr Who when he faces a new breed of monsters that bring terror to the North Sea: 5.45

The invasion that never was – England 1940: 9.20

Bandits at 8.15! A special showing for Battle of Britain Sunday

SUPREME COMMANDER TO 6 ARMY, JANUARY 24, 1943
Surrender is forbidden stop 6 Army will hold their positions to
the last man and the last round and by their heroic endurance
will make an unforgettable contribution towards the
establishment of a defensive front and the salvation of the
Western world stop   Adolf Hitler

Stalingrad – Hitler loses an army, the allies find new hope: 9.25

BATTLE SLOGAN OF THE
JAPANESE 32ND ARMY

1 PLANE FOR 1 WARSHIP
1 BOAT FOR 1 SHIP
1 MAN FOR 10 ENEMY
1 MAN FOR 1 TANK

Kamikaze v chewing-gum – impossible mission? Grand Strategy: 9.25

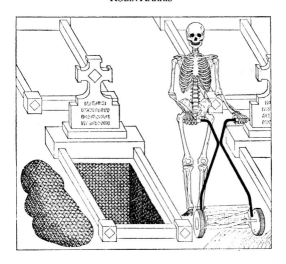

Most people drink. Few people really think about drinking. But who decides what you drink? Do you? Do your friends? Do you perhaps drink more than you thought? **What's Your Poison?** (Sunday 11.50 BBC1) is a new series presented by Brian Trueman, with an accompanying book (BBC Publications £1.75) designed to help you test how much you drink, and put your alcohol intake on a healthy footing.

Lorca's Lament for the Death of a Bullfighter: 9.20

'I killin' meself workin,' an' he sthruttin' about from mornin' till night like a paycock . . .' Juno Boyle's jaundiced view of her marriage to Jack, The Monday Play: 8.0

'Don't you glory in the thought of the child running in the free air . . . untrammelled, liberated . . .' The Renegade, *first of five stories by Penelope Mortimer: 4.35*

'You can make friends and life continues
as normal. But when you say to a friend at work,
"We had a super meal last night",
you can't exactly say
". . . and my husband was wearing a new dress".'

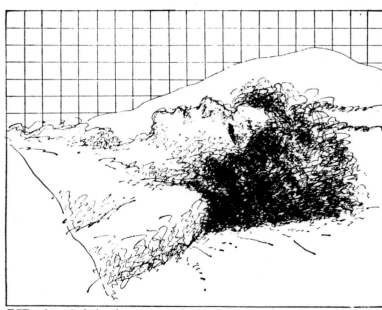

ECT – *does it help the patient? Inside Medicine* investigates: *9.55 pm*

Brenda Kidman talks about 'a subject that has to be brought out' in One Last Look at the Garden. *'I hope that it will help to more understanding of breast cancer.' She talks about her own mastectomy, the consequences and her present hopes and fears: 7.20 pm*

Georges Simenon: 'It's all a question of atmosphere'

8.0 pm Treat Me Gently. The operating theatre held no terrors for journalist **Tony Van den Bergh**, veteran of some 200 'ops' as an observer . . . until it was his turn to be the patient

'Hip-replacement? As a medical journalist I've seen the operation done twice. Nothing to it,' I'd told an arthritic friend. Then the hospital's questionnaire arrived for me. 'Next of kin?' 'Religion?' Did THEY believe I was going to die? Or that I would be one of the two per cent failure rate that end up as invalids? I waited for three days in the ward; examinations, blood-tests, X-rays . . . and considerable forebodings that were only stopped by the pre-med injection. Immediately after the operation I was awakened every two hours for bottom-rubbing, tea and sympathy. And, of course, the indignity, discomfort and pain of a bed-pan. The nurses were kind, considerate, efficient. But to me they all seemed very young ; and working in an orthopaedic ward, they must have regarded me as 'just another hip-replacement.' But to me, I am ME. The nights seemed months. Then a nightmare . . . waking-up, out of bed, crying in pain. Had I dislocated my new joint? I prayed not. Now it is over. My hip moves sweetly without pain for the first time in years. Soon I shall be saying: 'Nothing to it . . .' But not just yet.

BILL TIDY WAS BORN IN 1932 AT FRINTON IN TRANMERE. IN BETWEEN BOMBING RAIDS HE WENT TO SCHOOL AT ANFIELD ROAD, LIVERPOOL AND THEN AT THE AGE OF 11 TO ST MARGARET MARY'S, ANFIELD, WHICH HAD THE SMALLEST PLAYGROUND OF ANY SCHOOL IN ENGLAND. HE LEARNT TO PLAY CRICKET THERE AND, TODAY, HE PLAYS FOR THE LORD'S TAVERNERS

'I'd always been able to draw, always, since about the age of three. My mother encouraged me to draw. I'm sure she knew about my nicking sixpences from her purse but she never said anything. If I found one of my kids nicking from me I'm sure I'd batter them to death. I used to use the sixpences for buying copy books for drawing. I left school at 14 and joined a shipping company which exported railway engines to South America, which was an attraction to the boys of my school. I worked there for about 18 months, wasting time, but always drawing.

'In 1952 National Service came up. I had the choice of being called up or joining as a regular and earning an extra quid a week, so I joined up for three years in the Royal Engineers. I remember it was freezing cold and jam was at a premium and people were unsympathetic but on reflection it was great, all tolerable suffering is good for the spirit. Then I was sent to Germany which was terrible, there was still a lot of hostility, so I volunteered to go to Korea. Luckily, the maximum stay in Korea was a year and after that you were sent to the fleshpots of Japan. I was in charge of a dock in Kure and one of the men working for me was a little Japanese bloke who suggested I contribute some drawings to the local English-language newspaper, so I sent one in and they accepted it. When I saw it in print I realised my future lay ahead of me like a yellow brick road.

'When I finished my time, I came back to Liverpool and got a job in an advertising agency. While I was there I got my first drawing in RADIO TIMES in 1956. RADIO TIMES featured ads on the back page and I drew ads for greenhouses: about 800 words of copy and a drawing to go into a space of about half-an-inch square.

'The ads didn't get me anywhere so I decided to turn freelance. I went to London for a while and started selling drawings, cartoons, to *Picturegoer*, defunct now; *Everybodys*, defunct; *John Bull*, defunct: I was killing magazines. It was exclusively me–I killed publications like some terrible, terrible plague.

'However, I soon realised that there was no need to live in London, so I came back home and worked from there and got off to quite a good start–hit it immediately, you might say, with *The Daily Mirror*. I sold perhaps three

It's a Knock-Out!–1972
'They blow your brain
when they're being described'

drawings a week at five guineas a go, which wasn't bad dough then, and I was soon earning about £20 a week in 1958. It stayed like that for quite a long time until about 1965–I'd had no contact with RADIO TIMES since I left the advertising agency in 1956. However, I sold one or two drawings to *Punch*, which is a marvellous shop window.

'My professional life was still a bit of a struggle. However, in about 1966 it all seemed to click somehow; all the years of waiting were worthwhile. Hutchinson asked me to do a book of my gags which was flattering and, when it appeared, an old BBC programme ("Review" I think it was called, it went out on Saturday nights with James Mossman), decided to do my artistic life. Whether it was that exposure to the public on telly coinciding with publication of the book or not I don't know, but my wagon got on the move. I started "The Cloggies" in *Private Eye*; it became very popular.

'Round about this time Brian Thomas of RADIO TIMES rang me late on a Friday, just as I was off to my caravan in the Lake District–he always did this– and said can you do me a drawing by Monday? I thought, you swine! Soon after that Brian, popped up again to say would I do "It's a Knock-Out!" He had to describe one of their lunatic games over the telephone; I don't mean to denigrate the game because I've been involved in one for the Lord's Taverners, but they do blow your brain when they're being described to you. Then I had to make the famous "It's a Knock-Out!" trophy.

'Being enthusiastic but untutored, I made a super model out of plasticine of the preferred design but RADIO TIMES said we can't work from plasticine, you'll have to make it in something else so that a cast can be made, like Scopas wax. This is the wax used in the vanishing wax (*Cire perdu*) process, and it's bloody hard to work with–you have to heat it a little just to make it pliable enough to model. Anyway, the model was made, okayed by RADIO TIMES, so I asked who do you want the trophy made by? In the usual way RADIO TIMES wanted it yesterday so I got hold of a jeweller's in Birmingham and they gave me a deadline to which RADIO TIMES said "go ahead"–and gave the impression that there were unlimited funds available for this grotesque trophy. When the day came the bill was prodigious. Anyway, they were pleased in the end, and I still get a great thrill when I see it presented on telly to some unsuspecting mayor. You see, there are no handles so there's no way to hold it really, and it's very, very heavy. I've handled it since and it's obviously taken a fall or two because it's bolted and nailed, riveted, and looks as though it has been around. I reckon it'll probably be presented to me on my deathbed.'

Bill, you've not only drawn for RADIO TIMES, *but you've had numerous appearances on television–including your own 'Fosdyke Saga.'*

'Yes, and I was supposed to be on the cover when the series started so I was very flattered. I was a bit scared: I'd that only losers got on the covers of RADIO TIMES, but I went down on a Sunday to London to an address to meet a photographer. I had a piece of paper with the number "11b so-and-so street" written on it. So I went to 11b and asked for the photographer and was told, "He used to live here a long time ago but God knows where he is now," and I thought, "Hell!" So I went home next day and rang RADIO TIMES in a fury. Before I could get in a word they said, "Where were you?" To cut a long story short, the piece of paper said "116" not "11b". So I never made the cover, but pehaps I saved my career!'

A day in the life of Mr Average

7 am

Adrenal hormones at peak, being pumped through the blood

8 am

Sex hormones at peak – men usually more aware of this than women

8.30 am

Urine volume at peak – bulk excreted during morning

9 am

Body least sensitive to pain; ideal time too for slimmers to eat

10 am

Efficiency climbing – but extraverts work better in the afternoon

12 noon

Peak time for susceptibility to alcohol

2 pm

The 'post-lunch dip' – not caused by lunch but by the body's rhythm?

3 pm

Efficiency peak for most tasks – if you are an extravert

4 pm

Breathing rate at highest

5 pm

Sensory awareness – taste, hearing, smell etc – more acute

6 pm

Physical vigour at its greatest

7 pm

Blood pressure and heart rate near peak

8 pm

Body temperature and weight at peak

10 pm

Hormones running down, temperature dropping, heart and breathing slow

Midnight

Skin and other cells at work, building for next day

4 am

Sense of hearing very acute, otherwise the body at its lowest ebb

RadioTimes

Abbey

Page 14 *Christmas Cover* 19.12.24, **p.15** *Christmas Cover* 18.12.25.

Ardizzone, Edward
(1900-1979)

Edward Ardizzone was born in Tonking; educated at Clayesmore School. He went on to study art at evening classes at Westminster School of Art under Bernard Meninsky, 1921-26. In 1926 he left his job and turned freelance, and began contributing work to RADIO TIMES almost immediately. Contributed work to many other magazines; other commissions include poster work for London Transport etc, menus and wine lists and the birthday greeting telegram. Ted Ardizzone was an Official War Artist, 1940-45; exhibited at the RA; retrospective at the V&A, 1973; illustrated the staggering amount of over 150 books including 'In a Glass Darkly', 1929; 'The Local' by Maurice Gorham, 1939; 'My Uncle Silas', 1939; 'Peacock Pie', 1946; 'The Warden', 1952; 'Robinson Crusoe', 1968; 'The Little Fire Engine', 1973; books of his own that were published: 'Little Tim and the Brave Sea Captain', 1936; 'Baggage to the Enemy', 1941; 'Tim All Alone', 1956; Diana and her Rhinocerous', 1964; 'Sarah and Simon and no Red Paint', 1965; 'Tim and Ginger', 1965; 'The Young Ardizzone', 1970; 'Tim's Last Voyage', 1972.

Page 40 *Children's Hour Number* 26.2.37, **p.60** *Interview, A Passage to India* 21.10.55, **p.61** *Christmas Cover* 23.12.32, **p.62** *Conversation in the Train* 24.9.37, *Horty Mania* 20.8.37, *Old Music Halls* 3.6.38, **p.63** *Come Along Liza* 27.8.37, *The Lunatic at Large* 16.7.37, *Children's Hour, competition* 31.3.39, *Cavalcade* 12.5.39, **p.64** *Christmas Cover* 24.12.37, **p.96** *My Best Story for Christmas* 23.12.49, *Northanger Abbey* 14.1.49, *Whit Monday Picnic* 14.5.48, **p.97** *Christmas Cover* 24.12.48, **p.135** *A Dog's Life* 25.6.54, *King Lear* 9.11.51, **p.155** *Beggar's Opera* 3.8.61, *Falstaff* 30.4.64, *The Warden* 8.9.66, *Bloomsday* 4.5.61, *Below Stairs* 2.2.61.

Ayrton, Michael
(1921-1975)

Michael Ayrton was born in London, the son of Gerald Gould the poet and critic and Barbara Ayrton-Gould, suffragette and Labour Party Chairman. He was educated at Abinger Preparatory School but left at 14 to study art in Paris and Vienna. Exhibited from 1942 onwards in England (especially the Redfern Gallery), Europe and the USA. He designed the theatrical productions of 'Macbeth', 1942; Sadler's Wells Ballet, 'Le Festin de l'Araignée', 1944; Purcell's 'Fairy Queen', 1946 and 1951; he was art critic of *The Spectator* 1944-46; books published include 'British Drawings', 1946; 'Hogarth's Drawings', 1948; 'Tittivlus', 1953; 'Golden Section', 1957; 'Illustrated Poems of Death', 1945; 'The Duchess of Malfi', 1945; 'Summer's Last Will and Testament', 1946; 'The Unfortunate Traveller', 1948; 'Macbeth', 1951; 'The Human Age', 1956.
Page 94 *Les Troyens à Carthage* 27.6.47, *The Golden Bridegroom* 14.1.49, *A New Way to Pay Old Debts* 15.10.48, *William Walton* 12.11.48.

Bacon, Cecil W.
(1905-   )

Cecil Bacon was born in Battle, Sussex, educated at Sutton Valence School and St Lawrence College, Ramsgate, studied art at Hastings School of Art, 1923-25, joined a commercial studio in London, 1926-28, and at the same time worked for an advertising agency until 1929; worked both with an agency and as a freelance artist until 1941; short term in the RAF and then was transferred to the MOI, 1942-45; began full freelance career in 1946; drew for the RADIO TIMES from 1935 to 1968; contributed work to *The Listener*, other BBC publications, London Transport. Work exhibited at the Folio Society (London and USA) 1957; various exhibitions 1960, 1961 and 1971; illustrated book-jackets, illustrated several National Service posters, 1939; books illustrated include 'The Adventures of Dr Barnado', 1949; 'The Dune Boy', 'The Early Years of a Naturalist', 1940; 'Window on a Hill', 'Essays and Notes: Richard Church', 1951; 'Voyage Around the World with Captain Cook in HMS Resolution', 1953; 'World Outlook 1900-1964'

(maps and diagrams), 1968; 'English Barometers 1680-1860', (design and typography) 1968; 'Exploring Britain', 1971.
Page 87 *Christmas Cover* 17.12.43.

Badmin, Stanley Roy
(1906-   )

Stanley Badmin was born in Sydenham and studied art at Camberwell Art School. He received a free studentship to the Royal College of Art. He first drew for the RADIO TIMES in 1951 and his work has always been connected with trees and the countryside. One-man exhibitions in London, New York and Worthing. Books published: 'Etched Plates', 'Autolithoed Educational' books, 'Village and Town', 'Trees in Britain', 'Farm Crops in Britain'. Illustrations to: 'British Countryside in Colour', 'Trees for Town and Country', 'Famous Trees', 'Shell Guide to Trees and Shrubs', 'The Seasons', 'Trees in Britain', 'Ladybird Book of Trees', *Readers Digest* and Royles Publications.
Page 131 *Easter Cover* 18.4.54.

Bateman, Henry Mayo
(1887-1970)

Henry Mayo Bateman was born in Sutton Forest, New South Wales, educated at Forest Hill House, London, studied art at Westminster and New Cross Art Schools. He worked for several years in the studio of Charles van Havenmaet; he began to draw for reproduction when he was 19, and in the course of his career he contributed thousands of humorous drawings to most of the leading weekly and monthly periodicals; theatrical posters for 'Fanny's First Play' by George Bernard Shaw; 'Other Island' by John Bull; one-man exhibition in 1919 at the Leicester Galleries; also a show of his paintings in 1936; he contributed to the Royal Academy in 1933. In 1960 he published 'The Evening Rise', 'Fifty Years of Fly Fishing', he published several collections of drawings: 'Burlesques', 'A Book of Drawings', 'Suburbia', 'More Drawings', 'Considered Trifles', 'Brought Forward', 'Colonels', 'H.M. Bateman by Himself'. In 1949 he read a paper 'Humour in Art' to the Royal Society of Artists with the idea of starting a National Gallery of Humorous Art. However, to his eternal regret, the project failed due to lack of premises.
Page 50 *Whitsun holiday Number* 29.5.36.

Batt
(Oswald Charles Barrett)
(1892-1945)

Oswald Charles Barrett was born in London, educated at St George's School, Ramsgate and Old Camden School of Art. His first drawing was published in *The Bystander*, 1911; after the war in 1919 he studied art at Heatherley's; Goldsmiths' School of Art. He shared a studio with

Eric Fraser for a while; illustrated *Current Literature* from 1926 for two years; began work for the RADIO TIMES in 1930 and continued for 15 years. Most noted works were his portraits of 'Great Composers'– the first in 1934 was Beethoven. They were so popular that the BBC published special issues for framing; illustrated 'Astonishing Island' by Winifred Holtby; H. M. Raleigh's stories; 'How Should we Rebuild London' by C. B. Purdom; 'The Oxford Companion to Music' by Dr Percy A. Scholes. In 1965, 20 years after his death, there was an exhibition of his 'musical' work, including all the RADIO TIMES portraits, at the Royal Festival Hall.
Page 31 *Summer Number* 10.3.33, **p.34** *Schubert* 10.6.38, **p.35** *Beethoven: The Man and his Music* 28.4.39, **p.95** *Elgar* 27.12.40.

Bellamy, Frank
(1917-1976)

Frank Bellamy was born in Kettering, Northants, and educated locally. He was a self-taught artist; worked in a local studio until he joined the army, in 1939; demobbed in 1945 and went to work first for a local design studio and then moved to London, where he joined a studio in Fleet Street. Began his freelance career in 1953; first commission for *Mickey Mouse Comic*. Contributed work to *Swift; Eagle* (Dan Dare strip); *TV21* (Thunderbirds strip); *The Sunday Times* colour supplement; Garth for *The Daily Mirror*, 1971-76. Received Best Foreign Artist Award from the Academy of Comic Book Art, New York in 1973; work exhibited in London and Birmingham from the mid-60s onwards.
Page 232 *Grand Strategy – Attack from the West* 3.8.72, *Grand Strategy – Pearl Harbour* 26.7.72, *Grand Strategy – Total War* 23.8.72, **p.233** *Red Arrows* 25.5.72, *Biggin Hill* 21.5.72, *Blitzkreig* 28.6.72, *Europe Invaded* 4.6.74, **p.234** *Dr Who* 27.12.72, 10.4.71, 30.8.75, **p.235** *Dr Who* 30.8.75, **p.236** *Britain Under Siege* 5.7.72, *Battle of Britain* 15.9.74, *Grand Strategy – Stalingrad* 2.8.72, *Grand Strategy – Angry Pacific* 16.8.72.

Bentley, Nicolas
(1907-1978)

Nicolas Bentley was born in Highgate, London, educated at University College School, London, studied art at Heatherley's; Director André Deutsch Ltd, Editor Mitchell Beazley Ltd. Spent six weeks with a circus and worked three years for Shell publicity before beginning his freelance career as author and artist; for a short time drew a regular cartoon for *The Daily Mail* in the 60s; illustrated 'New Cautionary Tales', 1930; 'More Than Somewhat', 1937; 'Old Possum's Book of Practical Cats', 1939; 'Cautionary Verses', 1940; 'Baseless Biography', 1940; 'How to be an Alien', 1946; 'This England 1940-46', 1946; 'Stiff Upper Lip', 1958; 'On Drink', 1973 and many others. Publications include 'Die, I Thought I'd Laugh', a book of pictures, 1936; 'Ballet-Hoo', 1937; 'Gammon and Espionage', 1938; 'Le Sport', 1939; 'The Tongue-Tied Canary', 1948; 'The Floating Dutchman', 1950; 'How Can You Bear to be Human?', 1957; 'A Version of the Truth', an autobiography, 1960; 'The Victorian Scene', 1968; 'Golden Sovereigns', 1970; 'Tales from Shakespeare', 1972; 'An Edwardian Album', 1974.
Page 65 *Christmas Number* 24.12.37, *They're all Easy* 7.7.39, **p.66** *Light Music* 9.7.37, *Brahms at his Greatest/Tchaikovsky's Debt…* 28.10.38, *American Humour* 5.8.38, *Men Must Work* *24.6.38*, **p.67** *Cricket* 27.5.38, *Seaside Bandstand* 31.3.39, *Boomerangs 10.12.37*, *Ladies & Gentlemen* 3.9.37, **p.68** *An Orchestra arrives at Broadcasting House* 22.12.33.

Biro, Val
(1921-)

Val Biro was born in Budapest, Hungary, educated at the School of Cistercian Monks, Budapest, studied art at Central School of Arts and Crafts. Joined the Auxiliary Fire Service, 1942-45; worked for Sylvan Press, 1945-46; C & J Temple, 1946-48; John Lehmann, 1948-53, before turning freelance; illustrated over 300 books, contributed work to many publications including the RADIO TIMES. Author of the 'Gumdrop Series' books (12 in all) for children.
Page 170 Interview, *Christmas Heading* 18.12.59, *Sunday Half Hour* 25.8.50, **p.171** *Christmas Heading* 18.12.59, *Duke of Kent's Wedding* 8.6.61, *Rake's Progress* 26.10.61, *Proms Concert* 20.7.61, *Glyndebourne* 13.7.61, *Silver Chords* 3.12.61, *The Edinburgh Festival* 16.8.62, *Border decorations for TV* 18.12.53, **p.172** *Nelson* 23.2.61, *Nelson & Trafalgar* 12.10.61, **p.173** *Aida* 1.8.63, *Nelson* 23.2.61, *Trafalgar* 5.10.61.

Brookes, Peter
(1943-)

Peter Brookes was born in Liverpool; educated at various schools around the U.K. as his father was in the RAF; studied art at Manchester School of Art, for a year; moved to Central School of Art and Design in 1966; turned freelance in the early 70s. He taught at the Central School of Art and Design, 1976-78; tutor at Royal College of Art from 1978; contributes work on a regular basis to RADIO TIMES and *The Listener*, other magazines include *New Society, New Statesman, L'Expansion, Marie Claire* and *Cosmopolitan* in France, and work in Germany and USA; illustrates books for Hutchinson, Folio Society, W. H. Allen; book-jackets for Penguin, Fontana; one-man show Mel Calman Workshop Gallery, 1978; work shown in 'European Illustration', 1976-81; Association of Illustrators, 1976-81; Scottish and Welsh Arts Council shows; Art Work exhibition, National Theatre; British Illustrators, Belgrave Gallery, 1978; exhibited at Illustrators' Art and Mel Calman Workshop Gallery, London.
Page 185 *Chinese Week* 4.2.77, **p.186 Inverview,** *Inside NHS* 28.9.74, **p.187** *The Proms* 15.8.78, *Russian Week* 5.11.77, *Sheep/Spring Issue* 19.3.77, *Fireside Issue* 22.10.76, **p.188** *The Oil Game* 31.8.74, *Horizon: Washoe* 4.11.74, *Fireside Issue* 23.10.76, **p.189** *Ali/Frazier* 30.3.72, *Industrial Espionage* 23.4.72, *NHS: You & Yours* 3.10.74, *Your Witness: Sexual Equality* 5.9.73, **p.190** *The World in a Box* 22.8.76, *The Daughter-in-law* 12.7.71, *Search for Satan* 13.9.75, *Eventful Death of Mr Fruin* 11.10.72, *Tuesday Call – Gardening* 7.10.75, **p.191** *NHS: It's Your Line* 1.10.74, *The Health Food Boom* 23.6.71, *Say it in English* 29.3.78, *NHS: Child Development* 28.9.74, *Panorama – Med Holidays* 23.8.71, **p.192** *Anatomy of Melancholy* 8.5.77, *Twice round the Gasworks* 26.3.76, *Mrs. Jordan…* 5.12.76, *The Red Cockerel Crows* 4.2.74, *The Night Bathers* 6.7.75, **p.193** *Death in Venice* 17.12.75, *The Amazing Dr. Clitterhouse* 10.4.76, *The Barrier* 4.6.71, *A Collier's Friday Night* 16.8.71, *Monkeys* 28.7.74, **p.194** *Travels in the Far World* 8.6.77, *The Night the East Coast Sank* 30.1.78, *Analysis: Aspects of Profit* 14.11.74, *The Lost World* 23.1.75, *Holiday '72* 28.10.71, **p.195** *Money Programme – Middle Classes* 4.6.76, *Horizon: Teaching Methods* 26.4.76, *Man Alive: Ralph Nader* 20.10.71, *Animal Farm* 8.5.72, *Up the Organisation* 12.8.72, **p.196** *The Return of the Native* 15.2.76, *Alice in Wonderland* 12.12.77, *The Thirteen Clocks* 22.12.73, **p.197** *Well well well* 21.9.75, *The Fixed Smile* 21.1.76, *Witch Wood* 23.8.75, *P. G. Wodehouse* 15.10.74, *Storm in a Tea Cup* 31.7.76, *Silas has most of the Rank* 14.6.76, **p.198** *The Power of The Atom* 7.6.76, *Inventing of America* 30.12.75, **p.199** *NHS: Menopausal Problems* 30.9.1974, *Orders from Above* 22.11.75, *Moon walk One* 20.7.74, *Machines that Think* *12.12.75*, **p.200** *View: Parkinson* 17.11.79, *Panorama: The Next Deterrent* 8.12.79, *View: King* 21.4.79, *View: Suez* 24.11.79, **p.201** *View: Today from Peking* 22.9.79, *View: Circuit 11* 10.11.79, *View: Horizon* 14.4.79, *View: Women at Arms* 31.3.79, **p.202** *View: In the Post* 10.3.79, *View: Genuine Article* 12.5.79, *View: Week in Westminster* 3.11.79, *Island of the Dodo* 3.3.79, **p.203** *View: Devolution* 17.3.79, *View: Where we Live…* 23.2.79, *View: Horizon Sugar* 24.3.79, *View: Rating Game* 9.6.79, **p.204** *View: Football* 26.5.79, *View: Cricket* 15.12.79, *View: Match of the Day* 18.8.79, *View: Spaghetti Western* 7.7.79, **p.205** *View: The Persuaders* 28.7.79, *View: Tom Keating* 4.8.79, *View: Mainstream* 13.10.79, *View: Antique Road Show* 7.4.79, **p.206** *View: Tinker Tailor* 20.10.79, *View: Curious Cat* 5.5.79, *View: Dog's Life* 8.9.79, *View: Crufts* 10.2.79, **p.207** *View: Last Night of the Proms* 15.9.79, *View: Ascot* 16.6.79, *View: Bellamy* 1.12.79, *View: Flowers* 9.5.79, **p.208** *View: Panorama* 24.2.79, *View: Mastermind* 1.9.79, *View: Come Dancing* 21.7.79, *View: The Editors* 23.6.79, **p.209** *View: Blankety Blank* 6.10.79, *View: Fellini's Roma* 3.2.79, *View: The Archers* 30.6.79, *View: Hitchcock* 1.8.79, **p.212** *Wimbledon* 4.7.74, 3.7.74, **p.213** *Wimbledon* 25.6.74, 24.6.74, 29.6.74, **p.214** *World Cup* 22.6.74, *Soyuz/Apollo* 15.7.75, **p.215** *First Test versus India* 6.6.74, *Golf* 11.7.74, *Soyuz/Apollo* 15.7.75, **p.216** *World Cup* 18.6.74, 15.6.74, **p.217** *World Cup* 13.6.74, 14.6.74, **p.218** *World Cup* 15.6.74, 22.6.74.

Cosman, Milein
(1921-)

Milein Cosman was born in Dusseldorf and studied at the International School in Geneva. She came to England in 1939 and went to The Slade School of Fine Art. She went to the Proms at Queens Hall in 1940 where she drew her first portrait of a conductor, Sir Henry Wood; she met Douglas Williams who commissioned her first drawing for RADIO TIMES of Constant Lambert in 1946; exhibits work in Paris and New York; illustrated Neville Cardus's 'A Composers' Eleven' and published two books of drawings. She now paints portraits and landscapes and also does etchings.
Page 130 *Promenade Concerts* 31.8.56, 7.9.56, 31.8.56, 24.8.56.

Dodds, Andrew
(1927-)

Andrew Dodds was born in Gullane, Scotland, educated in England and joined the Junior Art Department of Colchester School of Art; at 16 he moved to the senior school and began the full-time National Diploma in Design course until 1944 when he was called up into the Navy. After he was demobbed in 1947, he joined the Central School of Arts and Crafts, where he studied under Bernard Meninsky and John Minton; first job was illustrating for *Eagle*, followed by *Farmer's Weekly*; first illustration for the RADIO TIMES was for the series, *The Archers* (he used his mother as a model for Doris). Also has contributed work to the *Eastern Daily Press* and does book illustrations; lecturer in Art at Suffolk College.
Page 154 *The Changing Village* 23.2.61, *November Day* 11.7.63, *All Through the Night* 14.3.63, *Fruit Picking in Kent* 26.7.62, *The Archers* 19.7.62.

Draper, Richard
(1949-)

Richard Draper was born in London, educated at Hillside Secondary Modern School, Hornsey College of Art and then East Ham Technical College and School of Art; worked on the staff of RADIO TIMES for three years from 1969 as an art assistant; he began his freelance career with Nigel Holmes before he began to draw on his own. He has also worked for the Central Office of Information.
Page 219 *Go* 30.5.74, *Whistle Test* 23.3.74, *Canada into Action* 28.10.75, *Farnborough* 8.9.74.

Dunkley, Jack
(1906-)

Jack Dunkley was born in Holloway, educated at Sir Hugh Middleton Central School; at 16 he got a job doing the subtitles for advertising films. While he was there he won an award to go to the Central School of Art and Crafts three evenings a week. He left the film studio in 1930 to work freelance, he got his first commissions from *The Daily Mirror* and RADIO TIMES in 1932; since then, both before and after the war, he has contributed work to many papers and journals, including *The Daily Mirror, News Chronicle, The Daily Express, The Daily Sketch*; his specialities are, and have always been, humorous cartoons and sports coverage.
Page 28 Interview, *Cricket Glossary* 27.5.38, **p.29** *Five O'Clock Follies* 10.9.37, *A Mr. Funf…* 8.12.39, *Gentlemen v. Players* 9.7.37, *Cartoon '… and now…'* 15.9.39 **p.90/91** *Radio Concentration Camps* 26.4.40.

Einzig, Susan
(1922-)

Susan Einzig was born in Berlin; educated at the Gertrauden Lyceum; in 1939 she was evacuated from Germany to England; studied art at the Central School of Art and Crafts; in 1945 turned freelance; contributed work to *Lilliput, Picture Post, Vogue, House and Garden, Home and Garden, The Tatler, Good Housekeeping, She, The Strand*; book illustrations include 'Mary Belinda and the Ten Aunts', 'Tom's Midnight Garden', 'Sappho' for the Folio Society, 'Jane Eyre', 'My Mother's House'; one-woman show Mel Calman Workshop Gallery, London, 1975; exhibited at RA, Leicester Galleries, and with the London Group.
Page 132 Interview, *The Trial of Marie Lafarge* 13.12.57, **p.133** *The Tragedy of Nan* 13.6.58, *The Seagull* 30.9.59, *The Golden Door* 23.11.51, *The Aspen Papers* 16.2.51, *The Importance of Being Ernest* 18.12.59.

Ellison, Pauline
(1946-)

Pauline Ellison was born in Keighley, Yorkshire, educated at Keighley Grammar School, studied art at Bradford and Cambridge Art Schools, came to London in 1967 and began a freelance career. Commissions include work for *The Times Saturday Review, Harpers, Good Housekeeping, Nova, The Observer, The Sunday Times*; illustrated 'A Love of Flowers'; and just recently completed 'Grimms Fairy Tales'; work exhibited in 'Design and Art Direction', 'European Illustration' annuals.
Page 247 *Christmas Cover* 24.10.78.

Fantoni, Barry
(1940-)

Barry Fantoni was born in London; studied art at Camberwell Art School (1953-58). He first drew for the RADIO TIMES in the 70s and has given up his artistic career for writing. His book 'Mike Dime', published in 1980.
Page 248 *Letters* 15.5.76, 12.6.76, 22.1.77, 22.6.77, 15.7.78, 28.9.77, 25.6.77, 17.4.76, 27.3.76, 14.2.76.

Ferrier, Arthur
(1891-1973)

Arthur Ferrier began his career in a pharmacy, but soon changed to drawing: he said 'the best medicine was laughter'. He began drawing for the *News of the World* in 1923 and continued until 1959; he created the 'dolly bird' and the 'mini skirt' before their time. During the war he drew for the army magazine *Blighter*. He drew for RADIO TIMES in the 20s and was also a portrait painter.
Page 19 *A Vision of the Near Future* 15.2.24.

Fraser, Eric
(1902-)

Eric Fraser was born in London, educated at Westminster City School, studied art at Goldsmiths' College, 1919-24. He taught at Camberwell School of Art, 1928-40; began drawing for RADIO TIMES in 1926, also contributed work to *Harpers Bazaar, Vogue, The Listener, Art and Industry, Studio, Lilliput, Nash's Britannia and Eve, London Mystery Magazine, Leader;* Folio Society; illustrated for the Golden Cockerel Press, etc; mural painting for Babcock House, 1957; work exhibited at the RA and The Society of Scottish Artists, and Brussels exhibition, 1958.
Page 20 Interview, *Aaron's Field* 10.11.39, **p.21** *H. V. Morton* 6.7.28, *Ultimatum* 29.3.29, *Listeners' Point of View* 18.2.27, **p.50** *Autumn News Number* 7.10.38, **p.56** *Legionnaires* 23.12.38, *Ithuriel's Hour* 30.6.39, **p.57** *Further Outlook Warmer* 1.9.39, *Youth at the Helm* 3.4.36, *Small Print* 25.10.35, *Round the World* 22.11.35, **p.58** *Complete Radio Home* 18.11.38, **p.59** *Dance Music* 5.11.37, *American Jam Session* 28.10.38, *Joyce Jamboree*, 23.6.39, **p.84** *Under the Crooked Cross* 6.12.40, *The Raft* 14.8.42, *Gestapo* 6.2.42, *Scrapbook 1919* 1.2.46, *Five Hundred Thousand Dogs* 20.12.40, **p.85** *War and Peace* 15.1.43, *Shipyard Worker* 20.8.43, *Marching On* 24.4.42, *Yes Mother–Heil Hitler* 7.6.40, **p.86** *A Giant Waits* 6.3.42, *The Father* 21.1.49, *Information from the Enemy* 16.8.40, *My Sister and I* 31.10.41, *Victory Celebrations* 10.5.45, **p.103** *Coronation Cover* 31.5.53, **p.134** *The Alchemist* 26.1.51, *Arsenic and Old Lace* 28.5.54, *Heart of Darkness* 23.11.56, *The Barren One* 12.12.58, **p.137** *Christmas Cover* 22.12.60, **p.138** *Hurricane* 29.6.61, *Henry of Navarre* 20.10.66, *Tamburlaine the Great* 12.3.64, *Don Juan* 14.1.65, *The Big Hewer* 10.8.61, **p.139** *1940* 9.9.65, **p.140** *Shakespeare and St George* 18.4.63, *Tennyson's Harold* 6.10.66, *National Theatre of the Air* 3.8.61, *The White Falcon* 18.8.66, **p.141** *Shakespeare's 400th Birthday* 16.4.64, **p.142** *Forty Years of Broadcasting* 8.11.62, *The Body-Blow* 19.7.62, *Dr. Faustus* 28.5.64, *Hedda Gabler* 14.10.65, *The Photo of the Colonel* 5.3.64, **p.143** *Saints Day* 12.10.61, *Persons from Porlock* 22.8.63, *Scoop* 14.11.63, *The Mortimer Touch* 16.8.62, **p.144** *Christ and Disorder* 27.6.68, *A Man's House* 4.4.63, *Caligula* 22.6.61, *Small World* 13.5.60, **p.145** *Christmas Cover* 20.12.62, **p.146** *Eastward Ho!* 27.6.63, *Restoration Comedy* 29.6.61, *Perspective on Handwriting* 28.3.63, *To Die a King* 8.2.68, *Butterfly in the Snow* 23.2.67, **p.147** *Education at Home* 3.10.63.

Gage, Edward Arthur
(1925-)

Edward Gage was born in East Lothian, educated at the Royal High School, Edinburgh, studied art at Edinburgh College of Art, 1941-42 and 1947-52; art master Fettes College, 1952-68; art critic for *The Scotsman*, 1967; President of the Scottish Society of Artists in the 1960s; senior lecturer, Napier College. First drew for RADIO TIMES in January 1953. He also contributed work to other BBC publications. Illustrated books for Bodley Head, Cassell, Michael Joseph, etc; published 'The Eye in the Wind' in 1978; he has had several one-man shows and his work is on permanent exhibition in Edinburgh, Glasgow, Aberdeen and Argyll.
Page 126 Interview, *Under Milk Wood* 19.8.60, **p.127** *Othello* 27.11.53, *The Wooden Dish* 29.10.54, *Oblomov* 17.9.54, **p.175** *Henry IV* 30.1.64, *Dr. Faustus* 28.5.64, *Rosmerholm* 9.3.67.

George, Adrian
(1944-)

Adrian George was born in Cirencester, studied at Harrow School of Art and the Royal College of Art, 1964-1967. Since 1967 Adrian George has participated in numerous group exhibitions in Britain, France, Germany, Japan and the USA; he has also contributed freelance work to magazines and newspapers including *The Times, The Sunday Times, Queen,* RADIO TIMES, *Nova* and, in USA, *New York Times* and *New York Magazine;* he has had four one-man exhibitions, two of which have been held at the Francis Kyle Gallery.
Page 238 *Death of a Bullfighter* 25.4.71, *The Selling of the Pentagon* 11.5.71, *The Last Resort* 5.10.79, *Juno and The Paycock* 26.1.76, *The Renegade* 29.3.76, **p.239** *French Railways Cover* 12.8.78, **p.240** *Crossing Over* 6.6.79, *The Autumn Garden* 22.7.71, *Inside Medicine* 6.9.76, *Wake!* 4.6.76, **p.241** *Breast Cancer* 3.1.78, *Simenon* 22.7.72, *Treat Me Gently* 3.2.77, **p.242** *Proms: Tal* 5.9.79, *Proms: Sibelius* 29.8.79, *Proms: Janet Baker*

3.8.78, *Proms: Mahler* 20.7.79, **p.243** *Jubilee Paintings* 4.10.77.

Gilroy, John
(1898-   )

John Gilroy was born in Newcastle, educated at Heaton Park School, Kings College, Newcastle. After the First World War he studied at the RCA, 1919; British Institute Scholar, 1921; RCA Travelling Scholar, 1922; exhibited Upper Grosvenor Galleries, 1970; created the Guinness posters 1925-1968. First commissioned RADIO TIMES in 1932. Since the war he has concentrated on portrait painting, including The Duke of Windsor when he was The Prince of Wales, The Queen, Prince Philip, The Queen Mother, Prince Charles, Princess Anne, Lord Mountbatten, Sir Winston Churchill, Pope John and many others. Illustrated 'McGill, The Story of a University', 1960; 'Rough Island Story'.
Page 44 *The Listener Family* 15.4.38, *Welcome to the Isle of Man* 9.6.39, *Time to Laugh* 31.3.39, **p.45** *Humour Number* 9.10.36, **p.83** *Christmas* 20.12.40.

Goodall, John Strickland
(1908-   )

John Goodall was born in Heacham, studied art under Sir Arthur Cope (1923) and Nicol and Harold Speed (1924), at the RA Schools 1925-29; he began work for RADIO TIMES in the 30s and continued contributing a drawing a week until the war. In 1968 he began illustrating his own children's stories. Published: 'The Adventures of Paddy Pork', 'The Ballooning Adventures of Paddy Pork', 'Shrewbettina's Birthday', 'Jacko', 'Creepy Castle', 'The Midnight Adventures of Kelly, Dot and Esmerelda', 'Naughty Nancy', 'The Surprise Picnic', 'An Edwardian Christmas', 'An Edwardian Holiday', 'An Edwardian Season', 'An Edwardian Summer', etc.
Page 55 *Memories Number* 10.9.37.

Greer, Terence
(1929-   )

Terence Greer was born in Surrey, educated in Kew and Richmond, studied art at Twickenham School of Art. In 1947 he joined the RAF for 2½ years, then continued his studies at St Martin's School of Art, Royal Academy School; turned freelance when he finished college, and joined Saxon Artists agency; contributed work to *The Economist; New Statesman; New Society* etc; work includes book illustration, book covers for Penguin, among others, and advertising; exhibited at Whitechapel Gallery, Redfern, RA, and with the Young Contemporaries; 12 to 15 years ago changed career from illustrator to playwright.
Page 180 Interview, *Romeo & Jeanette*, 20.6.50, *High Noon* 18.12.59, *Yeoman Hospital* 27.11.59, **p.181** *Tea on the Island* 15.6.61, *The Vodi* 15.11.62, *Wells Fargo* 19.1.61, *My People & Your People* 17.7.59, *Fairy Tales of New York* 28.3.63, *The Visitor* 8.10.64, *Philip Marlowe* 22.1.60.

Gross, Anthony
(1905-   )

Anthony Gross was born in London, educated at Repton School, studied art at the Slade School of Fine Art, under Tonks, and then at the Académie Julian and the Ecole des Beaux Arts, Paris. Initially sold his work to Deighton's in the Strand and a dealer in Paris. Worked for many years with Hector Hoppin on film cartoons; Official War Artist, 1941-45. Illustrated among many other works, Heinemann's 'The Forsyte Saga'. Taught at the Central School of Arts and Crafts, 1941-51. Exhibited at the RA and in Paris from 1924.
Page 110 Interview, *Point of Departure* 2.2.51, **p.111** *The End of Things* 9.3.51, *The Seagull* 9.1.53, *The Beech Tree is Red* 23.11.51, *The Gambler* 25.7.52.

Harris, Robin
(1949-   )

Robin Harris was born in London, educated at St Clement Danes Grammar School, studied art at Hammersmith College of Art, 1967-68; Liverpool College of Art, 1968-71; Royal College of Art, 1971-74. After college he went abroad; on his return to England he began freelance work; besides the RADIO TIMES he has contributed work to *Management Today, Manage* (in Hamburg), *New Scientist, The Times Saturday Review, Mimms Magazine, Esquire* etc. He also does book covers and book illustrations, record covers; one-man show of paintings at the Park Square Gallery, Leeds, 1975.
Page 237 *Stop the World* 14.11.79, *What's Your Poison* 9.5.79.

Herbert, Stanley

Page 23 *Outside Broadcasts Number* 4.6.37, **p.26** *Whitsun Number* 18.5.34, **p.27** *Open-Air Number* 3.6.38, **p.30** *Autumn Number* 8.10.37.

Hodges, C. Walter
(1907-   )

Walter Hodges was born in Beckenham, Kent, educated at Mount Pleasant School, Southbourne. He left at 13 but completed his formal education at Dulwich College; at 16 he went to Goldsmiths' School of Art, where he became interested in theatre design; his first job was with The Everyman Theatre; he then moved on to advertising and joined G.S. Roydes agency; at the same time he joined R.P. Gossop's agency, soon receiving his first commission for RADIO TIMES. He considers his first job for RADIO TIMES as the beginning of his professional career. After the war he re-established his links with RADIO TIMES; children's books published: 'Columbus Sails', 'The Flying House', 'Shakespeare and the Players', 'The Globe Restored' (for adults), in 1979 Walter Hodges became an Honorary Doctor of Literature at Sussex University. Today, he is involved with the Wayne State University in Detroit, who are proposing to rebuild an exact replica of the Globe Theatre, a subject on which Walter Hodges is an 'authority'.
Page 32 *Christmas Cover* 23.12.38, **p.33** *Macbeth Cover* 10.3.33.

Holmes, Nigel
(1942-   )

Nigel Holmes was born in Yorkshire, educated at Charterhouse, studied art at Hull Art School, RCA, 1962. He also did some freelance work while he was at college; after he graduated he went to America on a scholarship; he contributed work to *Woman's Mirror, The Observer, New Society,* as well as RADIO TIMES, 1969; worked on a freelance basis for Cornmarket Press, 1967. He did a series of illustrations with Peter Brookes for the RADIO TIMES in the 70s; Nigel Holmes now works for *Time* magazine in America.
Page 210 Interview, current programme symbols 1970s, **p.211** *The City's Millions* 7.11.74, *It's Your Line: Alcoholism* 5.11.75, **p.212** *Wimbledon* 4.7.74, 3.7.74, **p.213** *Wimbledon* 25.6.74, 24.6.74, 29.6.74, **p.214** *World Cup* 22.6.74, *Soyuz/Apollo* 15.7.75, **p.215** *First Test versus India* 6.6.74, *Golf* 11.7.74, *Soyuz/Apollo* 15.7.75, **p.216** *World Cup* 18.6.74, 15.6.74, **p.217** *World Cup* 13.6.74, 14.6.74, **p.218** *World Cup* 15.6.74, 22.6.74.

Hulme Beaman, Sydney G.
(1887-1932)

Sydney George Hulme Beaman was born in Tottenham. After leaving school he studied art at Heatherley's. He began his career by carving children's toys and then turned to drawing. In 1923 *The Golders Green Gazette* published his first cartoon series 'The Adventures of Philip and Phido'. Books published: 'Aladdin', 1924; 'Illustrated Tales for Children', 1925; 'The Seven Voyages of Sinbad the Sailor', 1926; 'Out of the Ark', 1927; 'Tales of Toytown', 1928; 'Tales of Toytown' was the first broadcast in 1929 in *Children's Hour* and he continued to write stories until his sudden death in 1932. There was a stage production 'The Cruise of Toytown', 1947; TV series was produced in the 1950s.
Page 41 *Dennis and Larry Interview the Mayor* 13.6.30, *Wreck of the Toytown Bell* 10.4.31, *The Mayor of Toytown's Christmas Party* 18.12.31, *The Babes in the Wood* 17.12.37, *The Toytown War* 17.2.39.

Jacques, Robin
(1920-   )

Robin Jacques was born in London; after leaving school at 15 he joined an advertising agency; received no formal art training; but after the war in 1945 he became a freelance illustrator. Art editor for *Strand* magazine; also contributed work to *Lilliput, Vogue, Punch, The Observer, The Sunday Times,* etc; illustrated over 100 books including 'Kim'. Limited Editions, New York and 'Vanity Fair' for the Folio Society; one-man show at Mel Calman Workshop Gallery; also contributed to Arts Council exhibitions; illustrated many childrens books, 20 of which were with the same author, Ruth Manning-Sanders; published; 'Illustrators at Work' and 'Studio Vista'.
Page 112 Interview, *Julius Caesar* 22.4.55, **p.113** *The Tempest* 22.2.52, 12.10.56, **p.114** *The Tempest* 29.5.53, *As You Like It* 13.3.53, *Julius Caesar* 22.4.55, **p.115** *Monserrat* 10.9.54, *The Yellow Book* 5.1.51, *The Gun* 25.3.55, *House by the Sea* 19.1.51, *Sarah Chandler* 9.3.51, **p.116** *The Leader* 24.4.50, *A Penny for a Song* 7.8.53, *The Raphael Resurrection* 24.8.51, *Meloney Hotspur* 21.11.52, **p.117** *South Wind* 8.7.55, *The Celestial Onion* 10.11.50, *The English Captain* 29.10.54, *Mary Rose* 14.4.50, **p.158** *Waiting for Godot* 22.4.60, *The Magic Barrel* 27.7.61, *The Duenna* 17.12.64, **p.159** *The Sign of the Four* 28.2.63, *Arms and the Man* 9.2.67.

Jaques, Faith
(1925-   )

Faith Jaques was born in Leicester, educated at Wyggeston School for Girls, left at 15 to study art at Leicester School of Art until 1942 when she joined the WRNS, wherein she was posted to Oxford and continued to study at evening classes at Oxford School of Art. Then, in 1946 she joined the Central School of Arts and Crafts; sold work while still a student and, on leaving, turned freelance; contributed work to various women's magazines; *Lilliput, World Review, Leader,* etc; illustrated over 100 books including 'Charlie and the Chocolate Factory', Hugh Evelyn's 'Pictorial History of Costume', Andrew Lang's 'The Red Fairy Book' 'The Torrents of Spring' for the Folio Society; exhibited at Mel Calman Workshop Gallery, London; David Paul Gallery, Chichester; New Ashgate Gallery, Surrey; published two children's books; 'Tilly's House', 1979; 'Tilly's Rescue', 1980.
Page 148 *Howard's End* 11.7.64, *The Storm* 9.6.66, *Poil de Carotte* 21.9.61, *Wuthering Heights* 10.1.67, *Alice of the Servant Problem* 15.10.64, *Tales of the Supernatural* 1.12.66, *Kim* 17.10.63, **p.149** *Pippa Passes* 13.2.69, *What Every Woman Knows* 19.5.66, *The Richest Man in the World* 8.7.60, *The Hunting of the Truffle* 30.5.63, *The Sacred Flame* 15.7.65, *Alice of the Servant Problem* 15.10.64, **p.150** *Without my Cloak/The Little Girls* 17.4.69, *A Hero of Whose Time* 4.8.66, *The Bostonians* 24.4.64, *The Story of Theron Ware* 17.3.66 *Bohemian Scenes* 5.9.63, *The Turn of the Screw* 24.2.66, *A Room with a View* 4.5.67, **p.151** *Conrad's Victory* 18.11.65, *The Constant Wife* 29.6.67, *Where Angels Fear to Tread* 27.8.64, *Major Barbara* 6.4.67, *Venusberg* 31.1.63, *Shaw's First Play* 16.9.65, *Smoke 30.12.65, The Wall of Silence* 11.2.65.

Kauffer, Edward McKnight
(1890-1954)

Edward McKnight Kauffer was born in Great Falls, Montana, USA; educated at American public schools; began working as a scene-painter in America; studied art at night classes; six months Art Institute of Chicago; six months in Munich; two years in Paris and settled in London early in 1914. He began poster designing with Underground Railways; work on show in London, and Washington DC; work exhibited, Ashmolean Museum, Oxford, 1926; New York Museum of Modern Art, 1937; books illustrated include 'Anatomy of Melancholy', 'Benito Cereno', 'Billy Budd', 'Elsie and the Child' and 'Venus Rising From the Sea' and 'Nigger Heaven'.
Page 11 *Christmas Cover* 17.12.26, **p.18** *Christmas Cover* 23.12.27.

Lamb, Lynton
(1907-   )

Lynton Lamb was educated at Kingswood School, Bath; studied art at Central School of Arts and Crafts. On staff of The Slade School of Fine Art, since 1950; Painting School, Royal College of Art, since 1956. Production Adviser, Oxford University Press. Member of London Group and Society of Wood Engravers. President of Society of Industrial Artists, 1951-53. Architectural decorations for Orient Liners 1935-50; first exhibition of painting, Storran Gallery, 1936; designed Commemorative Binding for lectern Bible, St Giles Cathedral, 1948 and for Coronation Bible, 1953; work in the Arts Council's Exhibition of Painting for 1951 Festival of Britain. Designed £1, 10/-, 5/-, and 2/6 postage stamps for the new reign, 1955 and the air mail stamp, 1957; designed Purcell Memorial, Royal Festival Hall, London, 1959; served as Camouflage Staff Officer, 1940-45. Publications: 'The Purpose of Painting', 1936; 'County Town', 1950; 'Preparation for Painting', 1954; 'Cat's Tales', 1959. He has contributed work to several magazines and journals.
Page 120 *The Judgement of Dr. Johnson* 16.5.52, *Edward My Son* 8.5.53, *The Voysey Inheritance* 18.5.51, **p.121** *The Eustace Diamonds* 7.11.52, *Tartuffe* 9.8.51, *The Holly & the Ivy* 14.12.51, *The Sweet Bird's Song* 26.12.52.

Micklewright, Robert
(1923-   )

Robert Micklewright was born in Staffordshire, educated in Balham, studied art at Croydon School of Art (1939), Wimbledon School of Art (1947-49) The Slade (1949-52). First drew for RADIO TIMES in 1954. Has exhibited in London, the provinces and the USA. Illustrated numerous books, especially for Oxford University Press. Work reproduced in several reference books including 'Artists of a Certain Line', 'Drawing for RADIO TIMES' and 'Royal Academy Illustrated'.
Page 122 Interview, *The Last Summer* 31.12.54, *In Town Tonight* 24.9.54, *Music Club* 6.2.59, *Quartet* 10.5.57, **p.123** *Virtuoso/Like my Father Told Me* 21.8.59, *Fair Music* 18.2.55, *Maigret* 4.12.59, *The Blood is Strong* 20.7.56, **p.160** *Flowering Cherry* 16.2.61, *Caramel for Carlota* 14.10.65, *Bright Shadow* 4.11.65, *The Move up Country* 23.9.60, *The Scapegoat* 27.1.66, **p.161** *A Smashing Day* 9.8.62, *Three Sisters* 20.5.65, *The Kings' General* 22.9.66, *A Dam Against the Ocean* 25.7.63, *A Farewell to Arms* 18.5.67, **p.162** *Hedgehog* 28.9.61, *The Cloister and the Hearth* 30.1.69, *The Murderer* 17.6.65, *Pillars of Society* 20.9.62, *Dark Origins* 5.12.63, *Jaunting with Johnnie* 28.3.63, *The Razor Edge* 25.3.60, **p.163** *Marriage Settlement* 13.5.60, *Three Sisters* 23.3.67, *A Kind of Loving* 5.3.64, *Jaunting with Johnnie* 28.3.63, **p.164** *At Home in History* 22.12.66, *Santa Cruz* 25.11.65, **p.165** *Inherit the Earth* 9.6.66, *At Home in History* 22.12.66, **p.166** *BBC TV Today* 26.10.61, *The Entertainer* 4.7.64, *A New Season at the Proms* 15.7.65, *Haydn in London 16.6.66, The Thunderbolt* 25.5.67, **p.167** *A New Season at the Proms* 15.7.65, *BBC TV Today* 26.10.61, **p.168** *BBC TV Today* 26.10.61, *Gilbert Harding* 14.11.63, **p.169** *Jaunting with Johnnie* 28.3.63, *BBC TV Today* 26.10.61.

Minton, (Francis) John
(1917–1957)

John Minton was educated at Northcliffe House, Bognor Regis; Reading School, Berkshire; studied art at St John's Wood Art School, 1935-38; and in Paris 1938-39; With Michael Ayrton designed the decor for 'Macbeth' at the Piccadilly Theatre, 1941. One-man shows: Leicester Galleries, 1942; Roland, Browse and Delbanco, 1945; Lefèvre, 1945, 1947, 1949, 1950, 1951, 1954, 1956; taught illustration at Camberwell School of Art and Crafts, 1943-46; Central School of Art and Crafts, 1946-48; tutor at Painting School, RCA, 1949-56; illustrated 'The Wanderer', 1946; 'Treasure Island', 1947; 'The Snail that Climbed the Eiffel Tower', 1947; 'Time Was Away', 1947; 'The Country Heart', 1949; 'Old Herbaceous', 1950; 'A Book of Mediterranean Food', 1950; 'French Country Cooking', 1951.
Page 119 *The Lady from the Sea* 19.9.52.

Nash, Paul
(1889–1946)

Paul Nash was born in London, educated at St Paul's, studied art at The Slade School of Fine Art. He exhibited prolifically from his first exhibition in 1912 at the Carfax Gallery to his last at Cheltenham Public Art Gallery, 1945; exhibitions include, War Paintings, Leicester Galleries, 1918; Wood engraving, Redfern Gallery, 1928; Painting, Leicester Gallery, 1928; British Representative Carnegie International Exhibition Jury of Award, 1931; exhibited International Surrealist Exhibition, London, 1936 and Paris, 1938; official artist Western Front, 1917; instructor of Design, Royal College of Art, 1924-25; at outbreak of the Second World War organised Arts Bureau in Oxford for War Service; Official War Artist to Air Ministry, 1940; Official War Artist, Ministry of Information, 1941; publications include 'Places, Prose, Poems and Wood-engravings', 1922; 'Room and Book' (essay on decoration) 1932; 'The Fleuron', 1927; 'Penguin Modern Painters', 1944; 'Outline', 1949.
Page 74 *Christmas Cover* 19.12.30.

Peake, Mervyn
(1911-1968)

Mervyn Peake was born in Kuling, Central China, educated at Tientsin Grammar School and Eltham College Academy Schools. He has exhibited in London, New York and Dublin; illustrated 'Alice in Wonderland', 'Treasure Island' etc; written and illustrated children's books 'Captain Slaughterboard Drops Anchor', 'Rhymes Without Reason'; written three novels, 'Titus Groan', 'Gormenghast', 'Titus Alone'; book of poetry: 'The Rhyme of the Flying Bomb' and a ballad poem with drawings, 1962. He gained the Heinemann Award for Literature.
Page 118 *Treasure Island* 24.12.48, *The Brushwood Boy* 7.11.52, *Rumpelstiltskin* 17.12.48, *For Mr. Pye–an Island* 5.7.57, *The Enchanted Cottage* 9.2.51.

Ralph & Mott

Page 55 *Women's Broadcasting Number* 16.11.34.

Reinganum, Victor
(1907-   )

Victor Reinganum, was born in London, educated at Haberdashers School, Hampstead; studied art at Heatherley's Art School, Académie Julian, Paris. While there he studied under Léger, returning to London in 1926 and started a freelance career; began drawing for RADIO TIMES almost immediately, also contributed to many other journals and magazines; exhibitions include Pandemonium Group, Beaux Arts Gallery, 1930-32; Art in Britain 1930-40, Malborough, London 1965; Britain's Contribution to Surrealism, Hamet Gallery, London, 1971; one-man show, Hamet Gallery, 1972; Aspects of Abstract Art in England, London, Edinburgh, Brussels, 1974, Germany 1975; City Gallery, Milton Keynes, 1974-75.
Page 38 Interview, *Au Lapin Qui Saute* 14.11.30, *Both Sides of the Microphone* 19.12.41, **p.39** *Time, Gentlemen, Please* 3.10.30, *Broadway Matinee* 15.10.37, *Big*

Night of Dance Music 26.2.32, *America Calling* 27.3.36, **p.50** *Variety Number* 13.9.35, **p.88** *Both Sides of the Microphone* 19.12.41, 17.1.41, 19.9.41, 16.1.41, *There's No Future In It* 18.1.46, **p.89** *Café Colette* 1.7.49, *So This is Man* 9.3.45, *Taking Stock* 28.10.49, *Plain Man's Guide to Music* 15.10.48, *Taking Stock* 4.11.49, *Picture Parade* 29.10.48.

Robinson, William Heath
(1872-1944)

Heath Robinson was born in Hornsey, Middlesex, educated at Islington and studied art at the Royal Academy Schools. He contributed illustrations to *The Sketch, The Bystander, The Graphic* and other magazines. He drew for the RADIO TIMES in the 20s. Illustrated 'The Arabian Nights', 'Hans Andersen's Fairy Tales', 'The Water Babies' and 'Don Quixote'. Published 'Uncle Lubin', 1902 and 'Bill the Minder', 1912.
Page 42 *Circus* 31.12.37, **p.75** *Christmas* 20.12.35.

Rosoman, Leonard
(1913-)

Leonard Rosoman was born in Hampstead, London, educated at Deacons School, Peterborough, studied art at King Edward VII School of Art, Durham University, Central School of Arts and Crafts, RA School. Exhibited work in London, Sheffield, Bradford, Edinburgh, Dublin, provincial galleries and New York; taught illustration at Camberwell School of Art; mural decoration at Edinburgh College of Art and was tutor at the RCA—he first drew for RADIO TIMES in 1951.
Page 104 *Marshall Ney* 20.3.53, *The Flashing Stream* 21.1.55, **p.105** *Not by Bread Alone* 15.11.57, *Danger, Men Working* 6.7.51, *Mr. Gillie* 19.12.52, *Distant Point* 15.1.54, *Professor Bernhardi* 14.8.53, **p.106 Interview,** *Golden Boy* 27.4.51, **p.107** *The Great Gatsby* 7.10.55, *Brideshead Revisited* 6.4.56, *A Ram in the Thicket* 13.6.52, **p.108** *The Mayor* 18.1.52, *The End of the Tether* 8.2.57, *A Street in Soho* 2.4.54, *Rutherford & Son* 21.11.52, **p.109** *Return to Tyassi* 31.8.51, *The Rising Sun* 15.4.55, *The Man from Thermopylae* 14.12.56, **p.174** *Bitter Waters* 31.1.63, *Fury in Petticoats* 23.1.61.

Rountree, Harry
(1878-1950)

Harry Rountree was born in Auckland, New Zealand, came to England in 1901. He contributed to *Punch* and *The Sketch*. He illustrated books on travel, animals and for children; he also illustrated posters and was president of the London Sketch Club.
Page 47 *Jack and the Beanstalk* 23.12.32, *Wind in the Willows* 19.9.39, 20.10.39, *Little Red Riding Hood* 19.12.30, **p.48** *Curious Critters No 5* 22.7.38, *No 4* 15.7.38, *No 1* 24.6.38, **p.49** *Curious Critters No 6* 29.7.38, *No 3* 8.7.38, *No 2* 1.7.38.

Russell, Jim
(1933-)

Jim Russell was born in Walsall, Staffs, educated at the Royal School, Wolverhampton, studied art at Birmingham College of Arts and Crafts (1951), where he gained his National Diploma in Design; after the war he returned to Birmingham to get his Art Teacher's Diploma, he then taught for a year at a comprehensive in Walsall, and during that year joined Saxon Artists

and began a freelance career. He first drew for RADIO TIMES in 1960.
Page 176 *My Friend Charles* 1.8.63, 18.7.63, 4.7.63, 11.7.63, **p.177** *The Wooing of Jonas James* 13.8.64. *The Snake is Living Yet* 22.10.65, *My Friend Charles* 29.8.63, **p.178** *My Friend Charles* 8.8.63, *The Travelling Smiths* 18.5.61, *Dynamite* 19.7.62, *My Friend Charles* 4.7.63, *After the Last Lamp* 1.12.62, *Children of the Archbishop* 3.8.61, **p.179** *Trouble with Lichen* 22.11.62, *My Friend Charles* 11.7.63, *The Reward for Silence* 31.1.63, *The Acknowledgement* 25.3.65.

Ryan, John
(1921-)

John Ryan was born in Edinburgh, educated at Ampleforth College, studied art at Regent Street Polytechnic, 1945-48; Assistant Art Master at Harrow School, 1948-54; exhibited at RA; Trafford Gallery; Royal Pavilion, Brighton. 'Captain Pugwash' created in 1950 for the *Eagle* magazine, first shown on BBC around 1958 and soon after drawn for RADIO TIMES for eight years. Cartoonist for *Catholic Herald* since 1965. Also created other TV cartoons: 'Sir Prancelot' and 'Mary, Mungo and Midge'.
Page 182 *Pugwash Letters* 2.8.62, *Pugwash Game* 14.12.63, *Pugwash Ahoy* 24.10.63, 23.6.61, **p.183** *Pugwash Ahoy* 18.5.61, 27.4.61, *Pugwash X* 23.2.61, *Christmas Pugwash* 21.12.61.

Scarfe, Laurence
(1914-)

Laurence Scarfe was born in Bradford; he studied mural painting at the RCA; taught at the Central School of Art and Design, 1945-70; worked in a freelance capacity, worked as an art editor and contributor on the 'Saturday Book'. He first drew for the RADIO TIMES in 1947; he has exhibited work both in London and the provinces, the USA and Italy. Published 'Rome', 1950; 'Venice', 1952; 'Alphabets', 1954; 'Italian Baroque', 1961; designer for the COI, BBC, GPO and lecturer, faculty of Art, Brighton Polytechnic.
Page 156 Interview, *Romeo and Juliet* 8.10.54, **p.157** *A Midsummer Night's Dream* 16.4.64, *Hero and Leander* 7.5.64, *Troilus and Cressida* 17.9.64, *Love's Labour's Lost* 20.8.64.

Searle, Ronald
(1920-)

Ronald Searle was born in Cambridge, studied art at Cambridge School of Art; humorous work first published in *Cambridge Daily News* and *Granta*, 1935-39; Prisoner of War in Siam and Malaya, 1942-45; contributed widely to publications from 1946; creator of the schoolgirls of St Trinian's, 1941 till 1953, cartoonist to *Tribune*, 1949-51; to *The Sunday Express*, 1950-51; special features artist, *News Chronicle*, 1951-53; weekly cartoonist, *News Chronicle*, 1954; contributor, *New Yorker*; designer of commemorative medals

for the French Mint since 1974. He has won many awards, had many one-man shows, designed film animations and produced countless books.
Page 98 *Frieda* 4.2.49, *Of Mice and Men* 28.1.49, *Old Soldier* 9.4.48, *Rope* 13.6.47, *Rain* 7.5.48, **p.99** *Christmas Cover* 19.12.47, **p.100** *Celia* 22.10.48, *I Have Been...* 1.10.48. *The Independence of D Thwaite* 25.2.49, *The Silver Box* 19.3.48, *Once a Crook* 15.10.48, *Escape Me Never* 10.12.48, **p.101** *The Enigma of the Japanese* 8.8.47, *The Undefeated* 14.1.49, **p.128** *There are Crimes and Crimes* 16.2.51, *Richard II* 20.4.51, **p.129** *The Emperor Jones* 25.1.52, *Cover* 12.1.51.

Sherriffs, Robert Stewart
(1906-1960)

Bob Sherriffs was educated at Arbroath High School, where he was an arts medalist and trained initially in heraldry. He began drawing for RADIO TIMES in 1927 but also contributed work to *Punch* and *The Tatler*, where his drawings of celebrities first brought him to notice. He was also a noted cricketer.
Page 16 *The Chief Engineer* 27.12.29, *Engineer 1929* 4.1.29, **p.17** *The Big Noise* 6.4.28, *Tommy Handley* 4.5.28, *Anthony Asquith* 21.10.27, *Musical Avolos* 4.11.27, *A.G. Gardiner* 11.11.27, **p.24/25** *Sherriffs Week-by-Week* 23.12.38, **p.76** *Henry Hall* 15.3.35, **p.77** *Song Number* 1.3.35, **p.78** *Whitsun Holiday Number Cover* 7.6.35, **p.79** *Both Sides of the Microphone* 25.6.37, *Carroll Gibson* 24.1.36, *Both Sides of the Microphone* 20.8.37, 19.5.39, *Cads College* 29.4.38, *Geraldo* 10.1.36, *Both Sides of the Microphone* 19.5.39, **p.80** *Both Sides of the Microphone* 25.6.37, 9.6.39, 10.11.39, 17.11.39, 30.7.37, 20.8.37, **p.81** *It's Rather Hard...* 4.9.39, **p.92** *Gracie Fields* 18.7.47, *Oi!* 24.5.40, *Merry-go-round* 3.10.47, *Up the Pole* 29.10.48, **p.93** *Radio Variety Number* 25.2.49, *Hi Gang* 11.2.49, *Eric Barker* 10.9.48.

Smith, May
(May Bethell-Jones)
(1904-)

May Smith was born in Manchester, educated at Manchester High School for Girls, studied art at Manchester Art School, came to London in 1925 and worked freelance for publishers. Contributed work to RADIO TIMES in the mid 30s, illustrated a book of children's stories from the radio and, during the same period, 'The Man who Caught the Wind'. She also illustrated her own verse for several publications.
Page 46 *Studio Hounds* 5.8.38, 19.8.38, 12.8.38, 3.11.39.

Spurrier, Steven
(1878-1961)

Steven Spurrier was born in London; at 17 he was apprenticed to a silversmith and studied art in the evenings at Heatherley's; contributed work

to several magazines: *Madam, Black and White* and *Graphic*; during the war served in the Port Police and the RNVR; was demobbed and joined the staff of the *Illustrated Evening News*; first drew for RADIO TIMES in 1928, exhibited at the RA from 1913; published two books in 1909; 'Illustration in Line and Half-Tone', 1933.
Page 36 *The Proms* 24.8.34.

Steadman, Ralph
(1936-)

Ralph Steadman was born in Wales, educated at Abergele Grammar School, North Wales; apprenticed to De Havilland Aircraft Company, but soon left to join an advertising agency. While there he began a correspondence course in art, which he continued during his National Service; first job was for Kemsley, working on the Northern Group newspapers; he still continued studying art at evening classes at East Ham Technical College; turned freelance on leaving Kemsley's newspapers; contributed work to *Punch, Private Eye, The Observer, New Statesman, The Times, Daily Telegraph, Rolling Stone, New York Times* etc; contributed work to the Labour Party Campaign, 1979; exhibitions include European Illustration, retrospective, National Theatre, 1977; Freud illustrations: Ireland, 1980/81. Illustrated 'Fear and Loathing in Las Vegas', 'Alice's Adventures in Wonderland', 'Through the Looking Glass', 'Emergency Mouse', 'Inspector Mouse', 'Hunting the Snark', 'Cherry Wood Canyon', 'Still Life with Raspberry', 'Ralph Steadman's America', 'Freud'.
Page 220 *Arena* 9.2.77, *Cricket* 11.6.77, **p.221/222/223** *Motor racing* 15.7.78, **p.224** *Cricket* 11.6.77, **p.225 Interview,** *Cricket* 11.6.77, **p.226** *Controversy: Defence Experiment* 16.8.71, *Kissinger* 15.1.77, **p.227** *Levin* 16.5.74, *The New Radicals* 22.7.71, *Oscar Wilde* 24.6.71, **p.228** *Smoking Report* 31.12.70, *Tuesday Documentary: The Modern Way* 13.6.72, *The New Radicals* 17.8.71, *Hair* 17.1.74, **p.229** *Panorama: Smoking* 4.1.71, *Tuesday Documentary: Be Fruitful and Multiply* 28.7.70, *Horizon: Due to Lack of Interest...* 4.3.71.

Thomas, Bert
(1883-1966)

Bert Thomas was born in Newport, Monmouthshire, he was educated in Swansea. He was a humorous illustrator and contributed work to several periodicals including *Punch* and *The Sketch*. He drew for the RADIO TIMES in the 20s.
Page 12 *The Philistine...* 7.11.24, *Does your Wife...* 3.12.24, **p.13** *Voice of Uncle...* 28.11.24, *Wireless Education* 5.9.24.

Tidy, Bill
(1932-)

Bill Tidy was born in Frinton, Tranmere, educated at a primary school in Liverpool, and at St Margaret's, Anfield; received no formal art training, but drew constantly from an early age, at various jobs and during his army service. First drew ads for the back of RADIO TIMES (1956), while working at an advertising agency; turned freelance in 1957; originally contributed work to *Picturegoer, Everybody's, John Bull, Punch*, etc; creator of various comic-strips: 'The Fosdyke Saga', in *The Daily Mirror*; 'The Cloggies', in *Private*

Eye; 'Dr Whittle', in *General Practitioner*; 'Grimbeldon Down', in *New Scientist*; 'Keg Buster', in *Camra*; 'Red Spanner', *Datalink*; books published; 'The Fosdyke Series 1-10', 1971-1981; 'The Cloggies', 1969; 'The Cloggies are Back', 'Tidy's World', 1969 and 'Tidy Again', 1970.
Page 244 Interview, *It's a Knock-Out!* 11.5.72, 23.6.72, **p.245** *What Time is Your Body?* 6.12.73.

Till, Peter
(1945-)

Peter Till was born in Manchester, went to Cambridge to read English (1964-67); started selling drawings to *OZ* magazine, 1969; joined Flies Revue, 1970; began to get commissions from 1973; wrote and designed storyboard for short film *The Beard*, which was animated in 1978, by Ian Emes; joined The Comedy Factory, London, 1979, for six months, performing monologues; formed a band, The Rumba Brothers, 1979, recorded in 1980; contributed work to *The Times; The Sunday Times; New York* magazine; *New York Times*; also magazines in Australia, Germany and France.
Page 230 *Clone Affair* 15.5.79, *The War Crime* 9.1.76, *The Manipulators* 31.3.79, *The Nose* 15.2.79, *Pawn takes Pawn* 22.12.79, **p.231** *Horizon: Happy Castastrophe* 28.7.75, *Bear Next Door* 1.9.79.

Tunnicliffe, Charles F.
(1901-1979)

Charles Tunnicliffe was born in Langley, Cheshire, educated at St James School, Sutton, received scholarships to study art at Macclesfield Art School; Manchester Art School 1915-21; RCA 1921-25; illustrated Henry Williamson's 'The Old Stage', 'Peregrine's Saga', 'The Lone Swallows', 'Tarka the Otter', 'Star Born' and 'Salar the Salmon'; Mary Priestley's 'A Book of Birds' etc; contributed work to *Country Life* as well as RADIO TIMES; published 'My Country Book', 'Bird Portraiture', 'Mereside Chronicle', 'Shorelands Summer Diary', 1948; exhibited at RA, Manchester Academy, Preston Harris Art Gallery, Johannesburg and elsewhere.
Page 124 *The World of Nature* 17.4.59, *The Thrush's Anvil* 9.1.59, *Look: Birds of Holland* 27.2.59, **p.125** *Easter Cover* 23.3.51, **p.152** *Woodpeckers* 16.5.63, *Look: Seal Rocks* 19.11.64, **p.153** *Unspoiled World* 31.1.63, *Waxwings and Crossbills* 7.2.61.

Watson, Clixby
(1906-)

Clixby Watson studied art at St Martin's School of Art; worked abroad for a time but returned to England to paint English people and landscapes. Began to work regularly for RADIO TIMES in 1932. His main desire was to paint large frescoes but the necessity of earning a living as a cartoonist pushed this into the background.
Page 55 *Summer Number* 30.6.39, *Woman's Number* 17.11.39.

Watts, Arthur George
(1883-1935)

Arthur Watts was educated at Dulwich—he studied art in Paris, Antwerp and The Slade. He drew his humorous illustrations for RADIO TIMES, for 'Both Sides of the Microphone' from 1928 until his death in an air crash on his way home from Italy in 1935.

Published 'A Painter's Anthology.'
Page 43 *Following the Lead...* 18,12,31, **p.51** *Wireless of Every Kind* 29.5.31, **p.52** *The World is Full...* 18.5.34, *We are Now Going Over...* 22.2.34, **p.53** *The World is Full...* 18.5.34, **p.54** *Summer Number* 29.7.32.

Whistler, Rex
(1905-1944)

Rex Whistler was born in Eltham, Kent; studied art at The Slade School of Fine Art (1922-26) and then in Rome; painted murals and portraits; book illustrator and stage designer; painted murals for the refreshment room at the Tate Gallery, 1926-27; killed in action in Normandy.
Page 37 *Christmas cover* 18.12.31.

Wilson, Mervyn
(1905-1959)

Mervyn Wilson studied art at the Royal Academy Schools. He showed a light-hearted drawing to the Art Editor of the RADIO TIMES in 1929 and became a humorous artist, despite himself, from then on. Mervyn Wilson had one standing joke for many years, which he shared with all the members of the RADIO TIMES staff, with one exception. From 1950 he incorporated a portrait of Douglas Graeme Williams, then Art Editor and subsequently Editor of RADIO TIMES, in his illustrations. Douglas Williams remained, until his death, ignorant of the fact that practically every week he published his own self-portrait. He also drew for *Punch* and *The New Yorker*.
Page 69 *Snapped in the Studio* 20.10.35, **p.70** *Superset* 25.6.37, **p.71** *Home Number* 18.11.38, *Green Fingers* 6.8.37, **p.72** *Regional Tour* 20.7.34, *The King Who Didn't Matter* 19.5.39, **p.37** *Outside Broadcast, the Wrong Way* 1.6.34, *Balloons* 20.10.39, *Down, Down, Down* 29.9.39.

Wood, Owen
(1929-)

Owen Wood was born in Whetstone, London; educated at several schools in London which were evacuated during the war; studied art at Camberwell School of Arts and Crafts, 1945-47; from 1950-55 exhibited work at mixed exhibitions, Young Contempories, London Group etc; first work commissioned in 1956; taught at Cambridge School of Art, 1960; left in 1964 and joined the Vocational Graphic Design Course at Colchester School of Art; ceased teaching in 1966, due to an increase in commissioned work from England and Europe; designed new banknotes for the Clydesdale Bank of Scotland; painted a series of 12 large canvases which form the main feature of the London Stock Exchange public gallery; illustrated RADIO TIMES covers, 1974, 1975, 1976; contributed work to the *The Economist, Harpers Bazaar, Homes and Gardens, Bride and Home, Esquire, Club International* etc; also illustrated many books, book covers, record sleeves, greetings cards and posters; has had several exhibitions in this country, Japan and the USA and published work includes 'The Owl and the Pussycat and Other Nonsense', André Deutsch 1978.
Page 246 *Christmas Cover* 20.12.76.

Zec, Philip

Page 50 *Fireside Number* 15.11.35.